AF352501

Investigative Creative Writing

Frameworks for Writing

Series Editor: Martha C. Pennington, SOAS and Birkbeck University of London

The series offers books focused on writing and the teaching and learning of writing in educational and real-life contexts. The hallmark of the series is the application of approaches and techniques to writing and the teaching of writing that go beyond those of English literature to draw on and integrate writing with other disciplines, areas of knowledge, and contexts of everyday life. The series entertains proposals for textbooks as well as books for teachers, teacher educators, parents, and the general public. The list includes teacher reference books and student textbooks focused on innovative pedagogy aiming to prepare teachers and students for the challenges of the twenty-first century.

Published:

Academic Writing Step by Step: A Research-based Approach
Christopher N Candlin, Peter Crompton, and Basil Hatim

Arting and Writing to Transform Education: An Integrated Approach for Culturally and Ecologically Responsive Pedagogy
Meleanna Aluli Meyer, Mikilani Hayes Maeshiro, and Anna Yoshie Sumida

Creativity and Discovery in the University Writing Class: A Teacher's Guide
Edited by Alice Chik, Tracey Costley, and Martha C. Pennington

Creativity and Writing Pedagogy: Linking Creative Writers, Researchers, and Teachers
Edited by Harriet Levin Millan and Martha C. Pennington

Exploring College Writing: Reading, Writing, and Researching across the Curriculum
Dan Melzer

Reflective Writing for Language Teachers
Thomas S. C. Farrell

Tend Your Garden: Nurturing Motivation in Young Adolescent Writers
Mary Anna Kruch

The "Backwards" Research Guide for Writers: Using Your Life for Reflection, Connection, and Inspiration
Sonya Huber

The College Writing Toolkit: Tried and Tested Ideas for Teaching College Writing
Edited by Martha C. Pennington and Pauline Burton

Understanding the Paragraph and Paragraphing
Iain McGee

Writing Poetry through the Eyes of Science: A Teacher's Guide to Scientific Literacy and Poetic Response
Nancy S. Gorrell, with Erin Colfax

Investigative Creative Writing
Teaching and Practice

Mark Spitzer

SHEFFIELD UK   BRISTOL CT

Published by Equinox Publishing Ltd.

UK: Office 415, The Workstation, 15 Paternoster Row, Sheffield, South Yorkshire
          S1 2BX
USA: ISD, 70 Enterprise Drive, Bristol, CT 06010

www.equinoxpub.com

First published 2020

British Library Cataloguing-in-Publication Data

A catalogue record for this book is available from the British Library.

ISBN   978 1 781797 17 4 (hardback)
       978 1 781797 18 1 (paperback)
       978 1 781797 19 8 (ePDF)

Library of Congress Cataloging-in-Publication Data

Names: Spitzer, Mark, 1965- author.
Title: Investigative creative writing : teaching and practice / Mark Spitzer.
Description: Sheffield, South Yorkshire ; Bristol, CT : Equinox Publishing
   Ltd, 2020. | Series: Frameworks for writing series | Includes
   bibliographical references and index. | Summary: "Creative writing
   pedagogy is enjoying a rapid expansion - college courses have rocketed
   from four courses in 1999 to 38 in the US, UK and Canada in 2016.
   Investigative Creative Writing builds on teaching theories of
   established writers and scholars as well as current innovators in the
   field. In laying out the theoretical foundation for an experiential,
   discovery-based learning approach, the book is primarily aimed at those
   who teach at college/tertiary level. It will also be useful for teachers
   and students practicing the craft of writing in related fields like
   English, writing, linguistics, communications, composition and rhetoric
   and education.Investigative Creative Writing can be envisioned as a
   practical tool for overcoming hurdles that impede writers from venturing
   into unknown territory where discoveries take place. In other words,
   beyond assisting in developing and honing more cutting-edge creative
   writing programs, this guidebook will be extremely helpful for curious
   intellects in getting to the meat of the matter, generating narratives,
   identifying arguments, fleshing out character traits, discovering
   direction for plots, and developing a host of other skills that foster
   and embolden a literal and literary freedom of the imagination. Examples
   of student assignments are included in the text as well as instructions
   for assignments from past classes which are intended for instructors to
   adjust according to their needs"-- Provided by publisher.
Identifiers: LCCN 2019024879 (print) | LCCN 2019024880 (ebook) | ISBN
   9781781797174 (hardback) | ISBN 9781781797181 (paperback) | ISBN
   9781781797198 (ePDF)
Subjects: LCSH: Creative writing (Higher education)
Classification: LCC PE1404 .S748 2020 (print) | LCC PE1404 (ebook) | DDC
   808.06/6378--dc23
LC record available at https://lccn.loc.gov/2019024879
LC ebook record available at https://lccn.loc.gov/2019024880

Typeset by S.J.I. Services, New Delhi

Contents

Part 3 Programmatic Discoveries

Part 4 Eco-Investigations

Part 5 Experiential Exercises

List of Images

Acknowledgements

I am glad to thank the brightest light in my life, my wife Dr. Leigh Graham (a.k.a. poet Lea Graham), for her encouragement and acute advice. I am also grateful to the extremely savvy Martha C. Pennington for being so supportive of this project, even in the aftermath of a hurricane that took its torrential toll. I've never been challenged by an editor this hard in my life, and she really made a difference in making this book as strong as it could be. Ryan Boudinot was helpful in the evolution of the polemical chapter, and his responses to interview questions are greatly appreciated. Thanks also to Dr. Janine Peterson for coordinating the various departments that led to the wild people/wilderness lecture at Marist College and the chapter that developed from that. Many thanks to the editors and support staff at Equinox Publishing Ltd. Thanks as well to the students who granted permission for their work to be used as examples in this book. But most importantly, a salute to the hundreds of students I've known throughout my teaching career who taught me about the teaching of writing.

Acknowledgements are due to the editors of the following publications and the organizers of the following events who influenced early incarnations of essays and articles that eventually became chapters in this book:

"Teaching Students to Show Not Tell" was first published as "Teaching Students to Show, Not Tell" in *The Chronicle of Higher Education*, September 27, 2012 (https://www.chronicle. com/article/Teaching-Students-to-Show-Not/134614). Reprinted in revised form with permission from *The Chronicle of Higher Education.*

"The New Weird: What Happens to Creative Writing When the Truth Is Stranger Than Fiction" was first published as "The New Weird: What Happens to Literary Realism When the Truth Is Stranger Than Fiction?" in *The Chronicle of Higher Education*, June 12, 2012 (https://www.chronicle.com/article/The-New-Weird/132121). Reprinted in revised form with permission from *The Chronicle of Higher Education.*

"Multiple-Personality Pedagogy: A Hybrid Teaching Tool for Varying Voice in the Classroom" was first published in *Hybrid Pedagogy*, Spring 2013 (http://www.digitalpedagogylab.com/hybridped/on-pedagogical-manipulation). Reprinted in revised form with permission from *Hybrid Pedagogy.*

"Extreme Puppet Theater as a Tool for Writing Pedagogy" was first published as "Extreme Puppet Theater as a Tool for Writing Pedagogy at K–University Levels: A Vehicle towards 'Something Else'" in *Writing and Pedagogy*, vol. 6(1), Spring 2014, pp. 121–126. Copyright owned by Equinox Publishing Ltd.

"May the Farce Be with You: Reflections on Extreme Puppet Theater as a Vehicle towards *Something Else*" was first published as "May the Farce Be with You: Reflections on 'Extreme Puppet Theater' as a Vehicle towards 'Something Else'" in Alice Chik, Tracey Costley, and Martha C. Pennington (eds.), *Creativity and Discovery in the University Writing Class: A Teacher's Guide*, Equinox, Sheffield, UK, 2015, pp. 233–245. Copyright owned by Equinox Publishing Ltd.

"How to Sell a Creative Writing Program Based on the Question 'Why Study Creative Writing?'" was first published as "Why Study Creative Writing? Speaking in the Language of the Other to Sell Writing Programs to the State" in *Writing for the Curious: Why Study Creative Writing?*, edited by Kishor Vaidya, The Curious Academic Publishing, Canberra, Australia, 2015, no page numbers (Kindle publication). Reprinted in revised form by permission from The Curious Academic Publishing.

"Experience Investigative Eco-Fiction" was originally a PowerPoint presentation at the Creative Writing & Innovative Pedagogies Conference (CWIP) at the University of Central Missouri in Warrensburg, Missouri, October 17, 2015. Copyright owned by author.

"From Wild People to Wilderness: An Education in Investigating Monsters in Our Midst" was originally a public lecture sponsored by the First-Year Studies Program, the School of Liberal Arts, the Department of History, and Medieval and Renaissance Studies at Marist College in Poughkeepsie, New York, on October 22, 2015. The original subtitle was "An Education in Researching Monsters in Our Midst." Copyright owned by author.

– Mark Spitzer
Mayflower, Arkansas
August 2019

Mark Spitzer is the author of 30 books which include environmental fish studies, novels, memoirs, collections of poetry, and literary translations from French. He has taught almost all genres of creative writing, World and American literature, and first-year writing at the University of Central Arkansas, Truman State University, Louisiana State University, the University of Louisiana at Lafayette, and the University of Colorado. He has also taught at the City University of Hong Kong, the University of North Carolina – Wilmington, Lake Forest College, and Marist College. He formerly held positions as Editor in Chief of the award-winning literary journal *Toad Suck Review*, Managing Editor of the *Exquisite Corpse Annual*, Assistant Editor of *Exquisite Corpse*, and Translation Editor of *New Delta Review*. He currently holds the position of Associate Professor of Creative Writing at the University of Central Arkansas. Spitzer's articles on writing pedagogy and theory have appeared in *The Chronicle of Higher Education*, *Writing & Pedagogy*, *Hybrid Pedagogy*, and anthologies published in Australia and the United Kingdom. Other works have appeared in *Studies in the Novel*, *Review of Contemporary Fiction*, *Ecotone*, *Black Warrior Review*, *Cimarron Review*, *The Hudson River Valley Review*, *The Louisiana Review*, *The Oklahoma Review*, *Minnesota Monthly*, *The Satirist*, *Rain Taxi*, *The Laurel Review*, *Crab Creek Review*, *ACM*, *The Journal of African Travel-Writing*, and many other magazines, newspapers, and journals.

A leading researcher of the reviled gar fish, he can be seen on the "Alligator Gar" episode of the Animal Planet series *River Monsters* and occasionally heard on the radio or seen on TV in defense of fish, amphibians, and water quality. His latest environmental book, *In Search of Monster Fish: Angling for a More Sustainable Planet*, was recently published by the University of Nebraska Press. Other recent titles by Mark Spitzer include *The Crabby Old Gar* (Subversive Muse Press, 2018), a children's literature title; *Viva Arletty! Our Lady of the Egrets* (Six Gallery Press, 2017), a novel; *Beautifully Grotesque Fish of the American West* (University of Nebraska Press, 2017), a nonfiction book; *GLURK! A Hellbender Odyssey* (Anaphora Literary Press, 2016), a poetry collection nominated for a Pushcart Prize; *The Genet Translations: Poetry and Posthumous Plays* (Polemic Press, 2015), a literary translation; and *After the Octopus* (Black Mountain Press, 2014), a memoir. See www.sptzr.net for more information.

Series Editor's Preface

As might be expected from a creative writer who used to edit a literary journal titled *Toad Suck Review*, Mark Spitzer's *Investigative Creative Writing: Teaching and Practice* is an unusual work. It is one of the most original and interesting books on writing and the teaching of writing that I have ever come across, for a number of reasons. It is also possibly the most important current work on writing and the teaching of writing

One, it contains many novel insights about the process of writing creatively, together with truly inspiring ideas for both doing and teaching creative writing – and, for some adventurous English Comp instructors, for teaching academic writing creatively.

Two, it is a book that all those who teach writing can relate to, full of experiential anecdotes about teaching and professional life in a university setting.

Three, it is well crafted, frequently amusing, and highly accessible in style, and so can be read easily and with pleasure, even while learning a great deal.

Four, it is illustrated with photos and other images related to its textual content, thus adding to the interest and pleasure readers will experience in going through this book.

For these reasons alone, I consider it a must-read for all those who teach writing, creative or otherwise, and who are likely to write creatively themselves.

But perhaps the strongest reason all teachers of writing should read this book is the central message of *Investigative Creative Writing*, that of using the power of writing to make a difference – in particular, to ensure the health and survival of the human race and all other species at a time of environmental degradation. Indeed, any other focus for a writer's work pales beside this one.

I am proud of the part I played in helping Mark to organize and elaborate his ideas on writing and the teaching of writing, and to set them in a context of his philosophy that our students, and all of us, can do what we love while making a contribution to the betterment of the world. I hope you will find the book as enlightening and inspirational as I have, and also that you, like me, find many valuable nuggets of wisdom and practical ideas that you want to apply in your own writing and to pass on to students through your teaching.

– Martha C. Pennington
Series Editor, Frameworks for Writing

Introduction
Discover Creative Writing Superpowers
through Investigative Teaching Techniques

Origins of My Investigative Creative Writing Practice and Teaching

This book hinges on an orientation involving the concepts of *investigation* and *discovery* in order to transform novice writers into investigators and discoverers who learn through their writing. This orientation also involves the mystery of the journey of writing, not knowing where it will lead, and the mystery of the destination – which relies on finding revelations that can happen almost magically when subject matter is examined creatively. And when I write "creatively," I mean it literally: through the act of creating something which did not exist before. Whether that something is a text or an experience or even a failure, the idea is that epiphanies can be hauled from the depths of our flashing synapses by directly engaging with processes which provide incentives for writers to explore areas they may have never ventured without some sort of driving factor that takes them outside of themselves.

What I'm talking about is playing with words and allusions, and interests and concerns, by shifting perspectives in order to actively engage *the imagination*: a concept that refers to the machinery humans use to create images and context, but also to all the other sensual and idea-generating mechanisms people employ to make their lives more meaningful. In other words, there are innovative ways to play with language and learning which can reward those who write with experiences that take them to places they never thought possible. And because the payoff in discovering new terrain is often immediate, the result is an enthusiasm for exceeding one's own expectations. If you ask me, there's no better way to learn than that.

Envisioned primarily as a guidebook for student writers and those who teach and aspire to teach creative writing, this text is just as much about teaching creative writing as it is about teaching writing creatively. The ideas that follow can be applied to any writing or creative writing course from grade school to the graduate level, and they can serve creative and critical thinkers in areas as diverse as English, journalism, education, first-year writing, profes- sional writing, technical writing, world languages, and rhetorical studies. The exercises and approaches in this book were designed to be adjustable according to the needs of instructors in any field that seeks to tap into the subconscious, promote group work, inspire dialogue, and get to the points which matter the most. In short, the general advice contained in these pages is relevant to any subject matter in which writing is used to discover, whether the explorers are in academic settings or whether they are artists, scholars, or curious individuals studying writing on their own.

Essentially, the narratives that follow are intended to help writers relate their own narratives. The trick, of course, is for writers to make the messages embedded in their narratives worth it for the audience, the discoverers of their texts, to learn about. When writers engage readers by prompting revelations which truly speak to an audience, that's an exciting and valuable asset for whatever those writers want to accomplish. When that sort of connection occurs, so does communication. Whether that communication be a personal discovery, an emotional expression, information which can be useful to others, or ideas meant to solve global warming, using language to communicate effectively provides a powerful platform to make something happen.

As history has proven time and time again, narratives make profound differences in peoples' lives. Just look at all the religious texts in the world and how those narratives are essential to forming identities that shape worldviews, start wars, provide for charity, and support beliefs passed on for generations. Consider all the novels, memoirs, poems, philosophical writings, and other published narratives that have inspired readers to travel, experience new cultures, meet people with different ideas, change their politics, and ask questions they might have never asked if not for the privilege of literacy. And then there are the narratives that find their form in movies, television shows, radio shows, opera, video games – which provide for forms of psychic escape. Songs contain narratives that make incredible differences in peoples' attitudes and outlooks every day. Whether those narratives reach audiences through the blues, country music, Gospel, Buddhist chants or hip hop, audiences have been finding meaningful context in verse for centuries that directly applies to their lives. For example, millions of people, who've been disappointed in not getting something in their lives, have looked to the lyrics of the Rolling Stones' "You Can't Always Get What You Want" (Jagger and Richards, 1969) for consolation. Given that, and given all the other narratives people tell each other on a daily basis (especially on cable news), it's obvious that narratives are central in affecting how individuals perceive and take part in the world.

Let's start with my own narrative, which is that of a creative writing polygamist. By this I mean that I am just as committed to poetry as I am to fiction, creative nonfiction, literary translation, and drama writing. I've practiced and published in all these genres, and I've had the good fortune to apply that experience as an editor of some extremely colorful literary journals, especially the legendary *Toad Suck Review*. As a creative writing professor, I've taught everything from all the standard workshops, forms, topics, and intro courses to classes in College Writing and in Editing and Publishing. I've started and advised student organizations, worked with community leaders, led protests, and I've taken my messages to the streets via television, radio, newspapers, podcasts, blogs, and public talks. I've designed and developed creative writing programs, worked closely with administrators and faculty to launch those programs, and I've witnessed the growing pains associated with sustaining writing programs. I'm also dedicated to educating audiences interested in fish and environmental subject matter, I'm a practitioner of some obscure postmodern aesthetics, and I've published numerous articles in creative writing pedagogy – which is why this book exists.

In poetry I have always been attracted to the experimental subgenre of "investigative poetry" as proposed by the American bard-historian Ed Sanders, who appropriated techniques from Ezra Pound, Charles Olson, William Carlos Williams, and other avant-garde poets to develop a twentieth-century form of poetics constructed from "undefiled high energy purely-distilled verse-frags" (Sanders, 1976: 11). Sanders' definition of investigative poetry is undeniably abstract, so I'll just define it here as a free-verse-based collage that incorporates data, history, politics, images, quotes, references, and other bits of textual information, all bound together by a biased sense of humor. To this mix I've added aspects of ecology, science, psychology, sociology, historical fiction, the oral tradition, and audio to develop my own stylistic voice in biology- and folklore-based poetry-portraits of natural and unnatural worlds.

Somewhere along the line, I came up with the umbrella term "investigative creative writing pedagogy," which is an elusive notion. Even though there may be some conceptual crossovers that relate to "investigative writing," "investigative journalism," or "experiential education," such established approaches exist independently from the theoretical framework of the practices and pedagogy I envision here. Simply put, I do not consider myself a patron of any specific school or tradition of writing pedagogy, but I do consider myself someone from the creative writing spectrum who feels no hesitation in applying the William S. Burroughs quote of "all is permitted" (Burroughs, Gysin, Corso, and Beiles, 1960: 61).[1] I took that statement as poetic license for the freedom to appropriate, and with that liberty I developed a vision for what I call "investigative poetics" based on Sanders' brand (which is commonly referred to as "investigative poetry" or "investigative verse"). I then developed a vision for "investigative eco-fiction" and "investigative nonfiction," which I see as subspecies of the investigative creative writing pedagogy genus which I now find myself promoting with minimal attention to what theories are trending or what those who've invested themselves in other writing pedagogies might think about my trespasses.

My idea of investigative creative writing, like Sanders' idea of investigative poetry, depends in part on combining different snapshots of a subject's totality in order to create a textual mosaic that tells a unique story. In investigative poetry, the result of Sanders' cut-and-paste approach is easily seen on the page; but in investigative creative writing, the collage approach is sometimes less visible because it's more philosophical than physical. That is, in investigative poetry the combining happens right on the page; but in investigative creative writing, the combining happens behind the scenes. I'm talking about a conceptual combining – a combining of approaches, tactics, and exercises that invites students in, directly engages them in the discovery process, and creates a playful experience to inspire context which resonates for readers. Or, another way of looking at this comparison is that whereas investigative poetry is a collage composed of different facets of a subject's nature, investigative creative writing pedagogy, like the investigative creative writing practice on which it is built, is constructed from a kaleidoscope of experiences bent on turning learning into an event.

Like the lyric essay (in which lyrical language is no prerequisite), investigative creative writing pedagogy is a concept that originated from propositions offered in previous historical literary contexts. The lyric essay was officially established in the Fall 1997 issue of the *Seneca Review* by John D'Agata and Deborah Tall and was characterized by them as a creative nonfiction mosaic stitched from narrative fragments (D'Agata and Tall, 1997). Like investigative poetry, the lyric essay is a multi-faceted hybrid form that can incorporate research, memories, technical information, images, verse, and various stylistic tricks. Both the practice and pedagogy of investigative creative writing share the intention of the lyric essay and investigative poetry to combine smaller parts of the whole in order to create a new and novel way of providing focus. The lyric essay, being just as much a collage experience as investigative poetry, then joins the latter as a conceptual model for investigative creative writing. In the Whitmanesque sense that the self "contains multitudes" (Whitman, 2004: 123), investigative creative writing does the same thing: It relies on the premise that its entirety is amassed from myriad experiences.

At this point, defining investigative creative writing admittedly becomes an abstract argument based on teaching experiences that I recall but the reader has limited access to. That, however, is another reason this book exists: to organize those experiences, to set them down in the form of chapters, and to offer itself as a starting point for other writers and writing teachers to add their own experiences. Meanwhile, the word "investigative" refers to the act of investigating for the purpose of discovery just as much as it harks back to the innovative ideologies in Sanders' vision of investigative poetry.

Investigative eco-fiction, on the other hand, is a construct that relies on a slightly different collage-oriented approach. As a method for montaging moments and memories from one's own experience into a body of fictional prose, I examine the concept of investigative eco-fiction in Chapter 12 and advocate for experiential investigations that immerse and directly involve fiction writers in environmental subject matter. This getting-out-there-and-doing-it approach ensures that writers have more of a stake in the research focus than if they were just sitting at their desks making stuff up. Investigative immersion provides writers the opportunity to gather real-life, real-world, real-time information, so their final products have the advantage of being narratives informed by genuine experience.

The concept of investigative nonfiction is also examined in this book, especially in Chapter 13, "From Wild People to Wilderness," which looks at how I combined experience with research in order to create a highly active nonfiction investigation. As I note in that chapter, when nonfiction-based discoveries happen in which writers lose or discover themselves, this is a prescription for investigative nonfiction.

In investigative creative writing, investigations can range from inquiries into experimental teaching methods and dramatic ways of learning to exploring questions in the creation and operation of environments that directly influence what the editor of this book and the anthology *Creativity and Discovery in the University Writing Class* refers to as "discovery-oriented pedagogy" (Pennington, 2015: ix). This brings up another previously established literary context that overlaps with and augments the investigative aspect of the pedagogy I proclaim.

Much of the conceptual grounding for this book was realized in connection with the workshops I taught for the 2013 Summer Institute on Creativity and Discovery in University Writing hosted by the English Department at the City University of Hong Kong, which was spearheaded by its Research Coordinator, Martha C. Pennington. The book which resulted from that conference, *Creativity and Discovery in the University Writing Class* (Chik, Costley, and Pennington, 2015), is without question a big sister to this book. *Investigative Creative Writing* follows in the spirit of incorporating exploratory aspects to learning, and it essentially grew out of and grew up with guidance from *Creativity and Discovery in the University Writing Class*. As Charles Bazerman suggests in the third chapter of *Creativity and Discovery*, "Creating Identities in the Intertextual World," there is great value in "teaching students how to claim their place and accomplish meaningful actions in the worlds they are growing into. Teachers need to invent the environments and tasks that will nurture the students' invention of themselves as powerful … writers" (Bazerman, 2015: 46).

What this means is that a revolution needs to take place in education and specifically in the teaching of writing. This is not to say that I'm calling for an armed rebellion. Rather, I'm referring to a need for pedagogical motion, for teachers to get the investigative wheels rolling so that vehicles to discovery can take students to new places. What I am calling for is a progressive pedagogy, the idea being to move forward, to develop, to improve, to advance toward a higher, more effective state. "Progressive" is a quixotic word, an idealistic word, a word that implies moving away from the past and looking toward the future, and it has an agenda: to make things better, to reach a full potential, to evolve into the best incarnation possible. I envision the idea of revolution as a *re-evolution* in which educators, as Bazerman suggests, create occasions that lead to inventions (or discoveries) which not only empower students, but lead them to "understand and participate more fully in the worlds of their chosen disciplines" (Bazerman, 2015: 57).

As a mode to create greater communication between academic disciplines, investigative creative writing pedagogy promotes a progressive alternative to what Shirley Goek-lin Lim observes in "Highways and Sinkholes" (Chapter 13 of *Creativity and Discovery in the University Writing Class*) as the standard writing-pedagogy approaches of "observing poetic form, producing narrative structure, the best choice of diction, the most engaging dramatic action, and so forth … [which] underlie much of contemporary teaching in the creative writing classroom" (Lim, 2015: 252). Lim has a beef with the "current creative writing textbooks so popular in college classes [which] model [and] repeat standard and usually un-interrogated maxims and dogma that have been generally valorized as 'lore'" (ibid.). That's a sentiment I wholeheartedly agree with.

Still, I'm not making the claim that the voices which dominate creative writing pedagogy should be ignored or discounted. Veteran creative writing teachers have vast stores of seasoned experience to offer, and that experience is balanced by a lot of new blood generated by the MFA industry, which is currently producing plenty of passionate mentorship for developing writers. To this mix, I decided to add my own narratives to the conversation about what has been effective for me in teaching creative writing based on nearly twenty years of pedagogical experience at both the graduate and undergraduate levels. At times, my voice may seem unorthodox, and at times, it definitely is.

As a writer whose work often contains an edge which some have labeled "quirky" or "radical," I've discovered that I can use these outsider qualities to reach a mainstream audience, especially with my monster-fish books. My intention isn't to toot my own horn, but I know that my obsession with fishing and my sincerity of tone appeal to readers eager to experience the grotesques I've met. The discovery here is that creating a following is an important result which investigative creative writing practices can lead to – not for self-validating reasons, but for the most progressive reasons that have ever existed.

I frequently tell my students that writing is an advanced form of talking, and I truly believe it is. If you can get your views and visions down as you see them and feel them and hear them in your head, that's an effective method to begin drawing readers in. Furthermore, when emerging writers connect with familiar voices, or voices that feel natural or playful or musical or rich in information, those connections provide effective examples of how to proceed. And if developing writers take those hints, and if their content is progressive in intent like the environmental chapters in this book, then those writers will have a better chance at making their environments more sustainable and productive.

Consequently, this book is my take on approaches that can stimulate student imaginations in order to help crystallize visions. It's also my take on successful practices that students and teachers and writers can apply in the classroom and beyond. And by "beyond" I don't just mean homework. I'm talking about writers feeling enthusiastic and confident when leaping into investigations that can yield rewarding discoveries in their lives and the lives of others. I'm talking about investigators challenging their intellects by turning the practice of writing into a transcendental experience that takes them to greater heights. I'm talking about getting to that place where writers can discover and harness the crazy coursing currents of the word-universe through authentic experiences in which they become antennas pulling in visualizations and associations to connect and smooth out later. I'm talking about getting into the mythic "Zone," which isn't really mythic at all because these experiences can happen automatically and every day.

That's what happens when I write. I leave myself, go out of myself, and I experience a quasi-omniscience which allows me the freedom to play with language and ideas to the point that the outside world does not exist except as a place to return to. When I'm in the Zone, discoveries come in fast and frequent ecstatic rushes. This is the great elation and satisfaction that every writer strives to achieve. It's the stereotype of the mad scribe pounding away, spelunking the depths of his or her genius to find long buried treasures seeking light. It's the ideal, the grail, the apotheosis – and I can tell you that the Zone is achievable and tangible, and it's there right now for the taking.

Even as I write this, I see that I've forgotten to eat lunch because I'm as involved in mining my own mind for geodes of connectivity as a human being can possibly be. And yes, I'm hungry, but a cream-cheese bagel can wait for this highly addictive process to work its divine process.

Investigative creative writing is what I have to offer, and it's what I want to share with others. I've seen where it can take me, and the results are visible in my list of publications, which includes thirty books. I'm not saying this to brag; I'm saying this to show that immersing oneself in the practice of investigative processes not only is an accessible mind-blowing experience, but it can produce discoveries for which there is a strong demand. Not only that, those discoveries can lead to job security, support for future writing projects, awards, and professional recognition. But those are just starting points for what writing discoveries can really do. Since writing discoveries have led to the dismantling of governments, treaties between nations, and constitutions and bills of rights, they damn well have the potential to strengthen communities, fund cancer research, expose corruption, and lead to the laying down of arms.

Investigative creative writing pedagogy articulates approaches designed to encourage writers to push themselves athletically and beyond what the Nike commercials recommend. To their general advice of "Just do it," I would add: "…via writing discoveries that provoke!"

But provoke what?

Laughter, that's what!

Or crying. Or catharsis. Or empathy. Or action. Or change. Or evolution.

Or insights that transform writers striving in isolation into leaders emerging from the shadows.

Or questions that drive writers to ask further questions, and questions that really matter.

But most of all, to provoke the discovery and the writing of original, imaginative works that are conscious of what they want to accomplish and effective in doing so.

One measure of effective writing is if an audience wants more from a writer. If that's the case, then that writer is doing something right. Having an audience that wants more from you is a powerful hand to wield. That power, however, needs to be handled wisely and with respect or else it risks being wasted or misused. As Spiderman points out, echoing Voltaire, "with great power there must also come – great responsibility" (Lee, 1962: 11).[2] And as Bazerman indicates, teachers can invent ways for students to invent themselves into powerful writers. This means students have the power to discover their own superpowers – like the power to communicate and the power to influence and inspire – which hold both psychological and political currency and can be used to bring forth illuminations. Of course, the more play there is in discovering these powers, and the more personally rewarding those experiences are, the easier it is to get to know and control these powers. And the more writers know and control their power to connect with others, the more they discover about their worlds and themselves and what they can do to preserve what I refer to in Part 4, "Eco-Investigations," as "the whole fracking enchilada."

As an activist eco-writer who recognizes that all life on this planet depends on the health of the environment, this is what I now find my words fighting for. Due to that idealism, and because I've discovered that a well-written letter to the editor can shut down City Hall, the goal of this book is to generate and model writing power in order to empower writers involved with the most vital work there is to do. Whether that work is making great leaps in the protection of human rights, civil rights, animal rights, the preservation and propagation of endangered species, disease control, or making progress in the common-sense work governing bodies need to do to increase everyone's overall quality of life, I envision writing power as the ultimate gift teachers can give to students so that they can discover their own superpowers. But as both comic books and real life have demonstrated, there is always a risk with superpowers. Power can be used for both good and evil and everything in between, and it has been used for such extremes. Nevertheless, I am firmly committed to the belief that creative writing superpowers can help save us from ourselves.

Overview of Contents

Let's take a look at how the chapters that follow cohere to the whole. Part 1, "Discovery-Oriented Basics," consists of chapters focused primarily on craft. In Chapter 1, "Teaching Students to Show Not Tell," I address the age-old question of how to encourage developing writers to substitute specific detail for ambiguous or abstract words so as to conjure vivid visions and associations that resonate with readers, thereby challenging evolving imaginations to make use of writing power. Similarly, Chapter 2, "The New Weird: What Happens to Creative Writing When the Truth Is Stranger than Fiction," investigates approaches for empowering fiction by making it more colorful and memorable. Chapter 3, "The Ten Commandments of Incorporating Dialogue," was designed "For Those Seeking to Inform the Unprepared, the Disengaged, and the Thoroughly Confused," just as its subtitle claims. That chapter offers more than just advice on how to use the power of dialogue; it also offers practical reasons to hone a power which can change lives for the better.

Part 2, "Investigative Theatrics," also aims to make use of power – that power being teaching methods which actively engage students so that they're psyched to investigate. I see Chapter 4, "Multiple-Personality Pedagogy," as a way to explain a hybrid teaching tool for varying voice in the classroom, and I explain why this dramatic approach ups the ante by bringing in diverse points of view through a method that at first seems ludicrous yet has always worked for my students. Chapter 5, "Extreme Puppet Theater as a Tool for Writing Pedagogy," also illustrates a theatric way to entertain and educate in order to arrive at discoveries that free students from the learning fetters of the past (i.e. exams, memorization, forced essay writing), which just aren't as functional as they used to be in this highly technological, fast-paced, short-term-attention-span world. Chapter 6, "May the Farce Be with You," reflects on the phenomenon of puppet pedagogy and addresses the concept of *something else*, a loaded term which authorities in the field of creative writing pedagogy have been touching on for years. Chapter 7, "Pointers for Performance of Poetry and Prose," then ends this section with a talking-point-based essay on how to make the spoken word (to borrow from Jack Kerouac) "burn, burn, burn like fabulous yellow roman candles exploding like spiders across the stars" (Kerouac, 1959: 6).

Part 3, "Programmatic Discoveries," also seeks to tap into writing power, but at a more institutional level, so that higher education can serve students and communities. For example, Chapter 8, "How to Sell a Creative Writing Program Based on the Question 'Why Study Creative Writing?'" is about establishing environments for students to pursue discoveries that create strong communities. Likewise, Chapter 9, "Nine Recommendations for Growing Creative Writing Programs," goes after that same power and provides perspectives to investigate further. These two chapters rely on my experience in designing and founding the Arkansas Writers MFA Workshop at the University of Central Arkansas, and they investigate ways to start and sustain progressive programs in the discipline. Chapter 10, "Dealing with Diverse Issues in Creative Writing Programs: A Polemic," ends Part 3 with a look at recent arguments by some controversial provocateurs, but with an eye toward making the workshop more user-friendly and relatable for its diverse clientele.

Part 4, "Eco-Investigations," is included because this is my primary research area, and since I know the subject matter well, I can comment with authority. It's also the battlefield in which I've been concentrating my own power, and can be viewed as an example of how to effectively channel creative writing superpowers. Still, my intention here has nothing to do with winning anyone over to any side; it's about showing how creative investigations can lead to discovering solutions so that future generations of writing teachers and writing students don't end up powerless. Chapter 11, "Introducing 'Eco' to the Homies," is a breakdown of my line of attack for doing the most I can do for this planet while I'm here. It's a call to action, which is understood in much more depth when paired with Chapter 12, "Experience Investigative Eco-Fiction." This chapter draws upon my experience applying what I've gleaned in the field to an increasingly popular subgenre that's now urgently calling for more eco-voices to reach more readers because the planet is going down. Chapter 13, "From Wild People to Wilderness," then deconstructs my own self-designed education in investigating monsters in our midst. That chapter examines how I developed a personal aesthetic through decades of research in art history and world lit. In a sense, this approach to investigative creative writing pedagogy and practice completes the triumvirate of the primary creative writing genres (poetry, fiction, nonfiction) by establishing an investigative nonfiction component to ride alongside my versions of investigative poetics and investigative eco-fiction. More importantly, Chapter 13 provides an example for students of how to discover meaningful direction through investigative processes that have the power to influence social consciousness.

The last section, "Part 5: Experiential Exercises," culminates with a series of observations on investigative exercises that have inspired hundreds of students to dive into their own writing and have a blast experiencing their own discoveries. Chapter 14, "Seven Investigative Group Exercises," recounts some of the most successful experiments I've tried in the classroom. Examples of student work are provided to show the results. Specific assignments are included in this chapter, as in Chapter 15, "Four Investigative Exercises for Individual Discovery," which is geared toward generating revelations through practices that foster creative interaction. That chapter incorporates examples by students as well as discussions of innovative approaches practiced by other teachers. And finally, Chapter 16, "Six Investigative Homework Exercises for Encouraging Literary Citizenship," wraps up this treatise by examining how creative investigations that lead to writing discoveries can make a powerful difference for individuals as well as communities.

When Learning Becomes *Something Else*

As noted earlier, this book offers prototypes of investigative creative writing pedagogy for teachers to tweak according to their needs. Still, this text isn't meant only for teachers and students; if anything, these meditations on investigative teaching techniques aspire to do what the root of the word "investigative" blatantly suggests: to *invest*.

But invest in what?

In communicating what matters the most for the sake of preserving what matters the most. In other words, investigative creative writing offers writers an effective way to invest in themselves for what's needed to progressively evolve as a species.

But how?

By offering an accessible, provocative pedagogy that breaks into new grounds, excites imaginations, and provides for the illusion of play when serious work is being done. When learning becomes an adventure, it has an advantage over conventional methods in hooking students and leaving them hungering for more. Also, when learning becomes *something else*, the interactive process becomes a transformative experience for teachers as well as students. That's why I highly value group activities that create solid bonds in the pursuit of mutual goals, which is why I've made a study of how to pump up the play in order to engage students in the learning process – because learning always works better when it's fun.

From being a student myself in four creative writing programs, I instinctually knew this when I began teaching: That to be as effective as I can, to impart as much knowledge as I can, and to inspire students to take off on their own self-propelled investigations, my courses needed to be *amusing*. That is, they should provoke the muse through unusual experiences which open new doors and invite discovery.

Hence, *Investigative Creative Writing* – which comes directly from investigating my own writing experience – is my discovery on how to turn learning into a series of transformative events that elevate writing processes into *something else*. And since investigative creative writing pedagogy is equipped to provide the power needed to make use of our collective, ever-evolving, discovery-seeking DNA in the most progressive way possible, and since power is a terrible thing to waste, let's get cracking now!

Notes

1   There is some confusion about this quote, which Burroughs originally attributed to Betty Bouthoul. According to Jeff Taylor's article "Notes on the Origin of the Phrase 'Nothing Is True, Everything Is Permitted'" (Taylor, 2017), this was the title of the thirteenth chapter of Bouthoul's book *Master of the Assassins* (Bouthoul, 1936), even though the book was never published in English.

2   Voltaire wrote "grande responsabilité est la suite inséparable d'un grand pouvoir" (Voltaire, 1793), which I have translated from the French as "great responsibility always follows great power." Other versions of this popular quotation have been attributed to Winston Churchill, Theodore Roosevelt, and Franklin D. Roosevelt.

References

Bazerman, Charles (2015) Creating identities in an intertextual world. In Alice Chik, Tracey Costley, and Martha C. Pennington (eds.) *Creativity and Discovery in the University Writing Class: A Teacher's Guide* 45–60. Sheffield, UK: Equinox Publishing Ltd.

Bouthoul, Betty (1936) *Le Grand Maître des Assassins*. Paris: Armand Colin.

Burroughs, William S., Gysin, Brion, Corso, Gregory and Beiles, Sinclair (1960) *Minutes to Go*. Paris: Two Cities Editions.

Chik, Alice, Costley, Tracey, and Pennington, Martha C. (eds.) *Creativity and Discovery in the University Writing Class: A Teacher's Guide*. Sheffield, UK: Equinox Publishing Ltd.

D'Agata, John and Tall, Deborah (1997) New terrain: The lyric essay. *The Seneca Review* 27(2) (Fall 1997): 7–8.

Jagger, Mick and Richards, Keith (1969) You can't always get what you want. *Let It Bleed*. London: Decca Records.

Lee, Stan (1962) *Amazing Fantasy* 15 (August 1962): 1–11.

Lim, Shirley Goek-lin (2015) Highways and sinkholes: Incorporating creativity strategies in the writing classroom. In Alice Chik, Tracey Costley, and Martha C. Pennington (eds.) *Creativity and Discovery in the University Writing Class: A Teacher's Guide* 251–276. Sheffield, UK: Equinox Publishing Ltd.

Kerouac, Jack (1957) *On the Road*. New York: Viking.

Pennington, Martha C. (2015) Editor's preface. In Alice Chik, Tracey Costley, and Martha C. Pennington (eds.) *Creativity and Discovery in the University Writing Class: A Teacher's Guide* ix–x. Sheffield, UK: Equinox Publishing Ltd.

Sanders, Ed (1976) *Investigative Poetry*. San Francisco: City Lights.

Taylor, Jeff (2017) Notes on the origin of the phrase "Nothing is true, everything is permitted." Retrieved on 28 April 2017 from https://my.vanderbilt.edu/jefftaylor/publications/origins

Voltaire (1793) *Collection Général des Décrets Rendus par la Convention Nationale* 72. Paris: Chez Baudouin.

Whitman, Walt (2004) Song of myself. *The Complete Poems*. New York: Penguin.

Part 1

Discovery-Oriented Basics

Chapter 1

Teaching Students to Show Not Tell

As described in the Introduction, investigative creative writing provides access to power. Whether such power is realized in an economic boost to the next socio-economic level, or whether it helps people realize there's lead in the water and solutions are available, strong writing depends on strong details to paint a strong picture. Therefore, a writer who wants to hold people's attention needs to paint a landscape which stimulates the imagination. The best way to do this is through injecting descriptions which provoke vivid visions or associations that resonate.

In his epic poem "A Season in Hell," the surly French poet Arthur Rimbaud proposes that the Devil likes writing which lacks "descriptive" qualities. Rimbaud then makes a stand in favor of descriptive writing by offering "these hideous pages from [his] notes of the damned" (Rimbaud, 2002: 67).

I wouldn't go so far as to say that non-descriptive writing is evil in any (religious or nonreligious) sense, but I agree that writing which fails to generate strong images or provoke significant feelings provides little incentive to be considered literary. Nevertheless, I've just indicted myself for the exact crime Rimbaud railed against. "Strong" and "significant" are examples of words that I have spent the past seventeen years advising college students to avoid.

When I encounter a vague word like "cool" or "good" or "bad" or "small" or "beautiful" in a student's creative work, I circle that word and ask how the writer can "show not tell" the details. After all, what's cool for one person is often not cool for another, and when something is qualified so ambiguously, it frequently means nothing.

So I ask students to rethink how the details can be shown. I explain that identifying words which fail the "show not tell" (SNT) test is an exercise in unlearning; that I'm challenging them to reimagine what they're aiming to articulate; and I'm trying to get them to take their descriptions to the next level in order to provide unique, colorful, action-packed images that provoke the imagination – a concept in which the role of the image is key.

Writing teachers from all disciplines and at all levels have been struggling with the issue of show not tell for centuries. I can't comment on how my colleagues encourage students to cast this demon out, but I can definitely remark on my own approach in introductory creative writing courses. For the first half of the semester, I put my students through a drill in which they write "portraits" of people, places, and things. I tell them that what I'm looking for are physical details, and I'm not interested in anything else. I don't care what their subject matter is, and I don't want any clever summaries to put anything in perspective for the reader. I just want pure description in 150 words. Then, after they hand in their portraits, I come along with my pen, circling words that "tell not show" like a tough-love tyrant.

Or a coach, because I'm getting them in shape. I tell them they're in training for their midterm – at which time we meet at the campus art gallery and each student picks a piece of art to write about in the form of a 100-word portrait. The grading is simple: An essay with no SNT violations equals an A+; one circled word equals an A; two is an A-; and so on. Showing not telling, I inform them, is a scientific measure of creativity that incorporates a critical and rigorous component. If they can weed out adjectives like "ugly" and replace them with phrases like "toothless, pus-covered, and puke-inducing," then they're on the right track (see Figure 1).

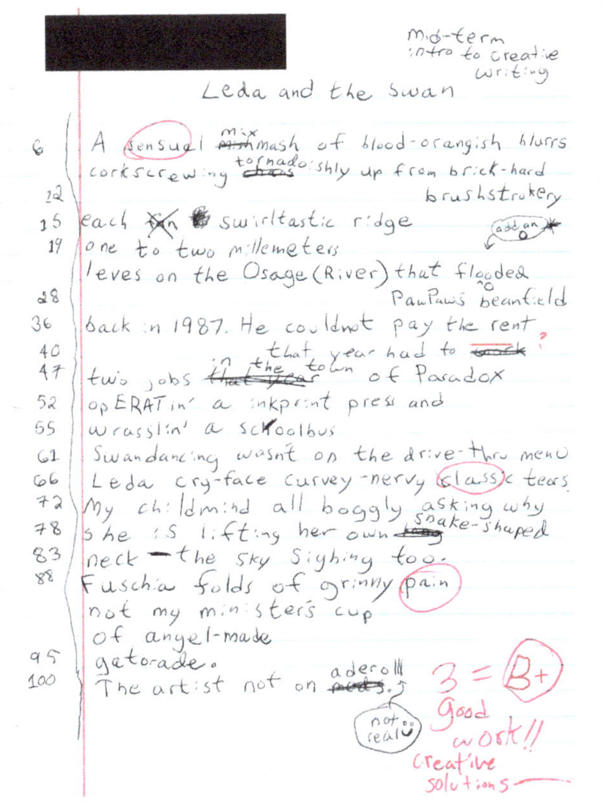

Figure 1. Example of SNT Midterm Grading.

During the first few weeks of the semester, I provide advice on how to avoid the tyranny of my red pen. Using the example of a student who describes a party as "the bomb," I explain why that phrase falls short. (Why is it the bomb? Don't tell me it's the bomb, show me it's the bomb.) I then ask students to brainstorm the details of what such a party involves by relying on the five senses. We discuss the subject in terms of sight, sound, taste, smell, and touch, and then I propose metaphors and similes as another technique in making writing more detailed. Then we move on to what I refer to as "wordular" inventions, which can add texture to text – because *creatifying creatures of contextio* is a quickish way to *frankenforge emotio-experience*.

But mostly I concentrate on encouraging students to expand with description rather than replace one vague word with another, which is what our instincts are programmed to do. In that sense, I take the Beat mantra of "First thought, best thought"[1] (Ginsberg, 1994: 17) to task by advocating the sixth or seventh thought.

Take, for example, the Hemingwayesque sentence "It was a good fish." Now let's expand that with detail: It was a healthy fish. It was a thrashing bass. It was a hull-slapping smallmouth bass. It was a hull-slapping, whoop-inspiring, Ozark smallmouth heading for my frying pan. It was a hull-slapping, "Yahoo!"-producing, green-gold-striped smallmouth from the Buffalo River whose filets would soon be dredged in a mixture of cornmeal, flour, and lemon pepper, and then fried on the calico shore. And so on.

The idea is for students to flesh out the details to the point that readers encounter a specific image, one which means something beyond a "good fish." Essentially, the more we see, the more we feel. That's what Rimbaud was talking about: employing details to conjure visions which trigger associations in the subconscious.

Rimbaud's theories on the "alchemy of the word," however, weren't intended to advance the dominant nineteenth-century literary trend now considered realism; he was aiming to create a much more visceral effect. This is the visionary poet who wrote "Voyelles" (Rimbaud, 1952: 89), a poem in which different vowels are ascribed different colors with different sensory qualities, a theory of synesthesia dating back to Greek antiquity then popularized in music study with input from Newton and Goethe. Rimbaud's vision of using physical details to create effects that play upon the senses later became a major objective of the symbolist movement, which eventually evolved into surrealism and became central to the postmodern aesthetic.

But for my intro students, I keep it simple. We work on physical details, then shift gears into writing poetry, and fiction after that. This progression provides for a background in description that prepares developing writers for more sophisticated explorations if they choose to move on to upper-level creative writing courses.

I also tell my students this method will help them on their college papers and in their careers, adding that if they don't believe my approach is worthwhile, then they can always reject it in the end. But once we're halfway through the semester, there's really no way they can look at their own writing without considering the hands-on process I've been putting them through.

The scrutiny of details carries through to their final portfolios, which tell it all: They hand in two versions of six pieces (one short story and five poems) in a standard cardboard folder. One pocket is labeled "originals" and contains texts full of words I circled, and the other pocket is labeled "revisions." In their final products, I see detailed descriptions, wordular inventions, and similes and metaphors. In short, I see their mental sweat. But most of all, I see students thinking critically about what they're composing – which is what the exercise is all about.

And the next one too, as described in Chapter 2, but in a way that makes the leap from embracing descriptive qualities to creating a strategic effect.

Note

1   The now common idiom "First thought, best thought" was originally proposed by William Blake, then ascribed to Jack Kerouac and eventually popularized by Allen Ginsberg.

References

Ginsberg, Allen (1994) Mind writing slogans. *The Poetry Ireland Review* 43/44 (Autumn–Winter): 17–20.

Rimbaud, Arthur (1952) Voyelles. *Œuvres de Arthur Rimbaud*. Paris: Mercure de France.

Rimbaud, Arthur (2002) Excerpts from *A Season in Hell*. In Mark Spitzer (trans.) *From Absinthe to Abyssinia: Selected Miscellaneous, Obscure, and Previously Untranslated Works of Jean-Nicolas-Arthur Rimbaud* 66–69. Berkeley: Creative Arts Book Company.

Chapter 2

The New Weird: What Happens to Creative Writing When the Truth Is Stranger Than Fiction

In the Introduction, I wrote that the creative writing process I envision actively investigates as it explores and communicates. The keyword here is the last one in the prior sentence: *communicates*. If a writer can understand an audience, and if a writer can speak to what that audience wants, then that writer can supply a demand. In other words, it pays to give audiences what they want – which is something unpredictable that pays off in an intriguing way.

Inspired by Edgar Allan Poe's concept of "the single effect" (Poe, 1983), which essentially means leaving readers with a single dominant feeling in the end (i.e., dread), I came up with my own version of a literary technique designed to hook readers. As I tell my students, there needs to be an element of the unusual in order for plots to interest readers. This usually happens through combining an ordinary character with an unusual situation or combining an unusual character with an ordinary situation. Better yet, I figured, why not double that effect by coming up with an unusual character in an unusual situation in order to create "the double effect?" This would "make it new," as Ezra Pound suggested (Pound, 1935)[1] – or at least the details would be unusual enough to make the result seem unique.

I've been hammering my Introduction to Creative Writing students with the theory of the double effect for over a decade and a half, and the more I do it, the more merit I find to this approach. So after laying this theory down, I tell my students that unusual characters have unusual names, so now we're going to invent a character with a memorable name. I tell them that since realism is old hat in this postmodern era, names like Mark and Mary just can't cut it anymore. I explain that readers want colorful characters with colorful names, and then I ask them to come up with some unusual possibilities for first names. For example, what did you have for breakfast?

I make a list of ten words on the board from names they volunteer, such as Waffle, Eggs, and Cheerios. "Okay," I say, "now let's make a list of ten possible last names." The possible names come in: Mountain Dew, Ornithology, Obamacare, Snooki, etc. Then we create ten combinations, like Waffle Mountain Dew or Eggs Ornithology, and eventually the students vote on the combination they like best (I like to give them two votes each, which usually makes ties less likely).

Figure 2. Mark Spitzer Teaching Unusual Characters Have Unusual Names. Photo by Scotty Lewis.

After the character's name is established, we think of ten unusual occupations, and if someone suggests something that's not so unusual (like a pimp), I ask them what can be added to make the job a bit stranger (like a pimp who is half-iguana). They vote on that, and then each student starts with the same unusual character in the same unusual setting, but then they all set out in different directions through an in-class assignment based on prompts. I tell them to take ten minutes to write a paragraph in which the character is considering a problem at the workplace. In the next class, I provide some class time for them to add another paragraph in which somebody from the character's past enters the story and complicates the problem. In the following class, I ask them to add some dialogue in which these characters plan how to tackle that problem. In the end, students are told to make those characters set out to enact their plan, but something goes awry.

This process takes students and their characters on a highly unpredictable and often absurd adventure, and they always end up with stories they never expected to write. Not only that, but because of the general unfamiliarity of the scenarios students create through practicing the double effect, most of them are rewarded with the creation of some weirdly intriguing flash fictions which are of interest to others.

Skeptics might wonder what's so great about the unusual. The point could be made that postmodernism has been playing with reader expectations for more than half a century, so shouldn't we try to do something a bit more novel than making up ridiculous stuff?

Tom Wolfe posited similar questions in his *Harper's Magazine* essay "Stalking the Billion-Footed Beast" (Wolfe, 1989), which the magazine billed as "a literary manifesto for the new social novel." I've taught this piece to graduate students as well as undergraduates in both fiction and nonfiction classes with mixed results. Wolfe's personal search for the cosmopolitan New York novel is of no interest to the current techno-video-texting generation, but students do relate to what I see as the meat of the matter. Wolfe (1989: 48), paraphrasing Philip Roth, states, "We now live in an age … in which the imagination of the novelist lies helpless before what he knows he will read in tomorrow morning's newspaper." Wolfe's and Roth's point is that the real world is so whacked out these days that fiction writers have to compete against journalists. In fact, Wolfe even wrote, "Unless some movement occurs in American fiction over the next ten years that is more remarkable than any detectable right now, the pioneering in nonfiction will be recorded as the most important experiment in American literature in the second half of the 20th century" (Wolfe, 1989: 56).

Whether or not such a movement has occurred is debatable. But what's not debatable is the fact that in the twenty-first century, creative nonfiction has become the most popular and most marketable literary genre there is. A New York agent recently told me that fiction is "the new poetry." Meanwhile, the term "autobiographical novel" has gone out of style, and "memoir" has become the fashion. Fiction has taken a backseat to nonfiction, due in part to the trend Wolfe saw evolving.

When it comes to what we're willing to accept in literature, the events of September 11, 2001, had a major effect on the communal consciousness of the United States. This is one fantastic story: at the dawn of a new century, a bunch of jihadist thugs highjack some jets; crash them into the Pentagon and two biblical towers representing world commerce; disaster happens; the economy crashes; anthrax follows; armies are snuck into a war that has nothing to do with the terrorists who attacked; an ambassador's hot wife is outed as a spy; Osama bin Laden goes on the lam; and the world is embroiled in a new millennial turmoil.

That story, of course, is more real than Americans ever wanted it to be, and the result is that all stories must now compete for sensationalist elements which readers know are just as realistic as a major American city being flooded (Heckuva job, Brownie!) This story also happened at a time in world history when habits of readers were changing due to advances in technology. This is no longer a planet where ordinary peasants visiting elderly relatives with tuberculosis can be endured for 900 Dostoevskian pages.

This is a world of action, explosions, conspiracy, war, porn, plastic surgery, rovers on Mars, and Olympic champs smoking bongs on YouTube because anything less is just plain boring.

Take our favorite Propofol-poisoned pop star as another example. Michael Jackson owned the publishing rights to the Beatles, tried to buy the remains of the Elephant Man, got hitched to Elvis' daughter, metamorphosed from ebony to ivory, dangled his child named Blanket out a window; and (here's the ultimate irony), after two serious allegations of child molestation, he died with the dream of building a children's hospital.

Because of stories like this, and hundreds of others we read and hear and see in the news and on the Internet every day, the extraordinary has become status quo. Just look at "News of the Weird" on a random day, January 1, 2012 (Shepherd, 2012): A man was arrested in Lexington, North Carolina, for trying to buy $475.78 worth of electronics at Walmart with a counterfeit million-dollar bill; he expected $999,524.22 in change. A drug dealer named Joseph Romano was busted for having his two-year-old son with him during an illegal transaction in Pennsylvania, and a rapist named Edward Chatman Jr. was booked for bringing his six-month-old baby with him when he climbed through a woman's window in Tennessee. Both of these events happened on Take Your Kid to Work Day. Meanwhile in Ontario, Canada, Doreen Wallace fell in the lobby of a hospital and broke her hip 150 feet from the emergency room. Following protocol, hospital workers called an ambulance, made her wait for an excruciating half-hour, then transported her to the front door.

Granted, there's not much unusual about these characters, but their situations are definitely out of the ordinary, which makes for an effect when reading these stories. That effect is a mixture of the tangible and the improbable; it's what makes us laugh or shake our heads or send links to friends or repeat stories to someone. It's what makes us say "stranger than fiction." It's what stimulates the imagination because of what it is: the unreal within the real. Or to put it in more literary terms: these elements of fiction in nonfiction make our lives more entertaining.

Just look at the *New York Times* best-seller list on January 3, 2012. In *The Girl with the Dragon Tattoo,* Stieg Larsson juxtaposes the odd couple of a pierced, Goth-hacker motorcyclist and a disgraced financial journalist investigating the death of an heiress in a sexual stew of violence and corporate malfeasance (Larsson, 2008). In Walter Isaacson's *Steve Jobs,* an acid-head Buddhist drops out but tunes in to the point that he affects twenty-first-century life for almost everybody on the planet with revolutionary innovations in personal computers, animated movies, music, phones, tablet computing, and digital publishing (Isaacson, 2011).

Of course, one of those books is fiction and the other is nonfiction, but that doesn't matter. What matters is that narratives like these incorporate unusual characters in unusual situations, so they're able to compete with the news. And in some cases, they *become* the news. In both of those books, and in thousands more, the authors recognized that the bizarreness of real life is not just something to compete against – it's also something to incorporate and reflect in a surreal reality which is no crazier now than it ever was.

What makes these times *seem* a bit crazier, though, is that writers are now combining the unusual with the unusual more than ever before because of a demand for a supply of the unusual, of which there is no shortage. But here's the twist: if that demand continues, the usual (meaning mainstream realism) will soon become extremely rare, so therefore extremely weird.

Beyond meeting the demand for the unusual, there are technical concerns, as the next chapter stresses, that can provide a writer the edge needed to send a submission up the ladder. Because no matter how unpredictable your plotline is, or how unusual and gripping your details are, if your presentation isn't as professional as possible with the technical details, then you're not taking advantage of an extremely vital component to boosting your writing power. And this – this isn't something to miss out on, especially if you are serious about affecting progressive change.

Note

1   Although the phrase "make it new" is attributed to Pound, and although he did name a collection of essays after that concept, the title of the book *Make It New* is deceiving. Pound actually recycled the idea, which he discovered in translating the twelfth-century neo-Confucian scholar Chu His (North, 2013).

References

Isaacson, Walter (2011) *Steve Jobs*. New York: Simon & Schuster.

Larsson, Stieg (2008) *The Girl with the Dragon Tattoo*. New York: Alfred A. Knopf.

North, Michael (2013) The making of "make it new." *Guernica* (August 15, 2013) https://www.guernicamag.com/the-making-of-making-it-new

Poe, Edgar Allen (1983) On the importance of the single effect in a prose tale. In Ann Charters (ed.) *The Story and Its Writer: An Introduction to Short Fiction* 1123–1124. New York: St. Martin's Press.

Pound, Ezra (1934) *Make It New: Essays*. London: Faber and Faber Ltd.

Shepherd, Chuck (2012) *News of the Weird* (January 1, 2012). Retrieved on 1 April 2017 from www.newsoftheweird.com/archive/nw120101.html

Wolfe, Tom (1989) Stalking the billion-footed beast. *Harper's Magazine* (November 1989): 45–56.

Chapter 3

The Ten Commandments of Incorporating Dialogue: For Those Seeking to Inform the Unprepared, the Disengaged, and the Thoroughly Confused

As I noted earlier, teachers can invent ways for students to discover their own power, and one of these powers is the power to communicate. As everyone knows, the best way to communicate is to have a conversation. And the best way for a writer to converse is to do it effectively, meaning with the correct punctuation and with an awareness of the dynamics of effective usage. So if a writer wants to communicate as effectively as possible, dialogue can be employed as a secret weapon to engage an audience. And the more natural that dialogue seems, and the more adept it is in not calling attention to technical details which distract, the more compelling the overall piece will be in satisfying its own agenda.

Recently, I took a look at a problem I've been having for years. Semester after semester, when I lecture my introductory creative writing students on the subject of employing dialogue in fiction, I've felt like the information I was relaying just wasn't sinking in. Perhaps part of the problem was that I was addressing too much in one class session by talking about the technical aspects of dialogue along with providing advice for its effective use, so it came in a rush that overloaded the students' circuit boards. Or maybe it was because I came late to an understanding of the mechanics of dialogue and was having trouble translating what I now know instinctively into a do-it-yourself format. Whatever the case, I figured that in this age of how-to lists and talking points it would be worthwhile to organize my ideas into a convenient top-ten list that clearly articulates how adding voices to fiction (or any genre of writing, really) can make narratives more diverse.

When a writer inserts dialogue into a piece of writing, the writer is injecting voices other than the narrator's, which breaks the story up and makes it more multi-dimensional via a variety of perspectives. This is why TV shows often include multiple characters with multiple plot lines in a single episode. This switching back and forth is sometimes necessary to hold viewers' ADHD-attention spans because the more action there is, the easier it is to keep an audience from drifting off. Same thing with fiction, which is why dialogue is an important tool to master.

The TV writers understand this, but the millennial college sophomore texting under the desk hasn't gotten the message yet. The messenger, of course, is the writing instructor, who may or may not understand what the TV writers have tapped into: the knowledge that to keep an audience from zoning out you need to offer a stew of voices made up from ingredients which synergize organically. Otherwise, you might as well just offer a menu with one item on it, like a baked potato. Because that's what narrative-driven fiction has become. One voice. One potato. So for that potato to be an experience worth having, it better be one hell of a spud.

Now that that's been established, let's start with the commandment which gives most people the most grief.

1. Periods End Things. Period

When I wrote earlier that I came late to an understanding of the mechanics of dialogue, what I meant is it took me thirty-something years to get a handle on where to put punctuation when dealing with quotation marks and dialogue tags (i.e. he said, she said). Why? Because I was so busy trying to express myself that it didn't matter where a comma or period went, which is why I can't fault students for making the same minor mistakes I used to make. Still, presentation matters, and since part of what creative writing programs are selling these days are students who can market themselves, it literally pays to demonstrate that one's self-editing skills can be applied to the work of others.

Here's the deal: In American English, the punctuation goes inside the quotation marks ninety-nine percent of the time. That's a given. What's less of a given, however, is what type of punctuation to use. But first, and as a general rule, you want to get that dialogue tag somewhere at the beginning of what a character says so that readers don't have to read through an entire chunk of discourse to know who said it. For most students, the problem arises when the dialogue tag is plopped somewhere in the middle or at the end of something somebody says, and if this is the case, here's what to do: if a character expresses something in its entirety, and the dialogue tag comes after that, then the quote should end with a comma and the final punctuation (periods or question or explanation marks) for everything should be placed after the dialogue tag. For example: "Hey man, I like ice cream," he said.

On the other hand, if a dialogue tag occurs before a sentence is completed, such that there is speech on both sides of the dialogue tag, then commas should surround the dialogue tag and the period should go where it always goes – as in "Hey man," he said, "I like ice cream."

This might seem like a no-brainer to some, but having spent seventeen years explaining this, I can attest that there's a semi-dyslexic function in most college students which causes critical thinking to start shutting down at this point. That's why I've always stated that if you are still confused with where to put the period or final punctuation in a character's speech, then the answer is to challenge yourself while reading books by paying close attention to how dialogue tags and punctuation are used together.

Wrong-O! For whatever reason, this self-supervisory approach has never worked. That's why I now have an in-class assignment (see Assignment 1 at the end of this chapter) in which I take students directly to the university library and tell them to collect six usages of dialogue tags from six different books published by American presses (to insure that the punctuation stays inside the quotation marks), which they hand-copy and turn in for credit. By actively placing dialogue tags, punctuation, and quotation marks onto paper, students begin the process of ingraining where that stuff is supposed to go. And to make sure that students take notice of how these components work together, they're charged with identifying dialogue tags with rectangles, drawing triangles around all commas, and drawing circles around all punctuation which terminates an instance of speech or a dialogue tag with or without any accompanying narration. After that, students are ready to supply three usages of dialogue tags of their own creation: one starting with a dialogue tag, one with a dialogue tag in the middle of a quote, and one with a dialogue tag following dialogue. Paying close attention to these details prepares students for placing punctuation in the right spot in their own fiction, and more times than not, what they discover stays with them.

2. Give Clowns Their Own Vehicles for Speech

Things get claustrophobic when two or more clowns are crammed into a single clown car. Same thing with two or more characters speaking in a paragraph. It just works better and it just looks better to not have all those quotation marks smooshed into the same space. Also, readers need some breathing room between speakers so that they can digest what's being said. So after you make somebody speak, hit the "Enter" button, drop down to the next line and keep on trucking. That way, dialogue won't run together chaotically and end up looking like this:

"See what I mean about complicating and confusing?" she asked. "Yes," he replied, tying his oversized clown shoes. "I totally see what you're talking about." "As do I," the editor chimed in. "Besides, it will up your chances of becoming a published writer if you can show you know how to play the game."

3. Divorce Dialogue and Narration

These two things should never be wed. The narrator has his or her own voice, and the characters have their own voices, so keep those voices separate so they don't interbreed. In other words, watch out for paragraphs that include both narration and dialogue because if you combine more than a single sentence of narration with dialogue, then you run the risk of one voice distracting readers from another. For example, notice how the narration in the following paragraph draws you away from what the character is saying and works to make you forget what was being discussed:

"That's really neat," she said. "I like ice cream too." She picked up her spoon, and then they both heard the sirens. The kid came running out of the alley. He was being chased by the dog. As the sirens got louder, it became clear why. The kid had just robbed the Dollar Store. Luckily, though, the dog was making sure that justice would prevail. "But," she added, "I don't like frozen yogurt."

To avoid such conflicts, just take the narration out of the paragraph and reorganize it either before or after the dialogue. With each voice having its own space (with paragraph breaks before and after), readers will be able to focus on the narration in its expected place and dialogue in its expected place and the story as a whole will flow in a much more user-friendly way.

4. He Said / She Said Has Gone to the Cows

Any tense of "said" in a dialogue tag can get old, so avoid that staccato repetition by mixing it up and utilizing other verbs, such as "he stated," "she screamed," "the clerk noted," "Bob remarked," "Beyoncé whispered in my ear." Because who wants to eat a bowl of bland rice with nothing on it for every meal? Or who wants to hear the same old song over and over again? In essence, "said" has become an overused, empty word which doesn't give us anything except the fact that when it's used sparingly it doesn't stick out.

Still, it's not so much about keeping yourself from hitting the same dull note again and again and again as it is about the variety of flora and fauna you can color your landscape with. You can have gazelles and penguins and coconut trees, or you can have a boring herd of indifferent cows who have nothing new to moo about so they keep on repeating the same dumb sound.

5. Dialogue Tags Are Your Underwear Friends

One of the greatest mysteries of the twenty-first century is why college students resist using dialogue tags. Numerous inquiries have failed to answer the question of what's at the core of this problem, but experts suspect that it has something to do with feeling intimidated by those pesky punctuation regulations which micromanage prose. Consequently, this phobia of dialogue tags has led to beaucoup students going commando, in a sense. That is, by not even trying to install such visible underwear in their prose, students risk exposing themselves for the technical skills they lack. When this happens, the result is that it's hard to tell who's speaking, so the writing comes off as not as strong as it could be.

The trick, therefore, is to step up to the task rather than letting something that you haven't even written yet bully you around. That's what needs to be stressed, along with the fact that dialogue tags can help a brother out. Or a sister. They're just simple things that ground readers and provide logistics. Dialogue tags are like underwear in that they lend support and cover our butts by making it clear who said what. So why not take advantage of their underlying purpose, which is to serve us?

But when doing so, consider what I call "piehole verbs" to make it clear who's speaking. These are verbs directly related to a character's mouth, like "yelled" or "told" or "snarled" instead of verbs that don't clearly show a character speaking – which is a common affliction often seen in fledgling fiction. For example:

Dialogue Tags Which Fail to Fully Communicate That Characters Are Communicating

"Let's go get a beer," Dwayne walked across the room.
Helen shot the bird, "Take that, stupid bird!"
"Would you like some fries with that," the cashier brought the order out, "or a life?"

Examples of Piehole-Verb Dialogue Tags That Clearly Show Characters Speaking

"Let's go get a beer," Dwayne sighed, walking across the room.
Helen shot the bird and spat, "Take that, stupid bird!"
"Would you like some fries with that," the cashier sneered, bringing the order out, "or a life?"

Of course, dialogue tags don't always need to be used, especially when two characters are volleying discourse back and forth. If the volley continues for more than three or four rounds, it's advisable to install a dialogue tag every once in a while as a friendly reminder of who's speaking.

6. Use Dialogue Tags to Pump Up the Sexy

Earlier, I encouraged divorcing dialogue from narration. That's not to say that they can't fool around a bit. In fact, they should – but only a little. Because let's face it, if there are lots of dialogue tags on a page echoing each other (i.e. "he said, he said, he said…"), they call attention to themselves. The danger in this is that readers might think the narrator is lazy, or unimaginative, or unaware, which isn't so good for connecting with readers.

More importantly, action is a strategic tool for engaging readers, which is why it's powerful – sexy even. And dialogue tags, they provide the opportunity to subtly insert more movement into fiction. So when you're plugging in a dialogue tag, throw in a gesture or a facial expression to provide another level of insight into what characters are processing. Or actually have them move locations physically – like driving in a car or swimming across a lake – to help propel the story into the next setting. Otherwise, it'll seem like the characters are just sitting there not doing anything, even if the writer believes they're obviously doing something. Besides, characters who just talk to each other without doing jack – well, that's about as dull as dull can get.

And as a general rule, keep dialogue tags simple so they don't complicate the paragraph and draw away from what's being said. Quick and dirty one-line dialogue tags are also recommended for momentum. For instance:

> "I like ice cream," he said, opening the freezer. "Hey, who ate all the ice cream?"

And embrace verbs, especially gerunds – despite that old school English teacher who once told you to avoid slapping an "-ing" on the end of a verb. Gerund paranoia holds no logic. Someone who can't stand action made up that bunk to keep promising writers from meeting their full potential. The Grammar Police then hopped on that blandwagon to enforce the edict. Yep, "blandwagon," with an "l" in it: a relatively motionless vehicle designed to keep fiction from carrying readers effectively. Because those who drive blandwagons want the rest of the world to drive just as mild-manneredly as they do.

7. Why Say "Yes" or "No" When You Can Say "Wang Dang Doodle?"

The question above is actually the question that's the test of all writing, but in order to keep things focused, let's get specific. When a character answers with a simple "yes" or "no," that's just lame – which is good if you want your character to come off as having this quality. But if you don't, then make the response more colorful. Does the Pope wear a pointy hat? Does a bear evacuate the contents of his large intestines in the wooded area? Hells No! Fer shnizzle!

See what I mean? It's called injecting attitude, or at least something that's not so commonplace so as to spawn yawns from here to Timbuktu. In the same way actual life is now way stranger than fiction (just look at this abnormal American presidency), dialogue, like fiction, must now compete with the reality that reality TV now prescribes what normal is. Consequently, fiction must provoke people's interest more than the network news if anyone's going to sit down and read it, which is why realism kicked the bucket. But dialogue, to grab the attention of an editor and even your average reader, not only has to compete with the reality of absurdity as well as a rampant twenty-four-hour news cycle, it has to beat out the phenomena of NetFlix, YouTube, social media, satellite, cable TV, Internet porn, and all the other steroid-driven bells and whistles of the digital day. So if you want what your characters say to be appreciated, it better have something *unusual* enough about it to make it a contender among all those other competitors for audience attention. If your words are not unusual in any sense, then you might as well just write "blah blah blah blah" because that's the translation anyone with any influence is going to give Wang-Dang-Doodleless dialogue in this over-hyped, over-sexed, off-the-chain reality show we've all become players in.

8. Dumb Dialogue Is Fun Dialogue

Remember the cheeseburger-in-France conversation from *Pulp Fiction* (Tarantino, 1994)? When Samuel Jackson and John Travolta discussed the McName of a ground-up bovine sandwich? That was really dumb.

But what wasn't dumb was that Quentin Tarantino used dumb dialogue for character development, and it worked by entertaining millions of viewers. It was also a moment that set the tone for the movie's quirky sense of humor. It was a moment that said, "Hey, here's some familiar pop-cult blather that's not too different from the stuff people really say to each other." And that, in turn, made a mass audience feel comfortable enough to laugh at the banality.

Since half the time you're writing a story and you don't know where it's going anyway, why not throw in some dumb dialogue to help find your way? Dumb dialogue can definitely function as a ludicrous, nonthreatening experiment to discover what your characters' views and values are. And so what if you waste time? That's how writing gets realized: by putting in hours and hours, and failing and failing, and revising and revising until you get it right. And if dumb dialogue helps you find what makes your characters tick, then you can always replace the stupid stuff with less stupid stuff later.

But here's the biggest secret regarding dumb dialogue. If readers connect with it, they'll think you did it for a reason, and that this premeditation indicates a sophisticated talent for playing with language at the deepest levels of perception. And that tendency, my friends, to give the writer credit, is something to milk.

9. Make Characters Talk Like Us But Don't Make Characters Talk Like Us

Paradoxes are good for us. They remind us that there are always exceptions to the rules. Rules like "Do not use contractions," which is another myth spread by bitter English teachers from a gone generation, were established to keep a sense of formality intact in the Queen's English. These days, though, there ain't no Queen's English – especially in the dialogue of American fiction, which has been evolving for centuries into a much more casual, less self-conscious tongue.

American dialogue, therefore, should reflect how Americans speak. Words like "don't" and "can't" and "shouldn't" are now natural usages, so use these forms for the dialogue of real Americans unless you're trying to show someone as being stiff, or severely British, or as an authority figure.

Of course, there are also different accents for different regions, and different vocabulary and idioms that vary according to subcultures, class, ancestry, and social identifications. Consider the verb of *axe* (as in "ask") and the *y'all*isms of the American South that also reflect how people speak. But when it comes to colloquial abbreviations like *'em* and *fishin'* and *bitchin' Camaro*, be careful with apostrophes, which can multiply like rats if allowed to scurry around unchecked. Apostrophe abuse is not only unsightly on the page, but it can sometimes slow an audience down by driving readers to pause to consider if the punctuation is being used correctly.

Meanwhile, go easy on the "umm"s and "uhh"s and "ya knows" of everyday language, unless you're trying to show uncertainty, hesitation, preoccupation, or nervousness. That sort of stuff just makes characters look dumber than the author intended.

And go lightly with repeating things because you don't need to make your point as much on paper as you do in real conversations with real people who don't listen well. I repeat, go lightly with repeating things – which can also create work for editors to delete. In other words, keep it simple and keep it smooth because what most readers want is an easy ride lacking clever speedbumps and excessive road signs to obey.

10. Commandments Are a Dime a Dozen

Any fool can make proclamations. Effective dialogue, however, takes a savvy ear and a shrewd eye, along with an aptitude for combining the creative with the critical. But what dialogue needs most is what all writing needs: risk, grueling failure, and an attention to detail that makes readers want to turn the page. These are things that everyone can master if they practice the above nine "commandments." But even if everyone could get a handle on mastering dialogue, keep in mind that it's still going to be only a small percentage of people whose work gets noticed, and that's the way it will always be. Because even if everyone on the planet could run a three-minute mile, there will always be a select few whose physiology and discipline make them the ones we want to see pull ahead of the pack.

That's not to say that thousands of literate human beings burning with passion and ambition shouldn't bother jumping into this metaphorical marathon – because excelling at dialogue isn't just for writers anymore. In this cyborg era of rapidly expanding media and communication systems, editors, educators, technicians, managers, administrators, journalists, translators, directors, producers, web specialists, software designers, business owners, myriad professionals, and support staff of all kinds are in demand everywhere. And those who develop a technical understanding of the written language of communication will have an advantage over those who don't. Not just in the job market, though. Understanding how we communicate isn't just a skill that's meant to pay off in marketing art. It's the key to finding solutions to problems as vast as world politics and as close to home as getting along with frenemies.

In fact, if we can use dialogue to help us treat our neighbors like we'd like to be treated ourselves, then we'd have less need for common-sense moral directives to honor thy mothers and fathers, or any of those other suggestions for getting along that Moses brought down from the mountain top.

Go figure.

Postscript

While drafting this chapter in the spring of 2017, I developed the assignment shown below. What I found, for the most part, was that it worked well for about half the students. After working in the library, we returned to the classroom where students were allowed time to finish up what they had started and then bring their completed assignments to me. I went through their work quickly with the students standing right beside me, marking any problems for them to go back and fix. This really got students thinking about how to use dialogue tags with punctuation and quotation marks.

By the time the final portfolios rolled in, however, it was clear that some students did not retain the lessons learned a few weeks before. Still, this is to be expected since intro courses in creative writing at my university had just been opened to first-year students, with no writing prerequisites required. I suspect that the demands of more technical courses of study, combined with the crunch of finals week, took priority for students who had gravitated toward majors which place less emphasis on language and communication. Nevertheless, the good news was that nearly fifty percent of those forty test subjects did retain what they had learned about dialogue and dialogue tags, and those students were successful in applying relatively error-free dialogue to their short stories.

Assignment 1.

WRTG 2310: Intro to Creative Writing, Spring Semester 2017 Incorporating Dialogue Library Scavenger Hunt Assignment

April 6, 2017: We meet in the stacks at PS3569.P558 C48 2001.

You are charged with finding six usages of dialogue tags (i.e. he said, she replied, etc.) in American English from six different books published by American presses (who use American English punctuation). The process is simple. Just pull books off the shelf, make sure they are mainly prose, and look at the copyright page.

If the book was published in the United States, then fill in the slots below (note: the first one is an example):

Title_______*Chum*________________________________

Place of Publication______Cambridge, MA____________

Instance of dialogue being used with a dialogue tag <u>"No way!"</u> <u>Yann says in disbelief. "No way in heck."</u>

____

Title____

Place of Publication____________________________

Instance of dialogue being used with a dialogue tag________

____

____

____

____

Title____

Place of Publication____________________________

Instance of dialogue being used with a dialogue tag________

____

____

____

____

Title____

Place of Publication____________________________

Instance of dialogue being used with a dialogue tag________

____

____

____

____

Title____
Place of Publication____
Instance of dialogue being used with a dialogue tag__________

____

____

____

____

Title____
Place of Publication____
Instance of dialogue being used with a dialogue tag__________

____

____

____

____

Title____
Place of Publication____
Instance of dialogue being used with a dialogue tag__________

____

____

____

____

____ Draw rectangles around all the dialogue tags (check off when done).

____ Next, draw circles around all punctuation (like periods, question marks, exclamation marks) that terminates a dialogue tag or the narration it's joined to (check off when done).

____ Then, draw circles around all punctuation (periods, question marks, or exclamation marks <u>inside quotation marks</u>) that terminates dialogue (check off when done).

____ Now draw triangles around all commas (check off when done).

Cool! Now create three instances of dialogue joined with dialogue tags from your own brain, but in three different ways:

1. Start a sentence with a dialogue tag, then supply the dialogue.

____

____

____

____

2. Place a dialogue tag in the middle of some dialogue.

____

____

____

____

3. Start a sentence with dialogue and end with a dialogue tag.

____

____

____

____

When you're finished, bring this assignment to me and I will check it. I might ask you to fix some things or not. When it's perfect, you can go.

Reference

Tarantino, Quentin (1994) *Pulp Fiction*. Los Angeles: Miramax.

Part 2

Investigative Theatrics

Chapter 4

Multiple-Personality Pedagogy: A Hybrid Teaching Tool for Varying Voice in the Classroom

Dialogue can be used on the page just as much as on the stage, and sometimes the classroom can be viewed that way to empower the instructor with "teaching methods which actively engage students so that they're psyched to investigate." That's what I wrote in the Introduction, and that's what I'm reaffirming now.

Teachers sometimes get tired of hearing their own voices. That's why they show movies, bring in guest speakers, and encourage discussion. In addition, teachers want to bring in other views to provide alternative perspectives. Otherwise, they're just recreating themselves in their students. Worse than that, a lack of diverse voices in the classroom can lead to boredom and indifference – so let's have some fun, and maybe even some inspiration.

That was my theory. So I put it to the test by adding a theatrical element to the English courses I taught when I was working at Truman State University. After all, as Pete Rorabaugh and Jesse Stommel note in their article "On Pedagogical Manipulation," "When we enter a classroom, we're stepping onto a stage …. [W]e all play roles: the teacher, the student … the reporter, the questioner, the dictator, the grader, the teacher's pet. It's in the careful modulation of these roles that we can actively control a learning environment" (Rorabaugh and Stommel, 2012).

With that in mind, I donned an old man hat and some Groucho glasses with thick eyebrows, a bulbous nose and an absurd mustache, then affixed a twisted sneer to my face and marched into my sophomore-level American Literature class. The next thing I knew, I was snapping at all those "whippersnappers" and "hooligans" to "zip their lips" and open up *Leaves of Grass* (Whitman, 2004). I told them that Professor Spitzer wasn't here today and that "Crabby Old Man" was substituting. They laughed, of course, and didn't take me seriously. Until, that is, I started ripping into Walt Whitman, attacking his politics, his stance on civil rights, and his "obscene" appreciation of the human body. "So what!?" I asked, scrunching my face like a hater. "Who cares!?"

To my surprise, the students shot back with sophisticated answers. They were playing along, actually defending a 150-year-old text. Not only that, they were into it, sometimes adding comments like "Whitman was espousing equality, something you can't even comprehend because you're too old school to get it, ya geezer!" Or "Whitman loved the 'body electric!' Male, female, whatever – he respected it as a vehicle for the Transcendental spirit, you old coot!"

In other words, those students were totally getting it, and they were totally getting what I was doing. Every time they shot me down, I'd respond with a cranky moan in which I'd lament the insolence of their generation, or how their parents should've paddled them more. The main thing, though, was that they were the ones raising the points. Therefore, they were the teachers. And since they were invested in their studies, they weren't about to let some ancient relic from a less enlightened era undermine their turf.

With a reaction like that, how could I not employ this technique in more college courses? So I did. I made it a point to use Crabby Old Man at least once per semester to rile up the students, who actually had glints in their eyes as they rushed to barrage a grumpy curmudgeon with arguments based on what they'd read. Even students who usually remained silent jumped onto the anti-Crabby-Old-Man bandwagon.

That's when it hit me: I'd struck a nerve. Because young adults are looking for excuses to lash out against outdated schools of thought. In public forums, however, there's usually a risk involved in talking back. But in this setting, the stakes were different. There was nothing to lose, and the constant laughing made things alright.

Then, when I went to the University of Central Arkansas to primarily teach creative writing, I came up with another persona: Big Dummy. His costume was simply crooked plastic teeth, but his shtick was even simpler. Big Dummy just sat there saying "duh" a lot, while asking students to explain stuff he couldn't comprehend – like plot points, character motivations, and use of symbols and metaphors. Big Dummy was also good for getting students to examine technical concerns in prose writing – like use of dialogue tags, which I'm always trying to get my students to embrace to clarify who's speaking. When I lecture in class that dialogue tags are your friends and you shouldn't be afraid to use them, it sometimes feels like I'm talking to a comatose community. But when melodramatically exasperated students explain to Big Dummy how dialogue tags can help ground a reader, then I know my advice is sinking in. And when students add that dialogue tags are best used near the beginning of what a character is saying so that readers immediately know who's talking (which is my advice they repeat), then I know I wasn't just speaking to air.

I've used Big Dummy in all sorts of classes. In fiction workshops, he's questioned how T. C. Boyle's various forms of narration (Boyle, 1995) affect empathy, and in creative nonfiction classes Big Dummy has helped make sense of how Lester Bangs' unconventional use of run-on sentences (Bangs, 2003) creates momentum. Big Dummy has also appeared in my Forms of Poetry class in which approaches to a confessional poem of Diane Wakoski (Wakoski, 1988: 44–48) is analyzed in basic terms that he can understand. The value in breaking things down for Big Dummy being: Students create simple algebraic equations to use as models on how to handle their own creative work. For example, if students can explain how Frank O'Hara's theory of "personism" (O'Hara, 2013) is actually just a bunch of fancy talk for writing a poem that directly addresses someone, then they see the process as easy and accessible – except for people like Big Dummy.

Then there's Cool Dude, who I use in my upper-level Poetry Workshop. I pass out copies of his poem entitled "I Am So Cool," then put a baseball cap on backwards and sport some cool shades. I announce to the class, "Now I'm one of you." They snicker and roll their eyeballs, and then Cool Dude reads his poem out loud. The mock workshop has begun, with the real me jumping in every once in a while by removing and replacing my disguise to guide the conversation. This flashing back and forth can get a bit schizophrenic, but for the most part the students do the talking and keep things level-headed. Meanwhile, Cool Dude gives a thumbs up whenever students compliment his work, and he waves their suggestions away whenever they offer criticism – because Cool Dude is just too cool.

My oldest and most often used personality, though, makes regular appearances in my Introduction to Creative Writing course to introduce the workshop procedure. I tell students how the dean called me into his office the other day and explained that a new student would be joining our class. I also tell them how the dean told me that this student had been kicked around from school to school, and how he's been in trouble with the law, but since his parents are big shots, he couldn't really say no. I then let the students know how I told the dean I'd let this student into our class under one condition: that he pioneer the workshopping phase of the poetry component. I add that after we workshop this student, it will be up to the class as to whether he can stay or not.

The students look around with bewildered expressions plastered on their faces, wondering where this new kid is, and then I explain that he'll be here soon. In the meantime, I hand out copies of his poem entitled "Loving to Love" by Tiger Nooodles. "Tiger Nooodles!" somebody inevitably shouts. "What kind of name is that?"

Then I break out Tiger Nooodles, who is an eight-inch-tall stuffed Grateful Dead tiger that I found on the streets of Baton Rouge following an LSU football game. Inevitably, the groans arise, and we get down to business. Tiger reads his poem aloud (me speaking

Figure 3. Tiger Nooodles and Crabby Old Man. Photo by Lea Graham, reproduced by permission.

in a squeaky voice), and then we do some basic workshopping. The standard method has already been explained, so students know that the poet is supposed to sit there silently and absorb the conversation. We start off with positive feedback, to which Tiger replies with some sort of chatter. That's when I pick him up and smack his head against the table. "I told you not to talk!" I scold him.

Predictably, gasps fill the air, and someone always pipes out, "Is that what you're going to do to us if we talk during workshop?" But I just laugh and continue. The students offer more feedback, Tiger nods his head, and then we get into constructive criticism. Suddenly, the students aren't speaking to me; they're speaking to Tiger – who tends to act out, sometimes shaking his fist at the class or wiggling his stripy butt.

After Tiger is thoroughly workshopped, I offer him a chance to reply. The students always have questions for him about his poem and his life, and they're eager to engage in conversation. Nothing like this has never happened before in any of their other classes, so nobody is dozing off or checking their cellphones. In the end I say, "Okay, let's play catch," and throw him out to the class. Tiger gets tossed around like a rag doll and eventually ends up on the floor with everyone laughing and bonding and debating whether or not he should be allowed to join the class.

Ultimately, and unconsciously, this exercise in multiple-personality pedagogy works to build anticipation. Students are enthusiastic to view workshopping as an event to look forward to rather than thinking of it as a "dissing session" in which judgmental peers slam each other's work. Similarly, students are excited to confront Crabby Old Man and Cool Dude and condescend to Big Dummy. But what all these instances have in common is that they provide occasions for applying dialectical methods which stimulate inquiry and debate in order to foster critical thinking.

The advantage of this mode of inquiry over others is that when students volunteer to engage in dramatic discourse, they're investing themselves in an active investigation rather than just sitting there absorbing info like a sponge. If one student takes a position, this increases the stakes for all the students in the class, no matter their degree of participation. As an audience that's savvy enough to recognize ridiculousness, discourse communities can't help but feel aligned when an Other challenges their reason for being in the room – which, in essence, is to not end up like intellectually stagnant stereotypes. If anything, this team bonding experience prompts a subliminal commitment to seriously evaluate the subtext under discussion. Because if they don't, then they don't have a position – which would, in effect, make them "losers." In a sense, these subtle manipulations steer students to respond in the texts they create to the nay-saying of Crabby Old Man and the ignorance of Big Dummy. And when students advise Cool Dude and Tiger Nooodles to "show not tell" or to avoid switching tenses, those students are prone to apply such approaches to their own creative processes. The result being: the uniqueness and quality of their work increases in direct proportion to how strongly they practice what they preach.

Of course, pretending to be somebody else is nothing new in pedagogy (e.g. playing devil's advocate), but it is something different for modern students who expect the same monotonous talking heads to drone on and on for an entire semester without attempting to make things entertaining. Thus, unexpected variation in voice provides dimension to the classroom experience and allows for the presentation of information in more involved ways. Or, as Rorabaugh and Stommel suggest, "encouraging them to recreate us even as they recreate themselves … is essential to understanding our hybridity" (Rorabaugh and Stommel, 2012). The way I see it, multiple-personality pedagogy is an effective type of hybridity which recognizes that teachers literally owe it to their students and themselves to reinvent the character and characters of all their different disciplines in order to transform the classroom experience into an event. That is, when teachers dare to apply such theatric elements to the classroom, learning becomes an amusing experience to look forward to, something in which discoveries are made through spontaneous, game-playing interactions – and ultimately, something which students feel they just gotta have more of!

Multiple-personality pedagogy, however, can grant even more access to writing power when students do the roleplaying – and that's the subject of the next chapter.

References

Bangs, Lester (2003) *Psychotic Reactions and Carburetor Dung*. New York: Anchor Books.

Boyle, T. C. (1995) *Without a Hero*. New York: Penguin.

O'Hara, Frank (1994) Personism: A manifesto. In Paul Hoover (ed.) *Postmodern American Poetry: A Norton Anthology* (2nd edition), 875–876. New York: W. W. Norton & Company.

Rorabaugh, Pete and Stommel, Jesse (2012) On pedagogical manipulation. *Hybrid Pedagogy* (April 9, 2012). Retrieved on 22 March 2017 from www.digitalpedagogylab.com/hybridped/on-pedagogical-manipulation

Wakowski, Diane (1988) The father of my country. *Emerald Ice: Selected Poems 1962–1987*, 44–48. Santa Rosa, CA: Black Sparrow Press.

Whitman, Walt (2004) Leaves of grass. *The Complete Poems*: 35–568. New York: Penguin.

Chapter 5

Extreme Puppet Theater as a Tool for Writing Pedagogy

In the Introduction, I stated that "the more play there is in discovering these powers ... the easier it is to get to know and control these powers. And the more writers get to know and control their power to connect with others, the more they discover about our world and themselves." In my experience, the teaching technique which illustrates this fact the most is that of "Extreme Puppet Theater," a concept I whooped up in jest, yet stand by now as the most playful and effective teaching tool for any subject matter.

There's an idea proposed by François Camoin (Camoin, 1994: 7) that texts can transform into "something else" – not a static thing, something more active and involving. Based on that notion, I extrapolated that if a text can become "something else" in this sense, then the workshop experience can become "something else" as well – a creative event that can work as a highly effective teaching tool. As an interactive learning experience, *something else* can test the boundaries of traditional pedagogy. Via Extreme Puppet Theater, I've found that undergraduate college students can be the creators of *something else*, which is not only engaging and empowering, but a hell of a lot of fun.

Birth of a Novel Approach in an American Literature Class

The idea first came to me when I was teaching a sophomore-level American Literature course at Truman State University. We were reading a book of short stories by William Faulkner, and I wanted to design a group project that offered students the opportunity to process information in a completely novel way. In a sense, I was aiming for a bizarre experience that would snap them out of their read-discuss-write-forget mindsets and into a more involved and creative application of knowledge.

When I announced the assignment, groans predictably filled the room. "What? A stupid puppet show?" was the anthem that arose. But as it turned out, these students in that initial, experimental class were the first to realize there's a lot to gain from "suffering together" (my term) in order to produce a "silly" (their term) puppet show. The puppet-show production experience then leads to a text that studies a text. Ultimately, students immerse themselves in studies of both texts, with their visions and imaginations acting as the driving force for the discovery of meaning.

For university students in their first or second year of college, these assignments work best at the end of the semester when brains are fried by the doldrums of Gen Ed studies and too many video games. All students need is a few class periods to work together, and if you can time it so their performances happen on the last day of class, a box of donuts can make the course end in a party.

In the particular English class in which Extreme Puppet Theater was born, the criteria for the show were simple. Each group had to put on a show lasting five to ten minutes, and in order for every member of the group to earn an A grade, they had to do the following: (a) everyone operates at least one puppet; (b) they describe the setting and plot of their story; (c) characters perform an excerpt from the story; (d) the viewpoint of a critic, book reviewer, author, or educator who is recognized as an authority on the subject must be incorporated (reader reviews from sources like Amazon and *Good Reads* are not allowed); (e) their overall group opinion of the text's underlying message should also be expressed; and (f) it has to be entertaining. Props and music were also encouraged.

After we went over the guidelines, I put them in their preselected groups and had them exchange contact information so they could work together outside of class (they received extra credit if they sent me a cellphone photo of their group rehearsing outside the classroom). They were also charged with deciding what sort of puppet-making supplies to bring for the next class (e.g. Should they use socks, googly eyes, paper bags, popsicle sticks?). Additionally, in order to be able to begin informal scriptwriting and make puppet characters in the next class, students had to study the story on their own.

When we met again, I found the students breaking out paper bags and scissors before class even started. The groups worked on their puppets and brainstormed ways to meet the criteria while one member drafted a collaborative script. Camaraderie happened, bonds were built, and serious discussions occurred having to do with motivations and metaphors. Work on the scripts, puppets, and performances went on for another class period, and in the last class we tipped a table on its side and adult students who'd been working like children got behind the makeshift stage and demonstrated what they had learned. As I later read in the course evaluations, this assignment was the highlight of a few students' college experience.

Developing the Approach for Writing Courses

Later, at the University of Central Arkansas, I tried this technique in a freshman-level/first-year composition course. We were studying argumentative writing, and I split the students into groups studying local eco-issues (e.g. the ivory-billed woodpecker vs. development of the Mississippi Delta, protecting the Ozark hellbender salamander, hydraulic fracking, etc.). I then charged each group with staging a puppet talk-show in which three specific arguments are debated by representatives from two different sides of the issue. The process was essentially the same as the Faulkner assignment in the American Literature class: They were given a set of criteria to satisfy; they wrote a script while constructing puppets; and then they performed a show in which a talk-show host offered the group view as a conclusion. In fact, here's the exact assignment:

Assignment 2.

WRTG 1310: Composition and Rhetoric, Spring Semester 2008 Persuasive Argumentative Puppet Talk Show Group Project

Here are the groups:

Group 1	Group 2	Group 3	Group 4	Group 5
Nikki	Kara	Howard	Bryce	Rebecca
Portia	Kristy	Cameron	Joe	Sharon
Steve R	Stephen H	Mary	Justis	Howard
Jonathan	Lauren	Chloe	Bethany	Jackie

Each group will be given an issue to study. On **Tuesday October 9** you will get together in class and split your group into two groups. One group will be the research group, which will go to the library and rustle up information on the issue (get on the computers, use Google, use the databases, ask a librarian) and be back by 3:40 with info that can lead to more insight on the dynamics of the problem. The other group will be the art group, which will make a list of what you guys need to make puppets and props for your production. This group will stay in the room and plan how to approach the show.

Expectations

On **Thursday October 11** you will meet with your group in class, make silly puppets and props, and begin drafting a script for your five- to ten-minute puppet show. There should be one puppet for each group member, including a talk-show host, a puppet representing one side of the issue, a puppet representing the other side of the issue, and one or two puppets for additional guests. The talk-show host should introduce the issue (the introduction) and then the puppets with opposing views will debate the issue (pros and cons). Each debating puppet should present three informed arguments that try to persuade the audience. The talk-show host will then make a closing statement (the conclusion). To get out of the classroom, you must show me your puppets and a rough draft of your script. If you want to kick butt on this assignment, you will meet on your own before Tuesday the 16th and rehearse your puppet show (send me a cellphone photo of your group at work and I'll give you **extra credit**). Your group will perform its puppet show on **Tuesday October 16ᵗʰ**.

Grading

50% of the grade will be in the category of entertainment/ workability. This means that half of your grade will depend on how well you engage your audience, how well you present both sides of the issue and inform your audience, and how well your show works overall. I will be looking for you to present serious issues through a ridiculous medium. The specific criteria are:

- the show should be five to ten minutes long
- an authority (critic, author, reviewer, reporter – but not *Wikipedia* or reader reviews from sources like Amazon) should be quoted
- three different aspects of the issue should be debated
- the host should supply statements that work like intros and conclusions
- each group member should operate one puppet

The other 50% of the grade will be technical. You will give me a typed and double-spaced copy of your script which has been worked on and proofread by everyone in your group. This script should have everyone's name on it and be free or errors. The script's format does not matter. What matters is that you all understand what to do. And don't forget to title it and staple it.

Additional Info

We will tip the table at the front of the room on its side to create a stage. Props add to the experience. So does music (or any other type of appropriate multi-media component) and food – so bring snacks if you like.

As usual, the students prepared and then performed. The audience was supportive, with a lot of laughter and donuts going around. Each group received their grade, and everyone left the class feeling that they'd been part of something useful and unusual.

Within a year I had a foldable puppet stage in my office, which I made out of plastic rods and purple fabric. Over time, other students and colleagues started coming to see the shows.

I later applied the idea of puppet pageantry to author presentations in my upper-level creative nonfiction courses. Having become just as bored as the students by having them stand in front of the class to rattle off biographical information and observations on voice and style, I decided to reinvent this component in a much more imaginative, hands-on way. I did this as well for a senior-level Environmental Writing class in which student puppeteers focused on the philosophies and politics of Edward Abbey's *Monkey Wrench Gang* (Abbey, 1975), Rachel Carson's *Silent Spring* (Carson, 1962), and Gary Snyder's *Turtle Island* (Snyder, 1974). And as the experiment continued, I began to see more and more how puppets could be used to stimulate sophisticated inquiries.

Now I'm using this component in my introductory creative writing course to introduce students to the genre of drama. After working in poetry and fiction, students read the Sam Shepard play "Cowboy Mouth" (Shepard, 1984) and employ it as a model to discuss the dynamics of scriptwriting. Then, after showing students a few select *Saturday Night Live* skits from the NBC website, they're prepared to embark on some group playwriting and puppet-making, resulting in a series of five- to ten-minute skits in which all students in the class collaborate to write, direct, produce and perform. And when they do, it's not for the purpose of satisfying a requirement for ten percent of their grade; they're doing it because they're invested in an investigation that they're psyched to see in the form of a dramatic production in which they each play a major role.

Watching these puppet shows for over a decade, I've seen three commonly repeated scenes. The first is the melee climax, in which all the puppets end up fighting each other in a battle royale. The second is the complete opposite: when puppets engage in orgiastic revelry to resolve differences. Then there's the occasionally repeated scene of a puppet of myself demanding that the other puppets "Show not tell!" But I don't mind if they make fun of me; if they meet their criteria and have fun along the way, then I've met my goal. And when every group in the class meets all of the criteria – which always happens – it's my pleasure to announce to the entire class, "A's for everyone!"

Reflections on the *Something Else* Approach

Of course, happy, clapping, cheering students lead to good teaching evaluations, but that's not why I'm a proponent of this strategy. It may seem childish at first, but as I've discovered, Extreme Puppet Theater taps into something which university students desire as they enter adulthood: they want to take their youth with them, and they want to play in ways that make intellectual sense.

I've tried this tactic with MFA students, and it works just as well as it does with undergrads, so I don't see why it couldn't work in any class on any subject from kindergarten to doctoral level. All a teacher needs to do is find a creative way to re-envision his or her conventional approach, establish criteria for an area to study, put students in groups, let them do what they do – and, in the end, bring donuts!

Consequently, puppetry has proven itself to me to be a highly utilitarian tool for transforming the classroom experience into *something else* – which is just as memorable as it is interactive. But most of all, it's something which motivates students and makes everyone in the room guffaw due to the realization that there actually is a practical place for something as absurd as Extreme Puppet Theater in the halls of academia. Still, the question remains: Can this method actually be applied by instructors who teach in other disciplines? Well, the answer to that question can be found in the next chapter because that's what it investigates.

References

Abbey, Edward (1975) *The Monkey Wrench Gang*. Philadelphia: J. B. Lippincott.

Camoin, François (1994) The workshop and its discontents. In W. Bishop and H. Ostrom (eds.) *Colors of a Different Horse: Rethinking Creative Writing Theory and Pedagogy* 3–7. Urbana, Illinois: National Council of Teachers of English.

Carson, Rachel (1962) *Silent Spring*. New York: Houghton Mifflin.

Shepard, Sam (1984) Cowboy mouth. *Fool for Love and Other Plays* 145–165. New York: Bantam.

Snyder, Gary (1974) *Turtle Island*. New York: New Directions.

Chapter 6

May the Farce Be with You:
Reflections on Extreme Puppet Theater
as a Vehicle towards *Something Else*

The last chapter argued that Extreme Puppet Pedagogy can help students discover more about the world and themselves. My classroom experiments showed that students can investigate environmental issues like habitat loss and hydraulic fracturing, and they can organize arguments in favor of social and environmental justice, which supports my statement above regarding discovery. Because when you learn about the world, you learn about yourself – especially when you find yourself changing your stance on political or philosophical issues. This was all evident to me back in 2013, but others required a bit more reflection to be able to regard this alternative writing pedagogy as solid enough to declare effective. Hence, I was challenged to support my claims in a way that would be convincing to others. This overview is the result.

Introduction

Puppets are often considered silly. This is a given. Still, they offer a creative way to communicate, research, present findings, and stimulate discourse and debate. In academia, puppetry is rarely used as a mode for discovery. Up until now, that is.

The inspiration came to me a decade and a half ago, when I was teaching a course in American Literature and was looking for an innovative way to encourage group work. I wanted students to be engaged in the process of analyzing a series of short stories, so I took a risk and debuted a concept that I jokingly termed "Extreme Puppet Theater." After putting students in small groups, I charged them with the task of putting on puppet shows that examined plots, characters, themes, metaphors, and underlying messages in the texts they were studying. Students were given a list of criteria to satisfy: their puppet shows should be five to ten minutes long, they should incorporate relevant research or criticism, excerpts from the texts should be performed, and ultimately, group opinions should be offered. Props and audio were optional. Students were given class time to work on this project and were expected to bring art supplies to class to make puppets while brainstorming a script.

Predictably, the groans arose. But in the next class, students got to work with paper bags and random socks, glue, buttons, yarn. We all knew this process was ridiculous, but what we found in the ensuing week was that serious research could be conducted through a forum usually reserved for children. For these young adults, the investigation proved to be an unusual, visionary learning tool in which intensive dialogue and hands-on experience promoted cooperation and creative problem-solving. In contrast to writing boring college papers that regurgitate information, this process allowed students to create something new – and, as it turned out, something valued by all those involved.

As the years passed, I incorporated guerilla puppetry into many of the other courses I taught. At the University of Central Arkansas, I had composition students work together to stage talk-show-type puppet shows in which characters debated local environmental issues. In essence, these productions illustrated a new twist on the outdated five-paragraph-essay format; the talk-show host presented the problem (the introduction), the opposing parties debated different sides of the issue (the arguments), and then the host provided a closing statement (the conclusion). The result was a highly memorable process of investigation unlike any college experience those students had ever had before. And because of their direct involvement with issues like preserving the Ozark hellbender (a giant salamander threatened by extinction) or protecting the controversial ivory-billed woodpecker from development, these students were not only better equipped to envision potential structures for college papers by fleshing out their most important arguments, their investments in their productions supplied them with studied perspectives on topics of current relevance that informed them as citizens as well as scholars.

After years of experimentation with this process, I eventually integrated Extreme Puppet Theater into both graduate and under-graduate creative writing courses. In my Creative Nonfiction Workshop, I used this method in the form of author presentations. In my Ecopoetics course, a fusion of puppetry and poetic license was employed to deconstruct and reimagine more advanced environ-mental issues like the use of dispersants for cleaning up oil spills.

The idea of using puppets to develop student writing was working and evolving. Students were using creative techniques to make sense of texts, and they were discovering meaning through improvisation, analysis, and writing. They were also developing skills that would be applicable to further studies and careers.

Because I still felt the need to make sense of the process, I wrote an article entitled "Extreme Puppet Theater as a Tool for Writing Pedagogy at K–University Levels" (Spitzer, 2014), which built on a vague but provocative concept in writing pedagogy proposed by François Camoin that texts can transform into "something else" (Camoin, 1994: 7). Camoin's implication is that a text can be something beyond what's visible on the page, something active that really speaks to people. Based on that notion, I extrapolated that if a text can become *something else*, then the classroom experience can as well. In appropriating Camoin's concept, I envisioned how works of prose, like works of drama, have the potential to be transformed into moments of action, or interaction. Because of this potential, the experience of creating *something else* can be applied as a highly effective, interactive teaching tool.

Given that group research is also a core part of the interactive process in Extreme Puppet Theater, I began to envision *something else* as a semi-living entity. Since puppet shows mimic life, in a sense, and since humans have a natural desire to create (consider the word "procreation"), it seemed to me that Extreme Puppet Theater provided the illusion, if not the actuality, of bringing something to life. That's why I wrote "As an interactive learning experience, *something else* can test the boundaries of traditional pedagogy …. [S]tudents can be the creators of *something else,* which is not only engaging and empowering, but a lot of fun" (Spitzer, 2014: 122). That statement occurred in an article published in the journal *Writing & Pedagogy* which received enough attention to elicit an invitation to teach pedagogy workshops in Asia for instructors in various disciplines. So a few months later, I was en route to the City University of Hong Kong, where the English Department was hosting a Summer Institute on Creativity and Discovery in Teaching University Writing. It was time to see if the theory behind the theory was really applicable to the vast range of ages and academic subjects I claimed it to be, and I was glad to have the opportunity to put my concept to the test. By subjecting it to such scrutiny, I figured that if my audience could find any weak spots in my approach, then that would be the equivalent of disproving the theory. If the theory was found faulty, then I'd have more work to do to. If it couldn't be disproved, then I'd be reassured that I was headed in the right direction.

But as I was to discover (in a forum focused on the theme of discovery), putting my method to the test was a moot point since the concept had already been accepted. I didn't know it at the time, but the participants who had signed up for my workshops were already motivated by the idea of playing with puppets in the classroom, and many colleagues I hadn't yet met were anxious to learn more about this unconventional pedagogical approach.

Description of Activities and Strategies for Implementation

I had no trouble getting through Customs with my suitcase full of glues, paints, scissors, markers, yarn, ribbons, pipe cleaners, buttons, sewing kits, googly eyes, paper bags, fabric scraps, and slightly defective dollar-store socks. I was also prepared with handouts and a lecture plan. On the day of the first workshop, I entered the room and met the class. They saw my suitcase full of stuff, and since they were there to make puppets and be creative, an eager participant immediately asked, "When can we start?"

Laughter arose, setting the tone. I then introduced myself, talked a bit about my experience with this teaching tool, and passed around the handouts to provide an outline of the process. I went through the argumentative assignment meant for first-year writing students, and pointed out the criteria I graded by. I explained that if students worked together to perform their show within the time limit while presenting information from authorities, and if they each operated one puppet and had their arguments and their introductions and conclusions in order, and if they were entertaining (which they always are), then their group would receive an A grade. I added that in all my years of assigning puppetry as a mode of investigation, no group had ever gotten less than an A. That's why, after student performances, I always announce, "A's for everyone!"

Chinese students being somewhat conservative and serious about their studies, this led to some questions on how the grade for this particular project can affect a student's overall grade for the semester: if everyone gets an A, what's the point?

The point, I explained, is to collaborate and have fun learning something which makes everyone involved a more critical/creative thinker. The fact that the group grade accounts for only a small percentage of the overall grade, I continued, means that not much is at stake. This, in turn, means the project isn't threatening. It would be highly unlikely that they would not all get an A grade. Hence, the point was to play, to create, and to "think outside the box" as a way to approach organizing ideas for writing.

I also explained that I usually schedule these assignments at the end of the semester when minds tend to be fried by academic pressure. In this sense, Extreme Puppet Theater is meant as a form of relief, which is why I usually schedule performances on the last day of class. At that time, I bring in soda pop and donuts and we have a party because "American students just love donuts!"

To give an idea of what was possible, I then showed the workshop a video made by upper-level undergraduates in an Ecopoetics class (see photo below). We then went over the following assignment, which those students had been charged with:

Assignment 3.

WRTG 4324 and 5324: Ecopoetics, Spring Semester 2013 Extreme Puppet Theater Ecologue Assignment

Yep, that's right: You'll be working in groups to put on silly puppet shows to be performed on the last day of class. The idea is that your group will decide on an environmental issue for puppets to debate through a talk-show format. As I noted at the beginning of the semester, an eclogue is a fifteenth-century poetic dialogue between shepherds on the subject of stewardship. Therefore, for the purpose of this class, we will envision the modern eclogue (sometimes termed "ecologue") as a conversation between differing parties about a contemporary eco-subject or eco-philosophy. Here's what you need to know and what you will do:

Group 1	Group 2	Group 3
Joseph	Courtney	Chelsae
Lisa	Erica	Chase
Alissa	Jessica	Scotty

Everyone should be involved and present for every class. Your group grade will be judged according to the following criteria:

- your performance must be 5 to 10 minutes long
- everyone operates at least one puppet

- timely and relative research is presented
- it's informative and provokes people to think
- it's entertaining (meaning you amuse your audience and there's lots of action)

Music and/or props are permissible and will be factored into your grade if they add to the experience.

Schedule

Thursday April 18: You will get together, decide on a topic, brainstorm approaches, then decide what supplies are needed and who brings what next time.

Tuesday April 23: You will make puppets in class and draft a script.

Extra Credit: If you can meet outside of class after April 23 and before April 25, and if you can send me a cellphone photo of your group rehearsing your performance, each group member will receive extra credit.

Thursday April 25: Come to class prepared to perform. I'll have a puppet stage (4 feet tall, 8 feet wide) set up for you and ready to go. Feel free to bring drinks and snacks.

In discussing the assignment with the workshop participants, I noted the criteria and timeline for making puppets, drafting a script, and scoring extra credit points by working as a group outside of class. The concept of "extra credit" involved a bit of explaining, since it wasn't a popular concept at Chinese universities. As I'd been told, Chinese students are assigned work and are expected to do it, end of story. But since this whole conference was about applying innovative teaching methods to foster creativity and discovery, I addressed the concept of extra credit briefly by stating that it's an incentive to encourage students to get together outside of class and fine-tune their performances so as to be prepared for their shows. I added that doing extra work together builds strong bonds, which results in more cohesive and imaginative productions.

This is where *something else* comes in. When groups begin to translate a text (in this case a script) into an event (Extreme Puppet Theater), individuals get excited and are naturally inspired to take off on their own. At this point, students become their own teachers and have little use for the teacher except as a symbolic deadline-enforcer whose grading mechanism is hardly as important as bringing their visions to crystallization. This is exactly what I'm aiming for: turning a mundane task into a self-propelled celebration that comes with its own momentum.

I then showed the YouTube video *In the Hot Tub with Sheila Tubman* (Birdsong, Ference, and Sexton, 2013) to the workshop, which my Ecopoetics students made. It's a pretty dang silly debate between an ExxonMobile executive and an environmental hippy over the 2013 Mayflower Oil Spill in Arkansas, near my university. Through the course of the semester, both graduate and under-graduate students in that class had been reading eco-nonfiction philosophy then responding via poetry. It had been unfortunate to have an environmental disaster in our midst, but it had also been a vivid eye-opener for many of the students in the class. Our own patch of nature had been defiled, and students in one particular group felt compelled to express their disgruntlement.

This video made for a good example of Extreme Puppet Theater, especially since the puppets were large and colorful and looked good on the projection screen. Still, the puppeteers behind the foldable puppet stage were even more colorful. They had music and props and a talk-show format in which puppets holding opposing viewpoints met in a hot tub forum moderated by a sassy host.

Figure 4. In the Hot Tub with Sheila Tubman. Photo by Mark Spitzer.

Also, the students had equipped themselves with sophisticated arguments. At one point the petrochemical CEO held up a graph showing tornado damage in the United States in comparison to damage from oil pollution, and then he asked, "Mother Nature, Exxon – who's really on your side?"

After the video, I went to the whiteboard and wrote the following talking point: "IN EXTREME PUPPET THEATER, RIDICULOUS ARGUMENTS ARE OKAY." This act, in a sense, made it official that students don't have to draft their scripts according to any expected language, and they can use their imaginations to order arguments according to what they want to express – which is a highly freeing process. Whereas one of the goals of my Extreme Puppet Theater composition assignment was to help students envision the structure of a basic argument paper or essay, the assignment (much like "slam poetry," which relies on fiery expression as a performance technique) was also geared toward utilizing emotional language as a political tool.

The message I was sending was that it's not only okay to take risks in creating biased puppet productions, it's encouraged. Being a creative writer at heart, my goal in academic writing as well as in creative writing is to promote discourse that strays from *the formal* and connects through *the informal*, an area where discourse is accessible to vast and diverse audiences. Because imaginations tend to connect at the informal level, where expected genre conventions aren't so important, risk-taking voices that speak to readers through *emotion combined with information* are often effective in providing perspective. Take hip-hop, for example, or punk rock as practical modes of communication, especially as acts of protest.

Some of the workshop participants clearly understood the value of using alternative forms of discourse in academic situations. I could see it in their eyes – most of which were focused on the suitcase full of puppet materials. The participants were ready to dive in and get cracking. Still, there were a few participants in the room who were having difficulty envisioning how to articulate what they wanted to express through playful tactics. One of the participants related that she was having trouble resolving how to unlearn the formal structures she had been trained to employ in teaching writing. Nevertheless, she was intrigued.

The next talking point I wrote on the board was: "CRAPPY PUPPETS ARE OKAY." The reason I strove to establish this also had to do with risk. First of all, if students know that their art skills won't be judged, they can quickly get past this self-conscious hurdle and get on to mapping the specifics of their puppets' agenda, which they might be more adept at. And secondly, I like to think of Extreme Puppet Theater as a type of "outsider art" that's open and accessible. This means you don't need to be Jim Henson to make a puppet. All you need to do is to have been a kid at some time in your life so you can call upon that vestigial innocence and wonder we all recall in order to apply these factors to the discovery process of learning from creative play.

I then put the workshop participants in groups of four so that they could jump straight into the process and see firsthand how it's applicable. As usual, I dictated who would work with who and charged each group with coming up with an issue in which a talk-show host moderated two puppets with differing views. This left each group in the position of trying to figure out a role for the fourth member, so they had to come up with a creative solution.

This is what Extreme Puppet Theater is all about: suddenly being charged with a mission, then looking for creative ways to transform discourse into something which is authentically *something else*. And that's exactly what happened. Some participants went directly for the supplies while others pulled their desks together to powwow about issues and brainstorm ideas for character positions.

The participants had one hour to come up with a show. Essentially, I was giving them sixty minutes to come up with what I usually give my students in Arkansas a week to accomplish. Thus, the mad scramble was on for each group to come up with a five-minute talk show based on a real issue.

As they worked, I went from group to group and asked them about their subject matter. As examples of their topics, one group chose obesity, another chose online dating, and another chose to look at the "fast fashion" retailer Topshop. Ten minutes into it, each group was working away, laughing out loud, and helping each other with gluing on eyes – which I had told them to start with since the glue needed time to dry. To speed up this process, I'd brought along a hair dryer from the hotel.

Toward the end of the workshop, I brought a table in from the hallway, turned it sideways, and set it up on top of the table at the front of the room so that the table top faced the audience. This was their makeshift stage – which they soon got behind, and like adults reverting back to childhood, presented sophisticated arguments through a ridiculous medium. The participants were animated, excited, and communicating with sincerity and optimism. Everyone had a knee-slapping time, and when the class was over, half of the participants stayed around for a while to discuss ways to apply Extreme Puppet Theater to other areas of study – like business, and even math.

Two days later, I conducted the same workshop again with the same inspired results, including one I didn't expect: When I left the room, I was buzzing hard, totally pleased with the enthusiastic response I had received and excited about the interest there was in applying this alternative pedagogy to extremely different disciplines. It's a feeling teachers rarely experience, when they feel they've made an impact not just on their students, but on themselves. Be it pride, a sense of accomplishment, or satisfaction in having successfully met a challenge, I felt an incredible self-indulgent rush to have taught something with such impact – which is the most that any educator can ask for. Because when something evolves into *something else*, it turns into something progressive, something validating, something truly transformative and transcendental. And that's what we're all striving for, consciously or not.

Reflections and Purpose

Due to the dramatic interaction that naturally occurs with Extreme Puppet Theater, one suggestion offered by workshop participants in their evaluations was to implement this assignment at the beginning of a semester rather than at the end. This would make the assignment operate as an icebreaker that could help introduce students to each other and promote a spirit of cooperation in the classroom. Several of the other overwhelmingly positive workshop evaluations also mentioned that Extreme Puppet Theater could work well to jumpstart more formal academic paper-writing assignments – which sounds good to me if it works to help realize the instructor's vision.

The way I see it, Extreme Puppet Theater is a flexible method that can evolve with the needs of any course. I therefore offer my own version as a prototype to be tweaked by other teachers according to their instincts and agendas. Nevertheless, what works for me may not work for others, and vice versa. Different subject matter might require different criteria or more background in certain areas before implementation.

As an exercise in creative problem-solving, I recommend that students be charged with at least one problem or mystery to solve. For example, if all the characters for a puppet show have been claimed, what type of support can an additional group member provide in order to play a valuable part in the event? Perhaps there are other kinds of technology that can add to the understanding of the discussion if incorporated in a creative manner. Or maybe the dialogue should touch on specific concepts, keywords, or the work of scholars with opposing views to make the investigation of an issue more focused.

I've also found that time is not a pressing factor. Whether students are provided an hour or a week to satisfy their objectives, they'll get the job done if the deadline is reasonable. Not only that, they'll go out of their way to get their supplies, and they'll even meet outside of class to iron out the details. Being accustomed to homework, students can predict what's required to get the job done. And since it's common knowledge that groups rely on individuals to literally play their part, everyone involved recognizes their level of responsibility and what is required of them.

Of course, the question remains of whether slackers will do their part. From what I've seen, this doesn't matter. In every group there are always those who take on leadership roles, and there are always those who are happy to be led or who remain more reserved. The benefit of staging these shows later in the semester is that it allows the instructor to gauge who the most ambitious personalities in the class are so that groups can be organized with a balanced number of "go-getters" and followers in each one. But that's not my point here. My point is that because Extreme Puppet Theater is an amusing group project, I've rarely seen students not play their part. Sure, some students might miss a class or two for various reasons, but for the most part, these teams develop organically and members carry their weight due to the inherent playfulness of the learning mode. Members of the group become invested in the process because they want to see what wacko form it will take in the end. The fact that they get only one chance to see the efforts of their labor, and the fact that they will also get to see others in the same bizarre situation, pretty much guarantees they will approach this process with more interest than class presentations in which droning monologues are the norm.

There's a big difference between mind-numbing class presentations and interactive dramas that rely on enhanced visual and oral elements derived through spontaneous play, which is why Extreme Puppet Theater is appealing to the imagination. In other words, the unpredictable nature of the process makes the ride a suspense-packed odyssey, which, to quote my own article, allows university students to tap into something they "desire as they enter adulthood: they want to take their youth with them, and they want to play in ways that make intellectual sense" (Spitzer, 2014: 125).

This brings me to my final talking point regarding this discovery-oriented teaching method. For the same reason I established that ridiculous arguments and crappy puppets are okay, I hereby proclaim that because it's impossible for instructors not to fly by the seat of their pants when assigning such a surreal, childlike process, "EXTREME PUPPET THEATER MUST BE A HALF-BAKED & LUDICROUS EVENT TO BE EFFECTIVE."

My advice, therefore, is to not even try to bake it all the way. Don't spoil it by preparing highly detailed lesson plans, assessment rubrics and the like. Just give them the keys to this vehicle, and see where they go.

As an educator, if this logic is perplexing or unconvincing to you, Extreme Puppet Theater might not work for you. But if the driving metaphor above seems clear, or at least puzzling in an intriguing way, then you have the sense of humor necessary to guide students through academic investigations via the machinery of absurdity – so why not go for it?

And may the Farce be with you!

References

Birdsong, Joseph, Ference, Lisa and Sexton, Alissa (2013) *In the Hot Tub with Sheila Tubman*. Retrieved on 3 April 2017 from https://www.youtube.com/watch?v=yrJ-oXl6aYc

Camoin, François (1994) The workshop and its discontents. In W. Bishop and H. Ostrom (eds.) *Colors of a Different Horse: Rethinking Creative Writing Theory and Pedagogy* 3–7. Urbana, Illinois: National Council of Teachers of English.

Spitzer, Mark (2014) Extreme Puppet Theater as a tool for writing pedagogy at K–university levels. *Writing & Pedagogy* 6(1): 121–125.

Chapter 7

Pointers for Performance of Poetry and Prose

Whereas the last three chapters examined the investigative theatrics of employing alternative forms of dialogue in the classroom, this chapter looks at how to apply some dramatic techniques to be used outside the classroom so that words can be as powerful as possible. The occasion arose during a graduate student reading at the Oxford American Annex at South on Main in Little Rock, Arkansas, in the spring of 2015. Our first class of graduating MFAs was essentially performing their greatest hits, and although their work was tight and well written, a discovery hit me that night: These students, who had inherited my creative writing genetics, were my intellectual progeny – but I had failed them. Not that their show was faulty or flawed, but because I, as their mentor and a more experienced performer, should've prepared them with what I knew from being coached by my own teachers, and from what I picked up along the way through my own teaching practice and performances. In other words, because they could've hit the ball farther out of the park, it bummed me out that I didn't foresee an important need regarding the wielding of word-power in live performance.

I therefore saw it as my responsibility to do better for the next batch of MFA students, and all those that followed. Using some of the role-playing strategies I'd developed for varying voice in the classroom, I made a short, semi-ludicrous video entitled *Pointers for Performance of Poetry & Prose* (Spitzer, 2014) and posted it on YouTube. Although I created it for students in the Arkansas

Writers MFA Program, it's still up and available to anyone who's interested.

The scene opens on me playing the role of the Tweedy Professor, who greets his imaginary audience with a melodramatic introduction of:

> "Hello students! Whether you're writing poetry or prose, there are some basic performance techniques that can pump up your work and make it resonate. After all, you don't just represent yourself on stage, you represent us, and we need you to blow your audience out of the water. So even if you know everything, take notes on the following pointers because there will be a test at the end of this video." (Spitzer, 2014)

Cut to Student Dude with his backwards cap and sunglasses, also played by me. Student Dude then reads from a poem of his own design in a staccato, machine-like delivery that fizzles into blah blah nothingness – to which the Tweedy Professor replies "No! No! No!" The first pointer is then introduced.

Pointer #1: Own It!

> "First of all, be proud of your words, even if you aren't. If you ain't, then fake it because every word is important and should Burn Burn Burn! You are a visionary! You are historical! Take your time and give your audience time to digest every living syllable. Make your audience feel the gravity of your intellect and imagination." (Spitzer, 2014)

Cut to Student Dude stuttering and bumbling his way through a poem. He coughs and has trouble with pronunciation as if he's never read his own work before, sometimes commenting on random things. Again, the Tweedy Professor replies: "No! No! No! That's half-baked!" (Spitzer, 2014). Which leads to Pointer #2.

Figure 5. The Tweedy Professor Professing. Photo by Mark Spitzer.

Pointer #2: Bake That Pie!

"Never bake a pie halfway. Coming off as human is not the goal. The goal is to be über-human, with an umlaut. So practice before reading aloud. Know what words are coming up and what ones you want to stress and what ones you want to plaaaaaay with. Plot it out.

"And if you're not sure about a pronunciation, or if you have trouble pronouncing certain words, then write yourself a note in the text. Like 'pasta.' I always think it's pronounced *pass-tuh* for some reason. I don't know why I think that, but I don't want to say it wrong when I'm performing, so I write myself a note that it rhymes with 'Rasta.'

"And say you say something wrong. Don't go back and correct it – just keep blazing away with confidence. If you speak with authority, nobody will ever know you screwed up. And pause for effect and emphasis at strategic places, like at the ends of paragraphs or stanzas where you can always easily find your place again." (Spitzer, 2014)

Figure 6. Student Dude. Photo by Mark Spitzer.

Cut again to Student Dude, who now stares down the camera with confidence as he proceeds to read Taylor Mali's "How to Write a Political Poem" (Mali, 2003) with fire and determination. He plays with his audience, projecting his voice and beat-boxing, and hamming it up like a spoken-word, slam-poet cartoon character, essentially dropping the mic.

Cut to the Tweedy Professor, pounding his fists in the air, responding "Yes! Yes! Yes!" Segue to the next pointer.

Pointer #3: Add Ham!

"The word 'ham' comes from *Hamlet,* from ham actors hamming it up. I'm not saying be cheesy, though. What I'm saying is don't just read – PERFORM! Incorporate theatrical *inflections* and gestures. Make eye contact with audience members and build to a CRESCENDO!" (Spitzer, 2014).

From there we move on to the next pointer.

Pointer # 4: Time Traveling and Rambling Do Not Mix!

Student Dude steps up on stage like a goofy doofus and goes into a rambling shout-out to a classmate followed by some arbitrary observations and the admission that the poem he is prefacing was an assignment for a class. Student Dude takes extraneous time setting the poem up before interrupting his own performance with comments on why he did certain things to the text while acting totally juvenile.

"No! No! No!" the Tweedy Professor breaks in again, clenching fists and teeth.

> "You're a time traveler. You're traveling through time. But more importantly, so is your audience. But you're driving, so know your destination. We don't want to be driven around in circles and up and down random streets. We don't want your ad libs, especially when there's a time constraint. If others are reading next, don't go throwing stories in there about what inspired your poetry or prose, just do it. There's nothing more annoying than a reader who takes seventeen minutes to fill a ten-minute slot and cuts into other peoples' mojo and makes everyone have to stay longer. So time yourself before you do it." (Spitzer, 2014)

Then we get to the final pointer.

Pointer #5: Stick a Fork in It!

Student Dude is ending a poem with dramatic profundity. Every syllable is loaded. All eyes and ears are riveted. As the heavy-duty nature of his syntax sinks in, he pauses for a moment of silence, then turns toward the audience, throws up his arms, and simply says, "Thank you, Little Rock! Goodnight!" He then introduces the next reader and steps off the stage.

"Yes! Yes!" the Tweedy Professor stresses.

"Don't just fizzle out and fade away. Let the audience know when you're done and the applause will happen on queue – because sometimes it doesn't always work that way. Especially with poetry. People never know when to clap for poetry."

"And oh yeah, if you're supposed to introduce somebody else, don't forget to do it during the fog that comes with finishing up and stepping down." (Spitzer, 2014)

Final Point

The video concludes with the Tweedy Professor stating:

"Now here's the test I told you about, and it's a take-home test, and you've got your whole life to work on it. The question is: What will you do with these pointers? Something? Nothing? Or will you get up there and do it for the children, the octopi, Walt Whitman, and ALL THE STARS OF INFINITY?" (Spitzer, 2014)

And that's where the video ends, with the question left in the students' court, where they can't help reflecting on it and hitting it back. Yes, it's a preposterous question, but its answer isn't. If anything, it's a challenge to performing writers that has to do with how far they'll go to set the stage for the reception of their writing – which is also the subject of the next chapter.

References

Mali, Taylor (2003) How to write a political poem. In Mark Eleveld (ed.) *The Spoken Word Revolution* (*slam, hip hop & the poetry of a new generation*) 174–176. Naperville, IL: Sourcebooks MediaFusion.

Spitzer, Mark (2014) *Pointers for Performance of Poetry & Prose.* Retrieved on 29 March 2017 from https://www.youtube.com/watch?v=9tgpQBwkqzk

Part 3

Programmatic Discoveries

Chapter 8

How to Sell a Creative Writing Program
Based on the Question "Why Study Creative Writing?"

The last section in this book dealt with factors of performance, and this chapter also considers audience reaction. As all politicians and writers know, there's power in tailoring one's voice to an audience, whether that audience is a bunch of green-haired punks at a protest or a department head reviewing academic documents. This was something I was aware of in 2008 when I began a three-year investigation of the question "Why study creative writing?" Or, more specifically, the question I was investigating was "Why study creative writing at the graduate level at the University of Central Arkansas?" because I was drafting a proposal for an MFA degree program. It was a question that I had to approach not as a writer or a writing teacher, but from the perspective of a university and the state board of higher education.

At first, my reasons for proposing the program were obvious. It was challenging to work with graduate students, and having come from an MA program in English at Truman State University in Missouri in which I directed creative writing theses, I found it rewarding to work closely with developing writers. Those, however, were personal reasons. As for my colleagues in the Department of Writing at UCA, their reasons for proposing the program were more along the lines of increasing our profile in the arts and becoming a player in the MFA industry. Still, I knew there had to be better reasons to launch a new graduate writing program, and I knew I'd discover those reasons once I immersed myself in the process. At this point, though, it would be a spoiler to spell out what I found, so let's save that for the end of this chapter.

When I began drafting the proposal, I was focused on selling the idea of why an advanced degree in creative writing was an important addition to the curriculum for an institution of higher learning to offer. After all, any proposal for any program is a response to the question of "Why should anyone study this subject?" So to study this question in terms of creative writing, I realized that to convince the university (whose administrators would be our first audience in the bureaucratic process), I had to think like a university.

That's why I went was to the mission statements of UCA and its College of Fine Arts and Communication in which the Department of Writing was housed. I knew that working the university's own words into the answer to the question would be an appropriate place to start the "Purpose of the Program" section. What I eventually came up with (with input from other faculty members later) was this:

> The primary purpose of this program is to advance UCA's mission to support "the intellectual, social and personal development of its students." This program will strengthen the University's dedication to the arts as well by advancing the College of Fine Arts and Communication's mission to establish a "learning community that is dedicated to the artistic, communicative, and personal development of the individual [which] prizes the artist's voice and vision." (Department of Writing, 2011: 2)

I was on the right track, but I still needed to justify why the artist's voice and vision, along with the intellectual and social development of students, were worthwhile investments not just for the university, but for the state. The Department of Higher Education would have the last vote on whether studying creative writing at the graduate level was an important enough ideal for the state to support. Taking the community-development route, I then added the wordage "this

MFA in Creative Writing will provide UCA with another powerful tool for enriching campus and community life … [and it] will nourish a blossoming literary culture … that has recently attracted national attention" (Department of Writing, 2011: 2).

This is where I began bringing in outside arguments for some good old fashioned persuasion rhetoric. Our literary journal, the *Exquisite Corpse Annual* (which later transitioned to the award-winning *Toad Suck Review*) had recently been recognized by the *Chronicle of Higher Education* as a factor lending to UCA's growing reputation as a "Cultural Hub in Central Arkansas" and as an "academic incubator for the arts" (Mooney, 2009: A17). Also, the state newspaper, the *Arkansas Democrat-Gazette*, had recently noted that the journal helped reflect UCA as a noteworthy player "in the fine arts 'big leagues'" (Martin, 2009: J1). These soundbites were good for showing that we already had the means to enrich campus and community life, but I still needed to get to why developing a literary culture was important to the question of what a graduate program in creative writing could offer students. As I found, each answer I provided only generated another question – which was essentially "Yeah, but why?" So I got more specific regarding the needs of the state by employing the following bullet points:

- Because this degree will develop a cadre of writing teachers, which Arkansas needs in order to maintain and sustain an acceptable level of literacy.
- Because this degree will produce writers with highly developed critical skills necessary to successfully communicate in the rapidly changing job market.
- Because, as Steve Healey's article "The Rise of Creative Writing & the New Value of Creativity" noted in the *Writer's Chronicle*, "An arts degree is now perhaps the hottest credential in the world of business" and "the most highly prized commodity in our economy" (Healey, 2009).

Incidentally, I backed that last point up with information incorporated from Healey's article to make the argument that "[s]ince 'creative workers' now make up almost thirty percent of the workforce, this MFA in Creative Writing will help students capitalize on the expanding market in which 'linguistic competence, knowledge, and imagination' are increasing in currency" (Department of Writing, 2011: 3).

More Healey arguments were subsequently capitalized on to stress that "creativity and 'thinking outside the box' have become primary tools for production in the American theater of the global economy" (Healey, 2009). I followed this argument by noting that developing this skill set would prepare MFA graduates in creative writing to compete in the global marketplace, where "the skills that have the most value in the new economy are … the ability to manipulate language, to affect audiences in powerful ways, and to craft evocative stories, characters, images, and voices" (Healey, 2009). I concluded the section by stating that an MFA program would "enhance the profile of this discipline in Arkansas, thereby increasing the state's reputation as a progressive advocate and producer of the literary arts while providing students the tools they need to excel in the new international economy" (Department of Writing, 2011: 3).

Admittedly, as someone who'd come to writing from an outsider perspective shaped in part by the anti-academic sentiments of *enfant terrible* Arthur Rimbaud and drunken curmudgeon Charles Bukowski, I felt like I was B.S.-ing my way through the document. I was using lifeless words and stiff and clinical jargon, but to paraphrase the notorious poet-thief Jean Genet (another anti-establishment influence), I was aware that it pays to write in "a language familiar to the dominant class" (Genet, 2004: 197). This quotation is frequently characterized as Genet's impetus to speak in "the language of the enemy," so that his "torturers" could hear him. Not that I considered the university or the state as nemeses, but I did consider them the audience, so for them to take us seriously we'd have to communicate in the expected language.

This is where the numbers came in. In the following section, "Need for the Program," I had to quantify the demand, so it would show what the return would be. I began by stating that "Creative writers, through the specialized knowledge of their craft, serve business and government by offering creative solutions and approaches to communicating with the public" (Department of Writing, 2011: 3). Then, I quoted Healey (2009) again: "Students are savvy enough to understand how powerful creative literacy has become in our current social context … [and] they want access to its power." It followed that since students demand access to that power, the university was in the unique position of supplying what they requested.

Hence, I conducted surveys with our own undergraduates as well as with students at other state institutions, both private and public, to measure the demand. The surveys showed that 91 percent of respondents had an interest in the proposed degree, and 57 percent were definitely interested.

I used other official statistics like that to make our case, then moved on to the "Job Opportunities" section, which provides the most practical answer for students on why to study creative writing. This is where I indicated that our graduates "will gravitate into teaching and editing jobs, and it is expected that some will move into a diverse array of other professions (i.e. areas such as journalism, theater, technology, management, and other fields in which a mastery of creative literacy is in demand)" (Department of Writing, 2011: 5). Some of these other fields included "advertising, architecture, design, fashion, music, the performing arts, software, television, radio, libraries, arts committees, literary guilds, law, professional groups, public arts commissions, the blogosphere, computer and video games, film and video, both public and private research, and other areas requiring a practical and/or stylistic command of language" (Department of Writing, 2011: 6).

After that, I focused on a big list of positions that MFA graduates were qualified for, which I'd been collecting from 2007 to 2010 from newspaper ads in the state. This list included calls for composition and writing instructors, developmental reading teachers, print production managers, page designers, assistant professors, a producer assistant for web design, a copywriter, a magazine office manager, a web content coordinator, a communications/publication assistant, a classifieds editor, a sports editor, a design editor, a technical writer, an education and instruction specialist, an education instruction coordinator, and a writer in residence. I named the employers as well: the *Arkansas Times*, the *Oxford American* magazine, the *Log Cabin Democrat*, the *Sentinel-Record*, the Searcy *Daily Citizen*, the Arkansas Business Publishing Group, Heifer International, Winrock International, the Clinton School of Public Service, the Clinton Presidential Center, Verizon, Acxiom, Aristotle, Web International, the American Cancer Society, the American Heart Association, the March of Dimes, the United Way, Habitat for Humanity, the Donald W. Reynolds Foundation, the Walton Family Foundation, the Arkansas Community Foundation, the Nature Conservancy, Pulaski Tech Community College, Arkansas Tech University, Hendrix College, Arkansas State University, the University of Central Arkansas, the University of Arkansas at Little Rock, the University of Arkansas Community College at Hope, Arkansas Baptist College, the American Composites Manufacturer's Association, Arkansas Educational Television Network, Hewlett-Packard and ITT Educational Services. What this extensive list clearly underscored, as the MFA proposal attested, was that it was true that "In the new global economy, the demand for creative, technically adept communications experts is fast outstripping the supply ... [making creative writing degrees] ideal training for a vast array of careers" (Department of Writing, 2011: 6).

Spotlighting these job possibilities was no doubt the most important part of answering the question of why anyone should study creative writing, but showing that employment possibilities existed on the national level was also key in making our argument. The 2010–11 *Occupational Outlook Handbook* of the U.S. Bureau of Labor Statistics became an important source to quote, since it projected 44,000 new job postings for writers and editors between 2006 and 2016. I therefore incorporated the following information:

> Employment of writers and editors is expected to increase faster than average for all occupations through the year 2010. Employment of salaried writers and editors for newspapers, periodicals, book publishers, and nonprofit organizations is expected to increase .... Also, online publications and services are ... spurring the demand. (U.S. Bureau of Labor Statistics, 2011)

Without question, my research into job possibilities revealed that technology was one of the biggest drivers for employing creative writers. Nonprofit and for-profit computer-related corporations, software developers, graphic designers, app publishers, website developers, online forums, and technical consulting firms were hiring not only graduates with MFAs in creative writing, but they were hiring graduates with MAs, BAs and BFAs in creative writing, writing, and English as well. Moreover, these companies were searching for creative writers during the worst financial disaster in American history since the Great Depression. In short, there was no shortage of technical jobs for highly literate college grads with creative problem-solving abilities, which is as good a reason as any to study creative writing: for a paycheck.

As for the teaching industry, here are two paragraphs from the proposal that also bolstered the faculty's position:

> Backgrounds in Creative Writing are currently a commodity in teaching, especially in community colleges, four-year liberal arts colleges, and universities. Since the MFA in Creative Writing at UCA will train graduates to teach composition and creative writing, the skills developed through this program will be especially valuable for positions in higher education where state teaching certificates are not a prerequisite (as they are in K–12). As the sample of recent job offerings below demonstrates, there have been a large number of educational positions available over the last three years just in Central Arkansas. For these positions, candidates with terminal degrees like the MFA have a clear advantage over candidates

with MA degrees. It should also be noted that the recent 5% rise in enrollment in 2010 … for Arkansas institutions of higher education indicates a "trend toward increased participation in higher education" (ADHE Director Jim Purcell, qtd. in Brantley, 2010). This trend, in turn, indicates a growing need for more composition instructors, which UCA graduates with the MFA in Creative Writing will be professionally poised to fill.

Graduates with an MFA in Creative Writing will qualify for many new teaching jobs in Arkansas, but in years to come there will also be hundreds, if not thousands, of teaching jobs offered throughout the United States. The National Center for Education Statistics "projects a rise of 10 percent in enrollments of people under 25, and a rise of 19 percent in enrollments of people 25 and over" (Institute of Education Sciences, 2011) between 2006 and 2017. This increase in enrollment will, of course, create a demand for more composition instructors. Also, considering that jobs for literature-based scholars were on the decline to the tune of 21% in 2008 (June, 2008), and that composition-teaching positions are on the rise and accounted "for about 20 percent of all jobs in languages and literature" (Johnson, 2010) in 2010 … graduates in writing- and rhetoric-based programs already have an advantage in applying for positions in higher education over graduates of English programs and programs in the humanities. Thus, the proposed MFA in Creative Writing will be most valuable as a gateway into the global teaching industry, and the experience offered in editing and publishing as well as new technology through this program will be an incentive for employers seeking writers with technical knowledge. Other incentives for employers to hire graduates of UCA's intensive 60-hour program will be the highly individualized mentorship and experience gained through internships, which will provide recipients of this MFA degree with a highly competitive edge.

(Department of Writing, 2011: 6)

Regarding that "competitive edge," the proposal went on to state that with coursework which includes pedagogy and publishing classes, graduates with this degree will have an advantage over their competition, since authority and articulation are often developed along with teaching skills, and technological skills are applied and honed in programs that emphasize publishing. As the ... *Occupational Outlook Handbook* notes, "writers and editors use desktop or electronic publishing software, scanners, and other electronic communications equipment in the production of their material ... [also] many writers today prepare material directly for the Internet, such as online newspapers and text for video games" (U.S. Bureau of Labor Statistics, 2011).

I then added more information from the Bureau of Labor Statistics, including how the MFA students trained by UCA's creative writing faculty will become knowledgeable in graphic design, layout, software and audio technologies, and how employers can expect graduates with this degree to possess such skills. Another incentive in hiring recipients of this degree would be that preparatory coursework necessary for such positions will be evident on applicant transcripts. Finally, I added, "Since internships develop a working knowledge of an involvement with numerous industries and their dynamics, this aspect of the degree will be an additional motivation for employers to hire MFA graduates with a practical and applicable set of real-world job skills" (Department of Writing, 2011: 6).

The creative writing faculty eventually assisted with the editing of the document, and those were the primary reasons we supplied for why students should study this discipline at the master of fine arts level. The proposal went through all levels of the process and the state signed off on it. The Arkansas Writers MFA Workshop was launched in 2012. A main reason it went through was because the proposal did not express the freedom-to-express-yourself aspect which is at the core of most writers' passion to manipulate language and tell stories. Such personal reasons to study writing were not part of building our case for our MFA program proposal. Rather, the arguments used avoided idealistic reasons to study creative writing and spoke the language of marketing.

Here's where we get to my most major discovery in studying the question of "Why study creative writing at the graduate level at UCA?" Having always been a personality who operates on the impulse of reacting against authority and the status quo, I have to admit that the main thing I learned through the experience of shepherding an MFA proposal into an actual degree program was that creative writing may be a visionary act of the imagination for the individual, but that's not the reason to study it – at least in the eyes of the state. State boards of higher education judge program proposals on the practicality of returns from investments. In other words, it doesn't help to use clever metaphors or colorful language or even a sense of humor because what the state is looking for are plans that make long-term business sense.

So if you're a creative writing faculty member and you want to start a creative writing program, be prepared to face the question of "Why study creative writing?" Be prepared as well to not rely on quixotic arguments about the power of the pen and empowering individuals to change the world through poetry and prose. Instead, stick to the exact opposite of that spirit and quantify the demand versus the supply. Use numbers, tables, graphs. Cite statistics and name-drop the most relevant authorities. But most of all, write critically and be flexible enough to create a voice that, ironically or not, contradicts what you've been teaching your students and yourself about writing creatively. The question of the value in studying creative writing has different connotations for different audiences, and if yours isn't made up of members intimately familiar with the impetus to create art, they will welcome projections for job creation in local and global economies – which, of course, can be articulated through writing skills developed in writing programs.

Postscript

As of this writing (August 2019), the Arkansas Writers MFA Workshop is heading into its eighth year of graduate studies in creative writing at the University of Central Arkansas. The Department of Writing has been disbanded, and the program is now housed in the newly created Department of Film, Theatre, and Creative Writing. Politics and realignments at the college level resulted in funding being cut for the internationally renowned *Toad Suck Review* literary journal, which used to be the cornerstone of the MFA Program as well as a powerful recruiting tool. Since this happened, enrollment has severely declined. This brings up the importance of establishing a respected brand and is discussed among other matters in the following chapter, which breaks down the basics for growing programs in creative writing.

References

Brantley, Max (2010) College enrollment rising. *Arkansas Times Blog.* October 4, 2010. Retrieved on 29 March 2017 from www.arktimes.com/ArkansasBlog/archives/2010/ 10/04/college-enrollment-rising

Department of Writing (2011) Proposal for a Masters of Fine Arts in Creative Writing. Conway, AR: University of Central Arkansas.

Genet, Jean (2004) Interview with Bertrand Poirot-Delpech. *The Declared Enemy: Texts and Interviews* (ed. Albert Dichy, trans. Jeff Fort). Stanford, CA: Stanford University Press.

Healey, Stephen Peter (2009) The rise of creative writing & the new value of creativity. *The Writer's Chronicle*, 41(4) (February 2009): 30–39. Retrieved on 3 January 2018 from https://www.awpwriter.org/magazine_media/writers_chroniclee_view/2444/the_rise_of_creative_writing_the_new_value_of_creativity

Institute of Education Sciences (2011) *National Center for Education Statistics*. Washington, DC: United States Department of Education. Retrieved on 15 February 2015 from http://nces.ed.gov

Johnson, Robert R. (2010) Rhetoric programs expand while humanities decline. *The Chronicle of Higher Education* (May 9, 2010). Retrieved on 15 February 2015 from http://chronicle.article/Rhetoric-Programs-Expand-While/655441

June, Audrey Williams (2008) Literature scholars face steepest drop in jobs in decades. *The Chronicle of Higher Education* (December 18,

2008). Retrieved on 15 February 2015 from http://chronicle.com/article/Literature-Scholars-Face/1417

Martin, Phillip (2009) Arts, culture… Conway. *Arkansas Democrat-Gazette* (March 1, 2009): J1, J6.

Mooney, Carolyn (2009) University strives to be a cultural hub in Arkansas. *The Chronicle of Higher Education* (February 20, 2009): A17–18.

U.S. Bureau of Labor Statistics (2011) *Occupational Outlook Handbook.* Washington, DC: United States Department of Labor. Retrieved on 15 February 2015 from www.bls.gov

Chapter 9

Nine Recommendations for Growing Creative Writing Programs

As mentioned in the Introduction, Part 3 of this book, "Programmatic Discoveries," investigates how to tap into writing powers at an institutional level so that higher education can serve students and communities. But for creative writing programs to empower individuals, they first need to work for themselves. What does that mean? It means that individual programs need solid foundations in order to develop their own specialized identities which can help literary artists become their own energy-generating turbines.

For example, the MFA program in creative writing at the University of Alabama at Tuscaloosa (https://catalog.ua.edu/graduate/arts-sciences/english/creative-writing-mfa) is a studio/academic program (same as studio/research) known for experimental aesthetics in connection with an innovative book arts program. This combination allows students to develop unique voices and styles as well as an appreciation and knowledge of the artistic craft of bookmaking. The MFA program at the University of North Carolina in Wilmington (https://uncw.edu/writers/mfa/index.html) offers its own valuable experience through their highly progressive publishing lab, which has created their identity as one of the most, if not the foremost, cutting-edge programs in creative writing in the United States. Then there's the heralded Iowa Writers' Workshop (https://writersworkshop.uiowa.edu), famous for being the oldest and most competitive creative writing MFA program in the country, which provides graduates with an advantage for acquiring teaching positions and literary agents.

But for programs to get to this point, where they're recognized for what they've accomplished and who they've trained, they need to get past the fundamental building blocks of establishing what and who they are and who they serve. That's what I was thinking about a few years ago when I attended a panel at the AWP (Association of Writers & Writing Programs) Conference on how to grow creative writing programs. This subject was of interest to me since I had recently assembled the proposals for a major and minor in creative writing and had spearheaded a program proposal for an MFA in creative writing at the University of Central Arkansas. Because of these experiences, I found myself looking for overlaps in ideas between the panelists and myself, but surprisingly, I found that there wasn't much intersection between their suggestions and the strategies I'd advise. This, in turn, led me to ask myself what I would suggest to departments invested in developing creative writing programs.

By the end of the panel, I'd created a list of nine recommendations for departments and administrators based on what had and hadn't worked for our institution and what could work for others.

1. Nothing Brings Students and Faculty Together Like a Literary Journal

At the undergraduate level, literary journals are community builders. Collaboration creates excitement and editorial experience offers a glimpse into the larger publishing world. The events that accompany literary journals (i.e. readings, poetry slams, conferences, fundraisers) work to publicly bind those whose art originates in isolation, which automatically creates communal catharsis. At the graduate level, lit journals are essential for recognition and the establishment of a serious literary culture. When outside evaluators look at creative writing MFA programs, they're basically united in the fact that if you want to be a relevant player in the industry, then you've got to have forums for creative outreach which extend beyond your own borders.

The question then becomes print, or online, or both? If a department decides to go with print, it's still going to need an online presence in order to be considered relevant. That presence could be a simple website or blog or Facebook page, or it could be a highly involved cyber version of the same publication, or something in between. Whatever the case, writers will look to the online component of a literary journal for the most up-to-date guidelines on how to submit.

Editing and publishing classes can also be built into creative writing program curriculums, and practicums can be designed in which students work on literary journals for credit toward their degrees. Such group experiences will bring writers together in an academic setting. This is what we do at UCA, designating our Advanced Editing and Publishing course as a required class to be taken during a graduate student's first semester in the MFA program. What we've found is that it's beneficial to mandate this coursework at the beginning of a student's tenure rather than toward the end because collaboration helps form strong bonds right off the bat when people don't know each other and are seeking to form communities. Also, as a side note, after a year or two in any program, complicated personal dynamics can arise that lead to tension not conducive to assembling the best product possible. This is a rare occurrence, but in my experience, I've seen it happen multiple times, so it's something to be aware of when the objective is bringing people together.

2. Build a High-Profile Literary Culture

Whether developing a reading series, or bringing in established writers for residencies, or spotlighting emerging local writers or putting on launch events, such events bring people together and reflect well on the organizers as being legit orchestrators of literary happenings. Even punk guerilla theater is a prescription for sophistication. Meeting in the flesh, of course, is harder for online or low-res programs, but it's also possible to interact via live performances or webinars on social media, or through sites like Reddit and YouTube – not to mention podcasts or old fashioned radio – in real time.

When a writing program builds a literary culture within and around the department, I see two main things being accomplished. First, in working together to secure venues, publicize events, collect cover at the door, and deal with whatever unexpected occurrences naturally come up, students gain valuable and applicable managerial experience. This is advantageous for CV-building and strengthening a program's standing in the community. Second, when writers are on stage, other writers actually slow down and listen to them, which is what students need to do to grow as writers. In order to be informed by a diversity of factors rather than the self-generated ideas that arise in their own private echo chambers, it can only help developing writers to witness the voices and approaches of their peers just as much as those who are already accomplished in their fields. It's a no-brainer that to be a serious writer one must read as much as one can, but watching and participating in literary performances is on the same level of importance for building writing communities. In addition, putting on events, attending events, and listening to other writers helps students become confident public speakers, which makes them more than just writers who write. That is, reading events provide guidance for writers to become just as skilled in communication as they are intriguing in craft.

3. Resources Are Imperative

Consistent and reliable funding is the most important resource any writing program can have. The more money a department can spare for stipends for writers, producing events and advertising its programs, printing classroom materials and supporting publication, computer equipment and software, the design and upkeep of websites, and travel expenses for faculty and students to take part in conferences, the more successful its programs will be. Passion is not enough to make a program brilliant or even adequate. A permanent budget is necessary, and arts fees can help with that, as can grants and endowments. Fundraisers, however, run the risk of bringing in less cash in subsequent years. They'll generate interest in the beginning, but after that initial rush of curiosity is over and the cause has become status quo, contributions can slow to a trickle. As an editor of the *Exquisite Corpse,* the *New Delta Review,* and the *Toad Suck Review,* I've seen this happen with numerous bandfests, variety shows, and readings organized by staff members. The new soon becomes the old and other needs and causes come along. If you decide to depend on funds you are able to acquire here and there or the occasional in-house grant or occasional philanthropist, it's going to be a long, frustrating, up and down ride. Nothing can burn out a faculty more than having to raise funds annually just to meet basic needs, so make sure you've got a reliable built-in budget for your program that can cover your needs as they change, or you might find yourself desperately scrambling for money. At the same time, it pays to incentivize faculty members who are willing to apply for grants, which may also be an appropriate role for the department head or other administrative staff to take on.

The second most important resource, and an unsung one at that, are faculty resources, which can play an important part in launching a program. When drafting the proposal for the Arkansas Writers MFA Workshop, our creative writing faculty foresaw that we'd receive pushback if we requested new faculty positions as a prerequisite for launching the program. Such resources would cost tens of thousands of dollars, and administrators, of course, are always looking for creative solutions to solving financial quandaries. Hence, we established that we already had all the faculty resources needed to start the program, but as the program grew and collected hundreds of thousands of dollars in revenue for the university, we would need more faculty resources to serve our growing student population. The fact that it wasn't necessary to provide any new faculty salaries in the first few years of the program was definitely an incentive which appealed to our dean and provost, and it gave us an edge over other departments in the university seeking to launch their own programs.

It also pays to look at resources that are already in place. The campus library, for instance, is already there, and it already has thousands of texts which pertain to writing. Some university libraries have annual resources available for purchasing books that students will need, so meeting with librarians during the drafting of a degree proposal is advisable to see what possibilities exist. One might also find unused space on campus that can be used to suit classroom or office space needs, or maybe there's a computer lab in another department which a limited amount of students could be granted access to. Offices of Sponsored Programs can also prove valuable in finding seed funds and private donors, and alumni associations can be strategic sources as well for securing in-house funds. At the University of Central Arkansas, our creative writing faculty often partners with the English Department at Hendrix College to bring established writers to both campuses. These are just some of a host of possibilities for making use of resources already in existence. If creative minds can write novels, plays, and epic poems, they can definitely write grant requests and discover creative ways to cut costs and capitalize on resources needed to maintain programs.

4. Faculty and Administrators Have to Really Want It

If there isn't a general consensus in a department that growing a writing program is an important curricular step to take, and if the leaders of such causes are not enthusiastic to take it to the next level and surpass faculty expectations, you might as well just give it up. Programs in creative writing need committed and excited champions who are zealots in their belief that creativity is critical, or else there will be a lack of vision and commitment.

When I drafted the proposal for the Arkansas Writers MFA Workshop, it definitely helped that the creative writing faculty members all had the same objective. When it came time to edit the document together, our faculty had weekly and sometimes bi-weekly meetings to go over the proposal section by section, word by word, until we worked out the kinks. Working so closely and articulating our arguments together also allowed us the chance to envision exactly what we needed to do and how to articulate our visions and requirements. The closer we got to our goal, the more excited we became at making it a reality. And the more excited we became, the more support we received campus-wide. It was ultimately a unanimous effort which involved some marketing to colleagues in other departments, and it paid off in the end.

On the other hand, I've seen creative writing faculty members at other colleges propose programs with fractured faculty support. I won't name these institutions, but I can tell you that when some professors are left out of the planning process, or not consulted, this feeds resentment and leads to program proposals going up in flames. It's a simple fact that a united faculty has more potential to get what it wants than a divided faculty, so the more faculty members you have on board, the greater your chances are of getting what you want.

5. Create a Brand That Stands Out from the Rest

Don't just come up with another standard BA or MA degree in creative writing, but consider the specialized areas and unique experiences and outcomes your faculty can offer depending on their backgrounds and expertise. Also, consider what resources are available on your campus. For example, UCA makes use of sharing faculty resources between disciplines. We have a professor who teaches in both professional writing and creative writing, and we have a screenplay writer who teaches in both film and creative writing, which has made for aspects of those subjects becoming part of the experience in our creative writing major and minor for the students who choose to go those routes.

As for graduate programs, most MFA degrees are studio/research (meaning half literature, half creative writing courses), whereas studio programs (writing-intensive) and research/theory/studio programs (theory-intensive) are less common. Consider what niches you can fill, especially in your region. Under whatever umbrella your department or university decides to create a program, you will also want to consider the specializations you can offer that will make your program unique. For instance, the creative writing MFA at the University of Arkansas (https://fulbright.uark.edu/departments/english/graduate/mfa-in-creative-writing) offers a focus in literary translation, the University of Wyoming's creative writing MFA (http://www.uwyo.edu/creativewriting/mfa-program) offers a dual degree in environment and natural resources, and UCA (https://uca.edu/ftcw/mfa-in-creative-writing) trains MFA graduates for jobs in publishing and pedagogy.

Still, there are other ways to establish a brand that stands out from the rest. The celebrated Wallace Stegner Fellowship at Stanford University (https://creativewriting.stanford.edu/stegner-fellowship/overview) is famous for producing legendary writers like Ken Kesey and Larry McMurtry, and it allows for students in their English department to interact with poet laureates and other world-class writers. Similarly, the Michener Center for Writers at the University of Texas at Austin (https://michener.utexas.edu) is one of the most prestigious and well-endowed MFAs in creative writing in the country. Every student in that graduate program receives $27,500 per year, and they don't have to pay tuition or fees, so they can concentrate on their work.

Since the programs students choose become part of their identities, who wants hamburger when you can have steak? As they say, "What you eat is what you are." I use this metaphor to make a point about brands that offer an unusual experience, which is a factor students consider in choosing programs to fit their needs. Unusual MFA experiences that lead to specialized MFA credentials can be advantageous for graduates whose competitors hold standard MFA degrees, a factor for any developing writing program to consider in marketing itself amidst the competition.

6. Broadcast the Fact That a Creative Writing Degree Is Currency

To sell creative writing programs to state boards of higher education in the United States, proposals typically need to include a section that describes what sort of jobs have recently been offered in the state for which graduates qualify. In assembling both the BA and MFA proposals for creative writing degrees at UCA, I had to do intensive research for jobs in Arkansas in which degrees in creative writing qualified graduates for jobs, and I found many more than expected. For candidates with writing degrees, there were positions for editors, reporters, software designers, and positions in management, marketing, graphic design, and teaching. Collecting relevant job descriptions in one's state or region provides for a realistic view of the jobs graduates will qualify for, and it's advisable to start on this list a year or two before any narratives are drafted for program proposals because the data will be vital for making the case that a creative writing degree is a valued commodity in the economic workforce.

You can also make the argument that the new global economy is not only looking for teachers in diverse areas of writing, but there's a solid demand for creative communicators with editorial and technical skills which are enhanced through creative writing programs. How to make this argument? By gathering articles and books that support such claims. Relevant sources can be found by simply going to Amazon or World Cat and doing a search that employs the words "creative writing programs" or "creative writing pedagogy" or going to Google or JSTOR and entering similar search words. When doing so, remember that currency is only currency when it's current, so any information that has been around for more than a decade might not be so pertinent in these rapidly changing times. Also, rely on articles in top trade journals like *The Writer's Chronicle* and *The Chronicle of Higher Education* to make your case for the value of creative writing programs because lesser known publications won't carry as much weight.

Students and parents frequently ask me what a degree in creative writing is good for, so knowing what jobs are out there and what the prospects are for graduates is extremely useful for advising. Additionally, when a degree proposal is going through the bureaucratic process, administrators and committee members from other departments will want an authority to speak directly to the currency of a creative writing degree, even if the facts are documented right there in the proposal. Knowing the jobs and knowing the projections for employment is just something those who make decisions will want to hear repeated for reassurance that if the institution invests in your department's vision there will be a return worth the effort.

More importantly, once a program is established, being able to list job opportunities will be valuable currency for recruiting students. Potential students as well as current students should know that committing to a writing program is a wise and practical decision to make. To spread the word about what your program can do for potential students, publish information on the program's website about graduates who've secured professional positions and maintain a blog or social network page that also includes such information. If your department prints literature to quantify the return of the education it offers, these are also inexpensive, effective ways to spread the message that creative writing degrees are currency. And if your institution has a visiting day where students and parents go to various tables touting different programs in different departments, be sure to supply your representatives with the job opportunities section straight from your program proposal.

Those who are dedicated to the study of creative writing will need little convincing. I've known plenty of business majors who, after some highly involved conversations with themselves, defected for poetry, and not for any business reasons. Of course, making money shouldn't be the goal in any profession; doing what you love should be the ideal. Still, for those considering a creative writing program, knowing that job security is possible can sometimes be a deciding factor. And if a creative writing program can provide scholarships, assistantships, tuition waivers, or any assistance landing jobs, that's currency too.

7. Appropriate Students from Other Disciplines

To grow writing programs by amassing more majors and minors, the key is to get students hooked on creative writing early in their undergraduate odysseys. This means, first of all, making intro-ductory courses easily accessible and available, and if possible, designating them as general education (Gen Ed) courses which satisfy core requirements and are open to first-year students. More students equals more interest, equals more degree applications, equals more departmental support from the institution.

And make it a department initiative for every creative writing faculty member in your program to give a quick talk at some point in every creative writing class about the value of your majors and minors. Let students know the currency of such degrees (see #7 above), and let them know there's no shame or dishonor in studying what they want to study rather than what they're expected to study. Odds are that in every creative writing course there will be some non-majors who are there to do more than score an elective. If students have gone to the trouble to meet the prerequisites for an upper-level creative writing course, that means they're interested in creative writing. And if that's the case, it could make a difference to let those interested students know that creative writing is interested in them as well.

Besides, it's good to appropriate students who have studied in other areas. They bring knowledge of other subjects with them, which can make a class more interesting for the instructor. I, for one, love defectors from biology. To make a stereotype, they tend to get all these wiggly little capillaries and Latin words into their descriptions that your average creative writing major has never experienced, which adds to the classroom experience. Moreover, if somebody is trying to decide if they should really give up their current major to practice their art – which was a question I was once faced with (do I choose literature at the University of Iowa or creative writing at the University of Colorado?) – and if they choose to go with their heart rather than what's practical, that's both a major (pun intended!) and scary existential decision. But if students choose creative writing like I did, the chances are extremely good that they will throw themselves into their passion. And what more devoted type of student can a writing program have than that? The point being: when creative students defect from other fields, they widen the playing field by introducing unique perspectives – which is good for communities.

8. Involve Hungry, Young, Idealistic Faculty

When forming committees to propose creative writing programs, it's more than practical to recruit new, ambitious faculty members who have something to prove compared to the tenured professors, who – having already fought to establish their place on the faculty – typically have less incentive to be involved in departmental development efforts. Also, younger faculty members, especially those just out of graduate school, will have a better idea of how other writing programs operate as well as what the concerns are at the student level. Of course, experienced, visionary faculty can work symbiotically with adjuncts, part-timers, lectures and visiting professors to fight for new programs, and that's always a bonus.

Still, the bottom line is if you don't have a dedicated frontline to lead your charge, you run the risk of ushering in a mediocre program with weak faculty support. Accepting such an outcome would be regrettable when the opportunity exists to attract and involve faculty members eager to invest in building the department and participate in new initiatives.

That's who I was and that's how I felt when I approached my dean in 2008 and outlined my plan of action. Knowing he desired a national literary journal to be published through the College of Fine Arts and Communication, and knowing I could negotiate a deal between UCA and Andrei Codrescu's long-established literary journal *Exquisite Corpse*, I communicated to the dean that Andrei was agreeable to publishing a print incarnation of the *Corpse*, which was only an online journal at the time. As an incentive, I offered to write the proposal for an MFA in creative writing – which I also knew the dean desired for the college. To my surprise, he didn't just accept my offer; he even provided the course releases necessary to launch the journal and draft the proposal.

I then threw myself into those projects and worked like a demon to actualize those visions. My enthusiasm was contagious, and I soon had my entire faculty on board. Together, we drew up the plans for a progressive MFA program in creative writing and created an award-winning, international literary journal.[1] This notoriety (which was mostly due to handing a new faculty member the keys to the family car) resulted in an explosion of positive attention for the department and college. Our accomplishments were reported on by the local, state, and national media, and just as the proposal promised, this ultimately increased the university's profile as an active and avant-garde force in the literary arts.

The point here is: Trust your young guns who have the energy and aspirations to take programmatic visions to the streets.

9. Offer a Progressive Curriculum That Values the Imagination

Designing courses geared toward creating art that challenges students to think in new and different ways rather than molding students into traditional scholars will open doors for creative communicators. What do I mean by that? Consider the graphic novel, for instance. Due to the current high-tech, visually oriented generation's demand to study this type of subject matter, more and more creative writing programs are teaching the genre of illustrated narratives. As postmodern texts like Art Spiegelman's *Maus* (Spiegelman, 1991) demonstrate, this genre is able to effectively address complicated issues like anti-Semitism and human rights in a way that's extremely popular with younger readers. It's probably safe to say that the graphic novel is preferred by developing writers over traditional writings on the diaspora. With apologies to the essay and to historical fiction, it's probably also safe to say that most creative writing students want to study writing modes which speak to them in the Now and can be seen as investments in their futures. So why not give students what they want?

In both the BA and MFA in creative writing at UCA, the creative writing faculty discovered that courses which employ contemporary literature as models for stylistic imitation to deviate from are not only more desirable for students over courses which dissect texts in order to analyze historical or social context, but they're more effective in providing evolving writers with the tools they need to reach their objectives (which, in most cases, is either publication, employment, or both). Studying Shakespeare or Victorian literature has its benefits, but for creative writers who are ready to get down to business practicing their craft, creative writing programs need to break away from the traditional read-this-discuss-that-receive-grade process typically taught in English departments which focus on the *study* of literature rather than the *writing* of it. Both creative writing students and creative writing programs will get more out of examining twenty-first-century works like the super-cerebral prose of David Foster Wallace's "Consider the Lobster" (Wallace, 2005) or the docupoetry of C. D. Wright's *One with Others* (Wright, 2010) rather than works by Hemingway or Stein – which, like it or not, are from another century.

Since most college mission statements state that fostering intellectual freedom and producing consciously aware citizens is an objective in educating students, implementing courses which nurture the arts rather than deconstructing prose or demystifying poetry is good for the creative neighborhood. What I'm talking about is teaching craft rather than teaching how to read and write like a professor. Or, in other words, to create creative writers it's just more useful these days to approach the writing process through investigations that lead to discovery than it is to rely on old school methods which are ultimately geared toward creating scholars rather than artists.

Take-Home Message

Take all of these recommendations, or even just some, and your writing programs will be in a better position to provide writers with the energy they need to generate their own power. After all, programs in creative writing don't exist to serve the needs of faculty members; they exist to advance the craft by passing on insights to aid in creating strong connections that speak to people – which is an awesome responsibility. Because if writing teachers look at their programs mainly as a means to feed their families or take off on summer vacations, then they've forgotten why they first got into this business. To spell it out: Writers are here to write, teachers are here to teach, and students are here to learn. But the one thing these groups have in common is that they all owe a debt to the muse. And that's where writing programs come in: to create the most progressive conditions possible to transform students into writers. Otherwise, students lose. And if students lose, then the question is how do we – as writers and writing teachers passing on the most powerful tool we know how to use – live with that?

Note

1   In 2011 the *Exquisite Corpse Annual* transitioned to the *Toad Suck Review*. In 2012, *Library Journal* honored the *Toad* with an award for being one of the ten best literary journals in the world published in 2011.

References

Spiegelman, Art (1991) *Maus: A Survivor's Tale*. New York: Pantheon.
Wallace, David Foster (2005) Consider the lobster. *Consider the Lobster*. Abacus: London.
Wright, C. D. (2010) *One with Others*. Port Townsend, WA: Copper Canyon Press.

Chapter 10

Dealing with Diverse Issues in Creative Writing Programs: A Polemic

I. How Can Programs in Creative Writing Serve Students Better?

In 2015, *The New York Times* characterized the creative writing industry as "explosive." Cecilia Capuzzi Simon's article "Why Writers Love to Hate the M.F.A." summarizes the growth of MFA programs in creative writing by noting that

> Iowa was the first, established in 1936. By 1994, there were 64. By [2014], that number had more than tripled, to 229 (and another 152 M.A. programs in creative writing), according to the Association of Writers and Writing Programs. Between 3,000 and 4,000 students a year graduate with the degree: this year, about 20,000 applications were sent out. (Simon, 2015)

These numbers are specific to the United States and do not include the rest of the BA, BFA, and PhD programs in creative writing around the world, which account for tens of thousands more. Because of such popularity, critics of these programs naturally exist.

I recall my own experience as a graduate student at the University of Colorado. Whereas everything that came along with being connected to an MA program in creative writing was inspiring for me, it was the complete opposite for my roommate. We were both living in the same duplex, taking the same classes, associating with the same students and faculty, but our outlooks were radically different. I saw the workshop as an exciting laboratory for experimentation and the gleaning of useful feedback, but he saw it as a humiliating torture chamber packed with smarmy egos and sadistic aggressors hell-bent on attacking each other and showing off. After two years in that program, I graduated with an optimistic confidence, and he sank into a jaded alcoholic stupor which he blamed, in part, on a dog-eat-dog culture that forces amateur writers to battle each other while shamelessly parading themselves and their work around as if they deserved pomp and acclaim.

That was his view of "the workshop," and a quarter-century later, he's still trying to recover from the trauma. But if there's one thing he got from that program, it was experience writing and teaching, which led to him becoming a professional editor. More than that, he's now a singing, songwriting, spoken-word advocate in the AA world who puts on local shows for people fighting similar demons. In other words, he's a critic of the workshop, but nevertheless a product of the workshop who was trained to communicate by the very system he condemns.

But that's the way it's always been. Programs are organized plans for people to follow, and since there's never a perfect plan, there's always room for improvement. Because people are always looking for improvement, every program in anything inevitably creates dissent, alienation, and criticism to varying degrees. And since writing programs churn out reactionary personalities with acute articulation skills, there are those who offer sound arguments for why creative writing programs fall short.

One of the most vocal critics of creative writing programs is Ryan Boudinot, whose essay "Things I Can Say About MFA Writing Programs Now That I No Longer Teach in One" (Boudinot, 2015) caused an uproar in 2015 when it was published in *The Stranger*. Boudinot railed against the MFA from the perspective of a disgusted former professor, claiming these three controversial bullet points:

- "Writers are born with talent;"
- "If you didn't decide to take writing seriously by the time you were a teenager, you're probably not going to make it;" and
- "If you complain about not having time to write, please do us both a favor and drop out."

His other observations were "If you aren't a serious reader, don't expect anyone to read what you write;" "No one cares about your problems if you're a shitty writer;" "You don't need my help to get published;" "It's not important that people think you're smart;" and "It's important to woodshed" (Boudinot, 2015). That last point, I should note, has more to do with the obscure definition of practicing on a musical instrument rather than taking somebody out back and whipping them into submission.

Contemplating Boudinot's article led me to investigate the complaints of some of the most visible contemporary critics of the creative writing goliath in order to find solutions for programmatic issues. My main question at the time was "How can creative writing programs better serve their students?" It was admittedly a vague and unfocused approach, but that's not uncommon for me, and in my experience, starting out scattered and unorganized often leads to specific discoveries which make sense in the end.

As usual, the process led me into terrain I didn't expect, which made the journey intriguing. As I went along, the road became more profound in what it revealed, and it eventually led to observing some dynamics that I had never considered so seriously before. This impressed me because I saw it lead to some intellectual growth in myself which could be useful for developing writers.

But back to Boudinot. He was open to responding to interview questions, so I asked him a few through the email ranging from whether he had come to any new conclusions regarding his arguments to whether there was a workshopping method he recommended. I tried to get him to elaborate on his characterization of what he termed the "Real Deal" students in comparison to the rest (whom he characterized as lazy, irritating, therapy-seeking wannabes seeking community), and I asked him if he thought MFA programs had any value in making the world a more sophisticated place by encouraging a respect for literature or preparing creative individuals for jobs in teaching.

What I received from Boudinot was a general response that challenged what he saw as my pessimistic depiction of his article. He went into great detail defending his stance that his arguments were a call for a deeper, more sincere approach to writing. He also expressed valuing his own MFA education while confessing to stereotyping the entire commerce of creative writing. He sort of responded to a question I asked about creative writing programs making the world a better place by confirming that MFA programs help to prepare teachers who should teach. The rest was about his vision of where literature was heading, what we have to lose, and what he was doing for the effort in his community of Seattle.

I wrote Boudinot back, thanking him for his generous reply and explained that what I was looking for were solutions to the problems he envisioned. Then, apologetically, I hit him with three more questions.

Predictably, I received no response.

II. The Investigation Begins to Take Shape

Another major critic of the MFA "guild system" is the writer and literary critic Anis Shivani, author of *Against the Workshop* (Shivani, 2011). His blog attack of 2010 in the *Huffington Post* (Shivani, 2010) definitely took the MFA to task. In his indictment, entitled "Creative Writing Programs: Is the MFA System Corrupt and Undemocratic?", he made statements like the workshop is "a hands-on learning so precious that rules of monopoly must be imposed to prevent its dilution" and "conservativeness in organization usually results in conservativeness of product as well" (Shivani, 2010).

Not surprisingly, these claims triggered questions from me. My main question was: But aren't there some teachers who act as progressive gatekeepers by discouraging mainstream writing, which dilutes the diversity of voice that the market is capable of spotlighting? This question was of interest to me because having gone through four programs in creative writing (a BA, an MA, an MFA, and a PhD), I'd had my share of rebel professors and activist rabble-rousers who encouraged risk-taking and stylistic acrobatics just as much as taking on the establishment or defying the PC police. These teachers ranged from Madelon Sprengnether, to Andrei Codrescu, Ronald Sukenick, Lorna Dee Cervantes, Ed Dorn, Steve Katz, Skip Fox, Linda Hogan, and more – all liberal products of the sixties in a sense, so therefore exceptions to Shivani's rule that graduate programs in creative writing are presided over by conservative practitioners.

I also had trouble with Shivani's (2010) contention that a new socially conservative writing arose in American culture during the eighties (Reaganism), and that writers like "Raymond Carver, Ann Beattie, Jay McInerney, Bret Easton Ellis, Amy Hemphill [*sic*], Mary Robison" became ascendant during the cultural popularizing of creative writing programs. According to Shivani, an "Inquisition" was formed and still exists in which "one is made to feel guilty and ashamed if writing compels one to move toward areas forbidden by the Inquisition" (Shivani, 2010).

Having gone to state schools and having taught at state schools for over half my life, perhaps I missed something. Sure, I've been fed a good amount of Carver, and I do see a lot of my colleagues pledging allegiance to the Inquisition Shivani suggests, but pressure from socially conservative writing was never part of my experience. Maybe a more East-Coasty education or going to a private college would have informed my inner-junior-inquisitor and so would've shaped my mentality as a more conservative writer. But because that didn't happen, I find it hard to accept Shivani's vision that an Inquisitional MFA pedagogy is now the absolute norm.

Still, I questioned my own questioning, wondering if I was missing his point. Maybe Shivani's Inquisition concept has more to do with competition at the commercial level, where most works by most writers have little potential to be lucrative when big-agented "lapidary"[1] authors receive attention for consistently grinding out work so minimalist that simplistic language and lack of metaphorical devices fail to elevate the author's voice and style to what is commonly considered "literary."

My questions about Shivani's arguments were undeniably embryonic at that point, and I had many. Shivani contended that "the monopoly of the craft" of fiction was "leaning strongly toward the confessional, memoiristic, autobiographical, narcissistic, and plainly understood," and I had questions about that point as well. I also had questions about his statement that "gone is the revolutionary, or even anti-establishment, potential of the reading; it functions these days not to stir or provoke or enlighten or anger or frustrate or cajole, but as an endorsement of the democracy of talent, and that alone" (Shivani, 2010) – a platform I challenged because I knew it wasn't always the case. For example, I regularly teach the poetics of the manifesto, and I've found that students, because they seek change, are predisposed "to want A.B.C., [and to] thunder against 1, 2, 3" (Tzara, 2001: 297). I've seen this impetus go into student work, and I've seen students get up on stage and thunder away, and having been there myself, I know that Shivani is wrong. When writers are sincerely strident about getting a message across, it's not about showing off.

But ultimately, I knew I was just picking around the edges of something even more important, and that the investigation was about to reveal something I had never expected. And then it did.

III. Race Reveals Itself as Major Part of the Investigation

The third critic of the MFA system I considered was the Pulitzer-Prize-winning nonfiction writer Junot Díaz. His controversial article "MFA vs. POC" in *The New Yorker* (Díaz, 2014) caused a shock to creative writing programs that the industry is still reeling from for reasons that go way beyond lamentations concerning the commercial technicalities of teaching craft. Díaz, looking back on his MFA experience, went right for the throat: The "standard problem with MFA programs," he claimed, and the problem he'd experienced with workshopping was: "That shit was *too white*" (Díaz, 2014).

This, of course, is something we can all see. Having embedded myself in creative writing programs for over thirty years, I can attest that you can usually count the number of minority students in a college creative writing class on one hand, and the faculty is usually just as Caucasian. It was Díaz who called this situation out to the woodshed (in the more common sense), and it's a discussion we needed to have – and still do.

Again I'm reminded of my experience at the University of Colorado. My disgruntled roommate and I were taking a poetry workshop with Reg Saner, and as in pretty much all creative writing programs across the country, the grad student population was dominated by descendants of the colonizers.

Esteban was the only person of color in that class. He was always quiet, he never volunteered to speak, and he watched the other students with a somewhat unnerving silence. Most students just figured he was anti-social, especially in the last class, a potluck at the professor's house. After we had our fill of everything from Esteban's spicy salsa (a big hit) to my carp dumplings (which didn't go over quite as well), the students gathered to perform one final poem each. The assignment was to read a poem appropriate to the occasion.

Appropriately or not, Esteban went last. I don't have a copy of that poem anymore, nor can I remember the exact wording, but he essentially told us he had urinated in the pico de gallo.

Whether that was true or not, Esteban finally cracked a smile. It was a smile that told us he was collecting what he was due. It was a smile that suggested some justice had been done. It was a smile that told us we ate pee. But most of all, it was a smile that made us reflect on something we needed to be aware of.

Díaz, I think, felt a lot like Esteban. As Díaz (2014) wrote, "neither the faculty nor the administration saw that lack of color in the fiction program … and neither the faculty nor the administration saw that lack of color as a big problem …. [M]y workshop reproduced exactly the dominant culture's blind spots and assumptions around race and racism." Díaz (2014) then described "an almost lunatical belief that race was no longer a major social force," after which he went on to explain how racial identities and the impacts of racial identities were never explored in his workshop and how he never got any instruction in that area. He added that race was never talked about in those classes unless an argument arose regarding how discussions of race should not be entertained by serious writers.

"In my workshop," Díaz (2014) wrote, "what was defended was not the writing of people of color but the right of the white writer to write about people of color without considering the critiques of people of color." Simply put, he saw himself as "a person of color in a workshop whose theory of reality did not include [his] most fundamental experiences as a person of color" (Díaz, 2014).

That's what I saw in Esteban's smile. He had been excluded. Maybe not intentionally, but because of the nature of who ends up in creative writing programs, the demographics are stacked in favor of those who are less conscious of how racial identities matter for some more than others. Consequently, what gets discussed in workshops are the concerns of the privileged class.

Díaz (2014), however, supplied easy solutions to this complex programmatic problem in his article. First of all, he advised students of color in programs that are just "too white" to "please hang in there. We need your work. Desperately." He also described a solidarity with other students of color that he was fortunate enough to discover, which he credited for saving his life. The Latino student movement Díaz joined had its influence on pushing "through our first fiction faculty of color in the MFA program" (Díaz, 2014), which led to his next solution: Students of color need faculty of color whose similar social experiences create bonds of understanding and support. Another suggestion was that it's vital to have successful role models of color right there in the classroom who can demonstrate to students of color that it's possible to break through ceilings and exist in environments which evolve slowly in casting off their antiquated ways.

But, I figured, there must be other solutions to this persisting problem – like just put it out there and start talking about it, like open up a conversation in order to get at what's important for the future of creative writing, such as a diversity of voices and perspectives. Still, one must be extremely careful when going down that path. These things need to be well thought out, unlike the diversity workshop recently offered in the MFA program in which I teach. Since three-fifths of our incoming class were students of color, the entirely white Graduate Writing Association (GWA) decided to invite the new students to open up a dialogue. Faculty were invited as well as the institution's coordinator of outreach programming, a person who was experienced in moderating such meetings.

To sum up what happened, the diversity workshop was a disaster. It began with a middle-aged white Southerner talking about his problem writing from the point of view of "the Other," and he wanted to discuss ways to go about this type of narration with proper sensitivity. This unfortunate framing set up an us vs. them dichotomy and a combative tension instantly arose. Things got heated and the outreach coordinator we thought could moderate couldn't keep the accusatory punches from flying across the room. At the end of the session, we were asked to state our goals, and the meeting was adjourned. And as I left that room wanting to run, I couldn't help overhearing some agreement about what a constructive conversation it had been – which it wasn't. It was a sloppy, embarrassing failure to communicate, and everything would've been better if we had just done our jobs and treated each other like normal human beings.

It was no surprise then when one of our new recruits, an African-American student, suddenly dropped out of the MFA program with no explanation whatsoever. Though other factors might have been involved, this proved to me that the exclusion Díaz noted was real enough to hit our small program.

A few months later, I discussed Díaz's article with a colleague who identified herself as a queer writer of color. She specialized in writing about racial identity, and I told her I was looking for solutions beyond what Díaz had suggested. She instantly promoted the idea of "sensitivity training," a notion some authorities are quick to claim as being faulty. The diversity workshop had essentially been just that, and, as an expert on sexual harassment that I'd heard on the radio noted, sensitivity training does not work. Her evidence was in what the #MeToo movement had accomplished. She pointed to a great wave of powerful men (Harvey Weinstein, politicians, hip-hop moguls, movie stars, sports stars, celebrity chefs – and, ironically, Díaz himself[2]) who all had the required sensitivity training of their industries because industries provide such training in order to not get sued. The authority on the radio asserted that sexual harassment is a constant in Western culture and will never be trained away, and I clearly saw a parallel point that racial insensitivity is just as much something not so easily trained away.

So maybe the question was how to come up with better training because, essentially, the professional sensitivity training faculty are required to do on an annual basis is a joke. All anyone has to do to pass the online tests is to keep hitting the first button seen on the screen, and eventually, without reading any instructional material, one can become a certified, non-harassing, non-racially divisive, culturally aware employee.

Be that as it may, I was again left with a growing list of questions.

IV: Student Involvement in the Investigation Leads to a Shocking Discovery

My graduate students, however, took a step in the right direction. Back in 2015, the GWA wanted to demonstrate their commitment to diversity, so they called a meeting to brainstorm solutions. Since collecting funds for a full scholarship was an unreachable goal, they decided they could at least cover waivers for grad school application fees for students of color. By working odd jobs, they were able to raise sufficient funds. They used a Twitter platform to get the message out, and though reimbursing applicants was reportedly a bureaucratic nightmare, their actions led to a 60 percent increase in newly recruited students of color in the Arkansas Writers MFA Workshop.

At that point in the investigation, I was having trouble getting responses from established creative writing pedagogues. That's why I decided to go straight to the frontlines and take an informal survey. The survey pool consisted of current and former MFA students I knew from multiple programs, the question being: What can MFA programs do to serve students better?

The first response I received was that the workshop was broken: students are not taught how to give worthwhile feedback, and there are no standards for quality of feedback. The student respondent suggested that students need to be held accountable for their feedback, but this brings up two more questions. First, how would standards for feedback be established, and wouldn't establishing standards lead to a backlash against such standards? Secondly, should creative writing teachers essentially become the Poetry Police, enforcing laws and cracking whips about what students say or write?

A recent graduate from an MFA program replied that a "master-apprentice style of study" would be beneficial, in which students work with professors whose specialties mirror student career goals. This student was not suggesting that the thesis or dissertation experience should be stretched out over a student's entire tenure in a program; he was recommending a less structured, more informal approach to mentorship. The problem with this quixotic approach is that professors don't have the time to provide individualized apprenticeships lasting two to six years, especially when there's no guarantee that a student who starts a program will finish it.

Another student veiled some complaints about a class she'd been required to take in a criticism of how MFA programs don't take the needs of diverse audiences into account. Her implication was that whereas graduate programs in other disciplines tend to take students straight out of college, a population from varied work backgrounds with more life experience gravitates toward MFA programs in creative writing where there's too much busy work which doesn't pertain to the non-creative-writing-oriented careers some students are already engaged in. She noted that homework assignments designed to find direction for career opportunities for MFA graduates are not useful for nontraditional students already ensconced in other fields, and this waste of time takes away from practicing craft.

More reading and more books was another suggestion, but to this I respond with another question: Is it the program's responsibility to drive students to read more, or is it the student's responsibility? If people are really invested in becoming serious writers, then they already have a growing pile of books which they're having trouble getting through. I would also argue that reading is one of the defining factors determining whose work gets noticed and therefore more widely distributed. The more writers that writers read, the more they train themselves to write in the language of the market. Since reading is done on one's own, and because this is something every writer needs to do to get ahead of the pack, reading, ironically, is a no-brainer.

That student also suggested a mandatory poetry class to be taken during the first semester of a creative writing program in which language is placed under the microscope in order to prep brains to dissect syntax. I believe there's some value in the idea that practicing poetry promotes placing sounds and context together more strategically, which can serve students when they jump into prose. But if it were to be mandated that all MFA programs should begin with linguistics, the ramparts would soon be stormed by angry, torch-wielding graduate students.

I received other responses as well, but these are the ones that were the most notable. As an environmental writer who is used to focusing on problems in fisheries and then offering practical solutions, it didn't feel very satisfying to end up with more questions than I started with. And the overarching question I was facing now was how to tie this all together: solutions from those supplying the demand vs. solutions from those demanding the supply; opinions on what creative writing programs can do to better serve their students vs. what the elusive real-world solutions are; and most importantly, questions of craft vs. questions of culture.

This latter consideration is the most problematic of all the questions I investigated. It might even be insulting to lump these very different questions together – as if the question of how to market vampire genre fiction is on a par with how to express complex cultural views from one's heritage when most students in a class might not have the inside knowledge to workshop such material with adequate sensitivity.

Then again, this discussion is meant to be a polemic concerning diverse issues, with which I expect and invite readers to take issue. So at this point, I'll just echo my earlier assertion that there are sensitive conversations which need to happen. But more than that, conversations about how to talk about race need to be approached in effective, proven ways or else they risk causing damage. What those ways are, I don't know – but since this is the twenty-first century, it's high time we figured it out. Because anything less is just plain racist.

V. Cutting through the Clutter and Getting to What I Can Comment on with Certainty

It was a shameful discovery: that a descendant of Holocaust survivors, who grew up with friends of all races, and who teaches and interacts with diverse people from all over the world had failed to recognize the importance of making under-represented students feel as included as possible. Not that I ignored the subject of diversity or didn't include texts by diverse authors in my classes, but I had definitely, in my teaching career, placed more emphasis on sustaining biodiversity on this planet than diversity without the "bio" prefix.

I am a white male, and because of that privilege, and because I had the luxury of not having to worry about my cultural experiences as a minority among a majority, I had overlooked an important responsibility in passing on writing powers: to make all my students feel as comfortable as possible expressing what they wanted to express.

Of course, some will look at this statement and say that teachers should just teach to the best of their abilities, and that taking special interest in a student just because of skin color is a form of racial profiling. And then there are the gay students, the transgender students, the older nontraditional students, the students with disabilities, and even the marginalized white students from disadvantaged backgrounds – all of whom I've tried to reach out to, but maybe not enough.

Maybe it was ridiculous for me to blame myself for not doing better when I was doing as well as I could and better than most. But here's what I recognized in myself and others from having been a white creative writing student in white creative writing programs: When the subject of race comes up in workshop, white students get defensive. There's often a silent communal groan that tends to shudder through the room when a minority student touches on an unjust experience. This groan comes from an attitude that race is something everyone should just get past because the more this scab is picked, the more it won't go away. And the reason this happens is because when white students who see themselves as socially aware suddenly hear narratives of oppression, they fear they're being attacked for the crimes of a previous generation. Hence, white students tend to wonder why minority students can't just write about the same things they do, that is, about "regular stuff." But here's the thing again: Those minority students writing about their experience are writing about regular stuff. Because for some, racial tensions are part of everyday existence. And for others, who don't have to contend with that on a daily basis, they sometimes think there's an aggression being directed at them. But it's not always the case that someone is pointing a finger; it's just that writers need to be real so they write about what's real for them. Then suddenly there's a misunderstanding regarding intention.

Those were the kind of thoughts I found myself dealing with while failing to get at what I could do better as a teacher. But at least I was looking into this matter, and considering the hypothesis that if race isn't an issue for me, then I'm part of the problem.

That's what I figured, and I was definitely out of my comfort zone and being challenged to look at something important through a new lens. But like many confusing realizations which slap people in the face and wake them up to what they couldn't see before, these things take time to process.

Luckily, at that point in the investigation, I got some input from an extremely savvy editor who looked at a previous draft of this chapter and asked me what the heck I was doing in combining all these scattered ideas. Her main question was "What is the whole that this amounts to?"

So here it is: The can of worms I opened had originally been labeled "How can programs in creative writing serve students better?" but what popped out was a hydra-head of diverse concerns: issues of race and inclusivity, what students want, what teachers want, what is, and what could be. It was an out-of-control mish-mash of questions, and it was time for me to start providing some solid answers.

So I did. By deciding to stop looking outside myself and resolving to start looking inside myself in order to identify the factor that had served me most in my own experience as a student in four creative writing programs. And here's what that factor is: there's truth to be found in the often applied cliché that "you get out of MFA programs exactly what you put into them" (Douglas, 2015). This line of thought led me to recognize my greatest personal discovery ever: If you're a student studying creative writing, you can't always depend on programs in creative writing to take you where you want to go, but you can depend on yourself.

Here's what I mean by that: When I was in those writing programs, they were only part of my experience and not the driving force. My driving force was me, totally obsessed with my own projects, my own research, my own experimentation, my own reading lists, and my own ambitions. Sure, I was able to discuss craft in workshop and interact with students and faculty because I was in those programs, but that was only a fraction of my writing life. With all the novels I was working on and translation research and marathon sessions pounding out memoirs in basements and sheds (isolation being imperative for years of failure and revision), creative writing programs provided extra support for what I was fortunate to already be up to my neck in.

I was also fortunate to land jobs in which I got paid while focusing on my own work. When I worked in factories, I listened to books on tape. When I worked as a parking lot attendant or a security guard, I'd stay up all night jamming away on laptop computers the size of suitcases. When I worked in libraries, I searched through the stacks for books and journals pertaining to the writers I was translating. I even took reams of paper to the streets as a deputized traffic director, and revised novellas and plays while standing in the middle of intersections. In other words, I managed to stay focused on my *real* work.

Double-dipping on quite a few independent studies also helped in making headway on the projects I was going to do anyway. From studying the Romantics, to translating French radio plays, to kicking out a totally unpublishable thousand-page manuscript that I eventually drove a one-foot spike through, I made my own writing projects count as credits toward my degrees – which is information most professors don't want advertised. Because if the value of taking as many directed studies as possible became something to widely exploit, creative writing faculties would find themselves overwhelmed by students vying for specialized supervised projects. And if professors supplied that demand, then classes wouldn't fill.

Another example of making my creative writing programs work for me rather than the other way around can be seen in how I used my time driving. When I lived in Baton Rouge, I used to commute an hour to work in Lafayette and then an hour back again. Crossing the Atchafalaya Swamp, I made it a practice to talk into a tape recorder, working out character traits, drumming up dialogue, and rehashing plot points I'd transcribe later. There were even a few years when I'd translate Jean Genet and drive at the same time, a makeshift desk duct-taped to my steering wheel, a stack of diction-aries, idiom books, verb-tense books, and print-outs of prison argot piled on my dash. That method, however, is not recommended, especially for curvy mountain roads, which I eventually discovered while skidding through a hairpin turn in Arizona.

I also expanded the mentors in my life by chasing down masters in the field and injecting myself into their lives in order to get insider perspectives. As a developing writer, I convinced Edmund White to assist me with my Genet translations; I barged in on the office hours of Anselm Hollo and Ward Churchill; and when my wanderings led to the infamous bookstore Shakespeare & Company in Paris, I imposed myself on a reluctant Allen Ginsberg as well as writers and editors who found themselves having to accommodate my eagerness or make their rejections known. I contacted experts through the mail and on the phone as well, bugging legendary translators and scholars for information, and because of that, some productive relationships developed. And from those experiences, I gained another nugget of writing-from-experience wisdom: Writers are basically altruistic, and if they recognize you as one of their peops, they just might let you in. And when you run with artists recognized for excellence, you learn how they invented themselves, how their work got to where it is, and how to apply their methods to your own situation.

I probably got more out of my three degrees in creative writing than ninety-nine percent of the hundreds of thousands of students who've ever studied in writing programs because I wasn't looking for those programs to prescribe my work for me. In sum, I was already immersed, and the creative writing programs I was part of were there to add to the numerous discoveries I was regularly making happen. Any disappointment I had with any of my programs wasn't worth a spit in a tin can because that wasn't what I was paying for. What I was paying for was the time to write, the space to write, and the company of people who were chasing the same dreams as I was. And that dedication to craft, that loyalty to crystalizing visions, that faith that the energy I was investing would pay off in the end – it finally did.

And that's the solution to all issues with creative writing programs: You need to work your ass off to the point that the workshop is secondary in comparison to the rest of the work you're doing. Because if you're writing and researching as effectively as you can, you're also getting direction from other sources: authorities and experts; people who screw up and lead you in the wrong direction; and people you don't even know reacting to what you send out, publish, fail to publish, ask, claim, and investigate as you become your own objective editor.

The moral of the story: Use creative writing programs as launching pads to get more experience. Then write from experience. Then, one day, come up with advice that's better than the following three talking points, which are based on what has worked for me in the past. They won't solve sexual harassment or racial insensitivity, but they can definitely help an evolving writer focus on what she needs to focus on to get to where she wants to be.

(1) If you have time to stress over problems with creative writing programs, then you're not working as hard as you can on what you need to work on to get to the next level.

(2) Expect problems, because they're going to happen, and you're not going to fix them. So instead of trying to make major fixes, find your own temporary patches, roll with the punches, and think of that as training for future injustices.

(3) Don't give up on the ideals that drive your obsessions because they can also be used to make the world a better place. Like the airlines tell you, if an oxygen mask drops from above, affix it to yourself first, then help others out. In other words, do what you need to do for yourself and don't stop in the middle and say "I can't do this," or "This isn't sufficient," or "This is getting in my way." In other words, when an issue comes up, deal with it. And if the issue is worth revisiting after you've seen the full picture, then take it to the real woodshed and keep at it until you get results.

The point I'm making is that what you put into a program in creative writing should be the same as what you put into anything you care about, including life itself. In most cases, you get back what you put in – which, in creative writing, can take decades before you see a return.

And remember this: Since the system is extremely competitive, it's only designed to recognize a micro-fraction of the macro-whole. Thus, for most students who go through creative writing programs, the returns will come in other forms – like careers and relationships. And if the process deforms you at any point, that's still a type of formation from which you can inform yourself.

Because if you can't build something progressive from your experience in a creative writing program, well – in the spirit of Díaz's view on the workshop, I'd say, "That shit is tragic."

Notes

1   The term "lapidary" was used by *Atlantic* staff editor Jessica Murphy Moo to describe Amy Hempel's aesthetic (Moo, 2006), which was formed in an era of commercial popular minimalism when editors like Gordon Lish favored writers like Raymond Carver, Ann Beattie, and Mary Robison. Referring to Hempel's work, Moo wrote: "This feast is neither lavish nor overwrought with sentiment .... The word 'lapidary' seems to be the most common – and apt – adjective used by reviewers to describe her stories." Moo went on to address how Rick Moody characterized Hempel's work as being "all about the sentences" (qtd. in Moo, 2006) and their rhythmic movement in paragraphs.

2   It is important to note, however, that after investigation Díaz was cleared to continue teaching at MIT (https://www.npr.org/2018/06/20/622094905/mit-clears-junot-diaz-of-sexual-misconduct-allegations) and serving on the Pulitzer Board (https://www.usatoday.com/story/life/people/2018/11/17/pulitzer-board-allows-junot-diaz-stay-after-harassment-allegations/ 2038471002/).

References

Boudinot, Ryan (2015) Things I can say about MFA writing programs now that I no longer teach in one. *The Stranger* (February 27, 2015). Retrieved on 12 December 2017 from https://www.thestranger.com/books/features/2015/02/27/21792750/things-i-can-say-about-mfa-writing-programs-now-that-i-no-longer-teach-in-one

Díaz, Junot (2014) MFA vs. POC. *The New Yorker* (April 30, 2014). Retrieved on 28 November 2017 from https://www.newyorker.com/books/page-turner/mfa-vs-poc

Douglas, Rory (2015) qtd. in Marta Bausells, Confessions of a creative writing teacher spark internet backlash: What is your experience? *The Guardian* (March 11, 2015). Retrieved on 28 November 2017 from https://www.theguardian.com/books/booksblog/2015/mar/11/confessions-of-a-creative-writing-teacher-spark-internet-backlash

Moo, Jessica Murphy (2006) Sentence by sentence: Short story writer Amy Hempel talks about forensics, seeing eye dogs, and her new *Collected Stories*. *The Atlantic* (April 2006). Retrieved on 29 March 2018 from https://www.theatlantic.com/magazine/archive/2006/04/sentence-by-sentence/304846

Shivani, Anis (2010) Creative writing programs: Is the MFA system corrupt and undemocratic? *Huffington Post* (October 23, 2010). Retrieved on 28 November 2017 from https://www.huffingtonpost.com/anis-shivani/creative-writing-programs-corrupt_b_757653.html

Shivani, Anis (2011) *Against the Workshop*. Huntsville: Texas Review Press.

Simon, Cecilia Capuzzi (2015) Why writers love to hate the M.F.A. *The New York Times* (April 9, 2015). Retrieved on 28 November 2017 from https://www.nytimes.com/2015/04/12/education/edlife/12edl-12mfa.html

Tzara, Tristan (2001) Dada manifesto. In Mary Ann Caws (trans. and ed.) *Manifesto: A Century of Isms* 297–304. Lincoln: University of Nebraska Press.

Part 4

Eco-Investigations

Chapter 11

Introducing "Eco" to the Homies:
A Liberal Professor's Activist Approach

Just as all ecosystems allow for biological communities to evolve, programs in creative writing allow for the growth of communities. Hence, Part 4 of this book, "Eco-Investigations," demonstrates how eco-investigations can lead to discovering solutions to environmental problems so that communities don't end up powerless.

I've been teaching environmental topics at both the pre-college, undergraduate, and graduate levels for over sixteen years. At first I taught Environmental Literature, then I taught Environmental Writing, and now I teach Ecopoetics. Back in 2002, the focus on environment was all about how cataclysmic climate change can be expected in ten to fifteen years. Now, the emphasis is analogous to trying to survive with a body in decline. In the decade and a half since I began teaching environmental subject matter, nature has radically changed. There are fewer glaciers and more sea rise. Species are going extinct on a daily basis, and a third of all species of wildlife are expected to be threatened during the next century. Global warming has ushered in more ticks and mosquitoes, more Lyme disease, chronic wasting disease, malaria, Zika, dengue – the list goes on. Still, the central messages in my introductory eco-lectures have remained the same. And since these talks never fail to fire up my students as well as myself, and since the wide eyes staring back tell me I've made a strong connection, I have an approach to offer other teachers. My hope is that this offering will be appropriated and revised according to instructor needs because the way I see it, there's nothing more important on this planet than the planet itself.

After introducing myself to my Ecopoetics class as a writer who studies fish and works on water quality issues, I establish that the ecosystem is important because it provides a place to have economies and exist with all our various problems. I add that they don't have to like nature to do well in this class, but they do have to educate themselves about what's going on in the environment in order to take a stand that matters in the discussion.

Then we go over the syllabus, in which the idea is to read and discuss mostly nonfiction, then respond via poetry. With poets like Charles Bukowski, Robert Hass, Denise Levertov, Gary Snyder and Mary Oliver addressing a wide variety of issues, Neil Astley's *Earth Shattering Ecopoems* anthology (Astley, 2007) provides solid models for framing responses. I also assign the first chapter of Bill McKibbin's *Eaarth* (McKibbin, 2011) to put current, excessive carbon dioxide levels into perspective. Later, we read Al Gore's Nobel Peace Prize speech (Gore, 2007) and the Edward Abbey essay collection *The Serpents of Paradise* (Abbey, 1996). For style and voice we look to parts I–III of Antler's "Factory" (Antler, 1980); Galway Kinnell's "The Bear" (Kinnell, 1967); Frank Stanford's *The Battlefield Where the Moon Says I Love You* (Stanford, 2000); and for illustrating landscape and characterizing place, we study the first page of Ken Kesey's novel *Sometimes a Great Notion* (Kesey, 1964). In the end, excerpts from the third edition of Dave Foreman and Bill Haywood's *Ecodefense* engender discussions on "monkeywrenching" philosophy (Foreman and Haywood, 1993), but we also watch the following documentaries: *The 11th Hour* with Leonardo DiCaprio (Conners and Petersen, 2008), *Gasland* (Fox, 2010), and parts 1 and 2 of *Cadillac Desert* (Else and Harrar, 1997).

I then explain that "green" is trendy and "eco" is hot and a new global consciousness is developing. Whereas the concept of "eco" and "environmental" are interchangeable, "nature writing" is not part of this equation. Nature writing, at least in American literature, evolved from a pastoral reverence for natural beauty found in eighteenth-century religious sermons. Nature writing is like, "Oh, look at that beautiful horse. Thank God for that horse." Eco-writing, on the other hand, has a consciousness and aspires to create change. It informs and has an agenda, and it comes from the left because all eco-writing comes from the left. If it comes from the right, it's not eco-writing but propaganda generated in defense of Big Oil. The scientific community is united on this. Some top deniers of climate change who used to be funded by the right-wing Koch brothers have even reversed their claims that global warming is not caused by humans.

By this time in the lecture it's clear that I'm definitely a lefty professor, which is fine for most students but can raise red flags for others. So I give my wary students an out. "In this class," I tell them, "you're going to get a liberal perspective from a liberal professor. If you don't like that, then drop this class as soon as you can and replace it with something more worthwhile."

Next, I talk about the roots of the prefix "eco," which comes from the Greek word "oiko" and the Late Latin "oeco," meaning "house" or "home." I bring up the French word "école" (school) and the English word "ecology" to make the point that the concept of "eco" is about schooling ourselves to find balance for our home. I then draw a circle on the board, and say, indicating the circle, that this is our home, and since we all live here, we are "the homies." They always get a kick out of that.

I then talk about the "ecologue," a perversion of the word "eclogue," a fifteenth-century text in which shepherds converse in verse about how to take care of the land. I also talk about the roots of eco-literature going as far back as literature itself. The *Gilgamesh Epic* (Sandars, 1972), written four thousand years ago, illustrated the clash between Wildness or Wilderness and civilization. King Gilgamesh, a city slicker, got into a fight with Enkidu, a wild man from the woods, but then they became bros and took on an evil giant who was cutting down trees.

"This clash between civilization and the Wild," I inform the class, "has reappeared in countless texts from the Bible, to the tale of the city mouse and the country mouse, and even perhaps to the sitcom *The Odd Couple*. The basic premise is that Wildness and civilization are separate, and that Wildness is for animals and civilization is for people. This was always the generally accepted view, but then Henry David Thoreau came along and capitalized the word "Wild" (Thoreau, 1993: 61), saying that this separation is baloney because the Wild is our home.[1]

My casual tone and playful language ease the students in. I'm a wacky professor who's clearly obsessed. I'm gesturing, marching around, and laughing at my own jokes – which is part of the show. In a sense, I'm playing the goof, but an amusing goof with something to say that's new to them. I'm relying on theatrics to make points like how the United States is a Wilderness nation, carved from the Wilderness, established in the Wilderness, and that American culture has always celebrated Wilderness as part of its heritage and identity. But I'm also saying that we're now grasping to hang onto what's left of the Wild. The jet streams are off, the seasons are messed up, and scientists predict that in a hundred years we won't have any ice caps left.

The fear-mongering has begun, but without the ominous music. In fact, it's almost as if there's comic music or a laugh track going as I deliver dire predictions while making fun of myself. I tell them how it blows my mind that we're losing one percent of our polar ice caps every year, and I communicate this with bugging eyes. This combining of the deadly serious and the absurd creates an effect, and it allows me to segue to how the Greenland ice sheet is melting five times faster than it was in the nineties, and the rate of melting is not slowing down. "Yep," I tell them, "it's melting at 'an accelerated rate'" (McDiarmid, 2012). Then gripping my head as if to keep it from exploding, I add that according to the 2013 documentary *Chasing Ice* (Orlowski, 2012), sea-level rise is happening sixty percent faster than predicted in 2007. And guess what? The year 2012 was hotter than any year on record, and every following year shows the same results.

But then it's time to shift gears. Clowning around has its uses, but the terrain I'm now taking them through requires sobriety. Or, in other words, now that we've had our laughs and feel comfortable enough to proceed, it's time to get serious. The question now is why we don't stop wrecking our home, and my answer to that is "Apocalypse" – a word which never fails to make students sit up and listen. I tell them that despite all the dystopian movies and shows they love to watch, the human brain is actually incapable of realistically envisioning true global disaster. As Brian Merchant explains in his article "Apocalypse Neuro: Why Our Brains Don't Process the Gravest Threats to Humanity," human grey matter just lacks the "ability to adequately process the concept of long-term, civilization-threatening phenomena …. [T]he human brain sort of malfunctions when it comes to navigating wide-lens, slowly-unfurling crises like climate change" (Merchant, 2010). So even when communities do get hit by floods and droughts and mass forest fires, we can't communally process these visions. It's like the right and left sides of our brains refuse to communicate because they just can't handle the reality of the situation in which we find ourselves. Why? "Because," I tell my students, "then you would feel guilty about driving to Taco Bell, and you'd regret the coal-burning electricity plants you don't have to see to watch TV, play video games, and charge your cellphones."

That's right, I indict my students, which directly involves them in the study of this subject matter. This makes them think, but this approach also runs the risk of alienating some, so again I quickly shift perspectives and go for the third person. "It's just much easier," I explain, "for people to accept the petro-chemical industry's marketing message that it's fine to power the industries and vehicles everyone desires, because it's our right. And as for all that misinformation out there coming from politically motivated deniers, this makes it seem like there's a debate among scientists as to whether global warming really exists, when in fact there's no debate whatsoever. But hey, that's okay. Four-wheelers, SUVs, RVs, V8s – that's the American lifestyle."

Call it reverse psychology, call it playing devil's advocate, or even call it sarcasm. Whatever the case, the barrage is on – a barrage of information gleaned from my research. But each little mortar blast has to be handled with a certain sensitivity. Because this is serious stuff. Serious enough to have pushed me outside my comfort zone, which drove me to action in writing and teaching. Still, if I scare my students too much, I could scare them away from examining what needs to be done in order to survive. So really, I can't dive too deep because that would be terrorism. I have to keep things on the surface, shifting the focus as quickly as I can.

I've also found that it helps to directly indict myself for being part of the problem. This lets students know that they can also look to their own behaviors and question how to own what they're guilty of as the world continues to burn through natural resources – which leads to greenhouse gasses, convection, ozone depletion, and acidification of the oceans. All this happening in the eleventh hour, at a time when the polar ice caps (a.k.a. the "air conditioners of the earth") are literally melting away.

But as I said, the human brain is not equipped to envision total, full-on planetary disaster. That's why I call attention to all the hurricanes, tornados, typhoons, and forest fires happening right now rather than in the future, and with increased force because of warmer skies and waters. Take Hurricane Katrina and Superstorm Sandy, for example. Look at Puerto Rico and sea-level rise in Florida. Look at Venice. Look at Alaska.

Overpopulation then goes on the chopping block. I cite various figures like the planet's population doubling every fifty years, and I note how the World Wildlife Fund states that we'll need as much food in the next forty years as we've produced in the last eight millennia to feed an estimated nine billion humans (Agence France Presse, 2011).

This is where I get to what comedian Stephen Colbert refers to as "the nutmeat of the matter." As poet laureate Amiri Baraka observed in his controversial poem "Somebody Blew Up America," "who need fossil fuel when the sun ain't goin' nowhere?" (Baraka, 2001: 8). He means drilling and spilling for more oil is just plain nuts when we have plenty of reliable, less damaging, alternative energy sources. Still, humans depend on fossil fuels, even though fossil fuels are suicide. "But what are fossil fuels?" I ask my captive audience, and then I answer my own question: "They're algae, that's what, crushed and cooked under the crust. And that, my friends, is Prometheus." And they get the metaphor. Playing with fire. Playing with death. "But thankfully," I go on, "we now have the technology to turn algae into a greener, cleaner fuel, so we don't have to ravage the planet for oil. In fact, we've already made this fuel, so we know how to do it. But the infrastructure changes needed for homo sapiens to progress as a species aren't being made. So why aren't we doing that? And why are we letting our seasonal cycles get so out of whack? With earlier springs and later falls, the birds aren't hatching in conjunction with the larvae they eat, so millions of anemic organisms are being thrown out of balance as they search for new food sources." That's the gist of my message.

Then we go back a few presidents, which is difficult to imagine for a generation in diapers during 9/11. The Bush administration is ancient history, but since I was there and remember how official climate change information was cut from the Environmental Protection Agency's annual reports and how the United States wouldn't join the Kyoto Protocol, this is something that needs to be reviewed so the same mistakes aren't made again. Students should also know how a funny-looking bird, the spotted owl, became the symbolic sacrificial goat for choosing jobs over the environment. "Would you wreck your house for a paycheck?" I put the question to my students. "Then you wouldn't have a house. And another thing: When George W. came into office, the first thing he did was dismiss indictments for pollution against 150 coal-burning power plants. And what was the result of that? Asthma is up eighteen percent" (Kennedy, 2007).

At this point, involving students directly in the conversation always seems to draw them in. I ask, "How many people in this room have ever been affected by cancer in their lives?" Every single hand goes up. "Well," I tell them, "a third of us will get cancer. Maybe even half of us. That's the way things are going. And oh yeah, have you heard the one about 'voluntary self-regulation?'" "Nope," they reply, so I give them the punchline: "Industries spewing fly ash, lead, mercury, PCBs. How do you think that worked out? And oh yeah, our national treasures, the National Parks, are now open for development."

The questions continue. "How many people here have kids, or plan on having kids?" I ask. At least half the hands in the room go up, followed by the information no parent wants to hear: Prozac in the water. Toxic retardants in human breast milk along with DDT, benzene, dioxin, trichloroethylene, perchlorate, arsenic, and a whole host of other poisons. According to the *New York Times Magazine*, we're also feeding babies "paint thinners, dry-cleaning fluids, wood preservatives, toilet deodorizers, cosmetic additives, gasoline byproducts, rocket fuel, termite poisons, [and] fungicides" (Williams, 2005). The result? Acid rain. Neuro-defects. Millions of fetuses with cellular damage.

That's how the lecture goes. And then I get to what I know best: The salmon crash of 2008 and 2009. The sturgeon crash. The snapper crash. The cod crash. Our food supply in constant danger. Deforestation, desertification, lack of clean water, nuclear proliferation.

By this time, I know I've inspired dread, so I have to tone it down a bit and give them some space to breathe. I'll tell a joke, or answer some questions, then assign homework. And that's how the semester begins: from a highly personal, activist stance.

Some colleagues, no doubt, will condemn me for thrusting my politics on impressionable minds – as if teachers are supposed to remain objective and just roll over for the bulldozers, the pipelines, the whole fracking enchilada. But my job is to teach in an institution whose mission is to mold responsible citizens – so I teach what I know. And the main thing I know is that we have an entire global ecosystem at stake. And since I'm not the type of homie to sit back and watch that happen, and since every student in the classroom is now aware of what they have to contend with, the question becomes "So what are we going to do about this, something or nothing?" It's a question I ask the entire class, but no one has to answer it because it's not a question that's meant to be answered. It's a question that hangs in the air like Beijing smog, which is the way it works best.

It's also a question which the next few chapters examine through challenges I've experienced. Because if I can discover the power to be good for something, and if I can write something or teach something that's progressive for species on this planet, then others can definitely do that, too.

Note

1   These points are further elaborated in Chapter 12.

References

Abbey, Edward (1996) *The Serpents of Paradise: A Reader*. John Macrae (ed.). New York: Henry Holt and Company.

Agence France Presse (2011) Planet could be "unrecognizable" by 2050, experts say. Yahoo News (February 20, 2011). Retrieved on 20 February 2011 from http://news.yahoo.com/s/afp/20110220/tsafp/scienceuspopulationfood

Antler (1980) *Factory* 3–16. San Francisco: City Lights.

Astley, Neil (2007) *Earth Shattering Ecopoems*. Northumberland, UK: Bloodaxe.

Baraka, Amiri (2001) *Somebody Blew Up America*. Oakland: blackdotpress.

Conners, Nadia and Petersen, Leila Conners (2008) *The 11th Hour*. Burbank, CA: Warner Home Video.

Else, John and Harrar, Linda (1997) *Cadillac Desert*, parts 1 and 2. Arlington, VA: PBS Video.

Foreman, Dave and Haywood, Bill (eds.) (1993) *Ecodefense: A Field Guide to Monkeywrenching* (3rd edition). Chico, CA: Abbzug.

Fox, Josh (2010) *Gasland*. Brooklyn: Gasland Productions LLC.

Gore, Al (2007) Nobel lecture. *Nobelprize.org* (December 10, 2007). Retrieved on 28 March 2017 from https://www.nobelprize.org/nobel_prizes/peace/laureates/2007/gore-lecture_en.html

Kennedy, Robert F. Jr. (2007) Farris lecture. University of Central Arkansas. Conway, AR.

Kesey, Ken (1964) *Sometimes a Great Notion*. New York: Viking.

Kinnell, Galway (1967) The bear. *Body Rags* 60–63. Boston: Houghton Mifflin.

McDiarmid, Margo (2012) Greenland glacier melting 5 times faster than in 1990s. *CBC News* (November 29, 2012). Retrieved on 29 March 2017 from www.cbc.ca/news/politics/greenland-glacier-melting-5-times-faster-than-in-1990s-1.1194070

McKibbin, Bill (2011) A New world. *Eaarth* 1–46. New York: St. Martin's Press.

Merchant, Brian (2015) Apocalypse neuro: Why our brains don't process the gravest threats to humanity. *Motherboard* (June 10, 2015). Retrieved on 18 June 2018 from https://motherboard.vice.com/en_us/article/qkv5a3/apocalypse-neuro-why-our-brain-cant-process-the-planets-gravest-threats

Orlowski, Jeff (2012) *Chasing Ice*. Boulder: Chasing Ice, LLC.

Sandars, N. K. (ed.) (1972) *The Epic of Gilgamesh*. London: Penguin.

Stanford, Frank (2000) *The Battlefield Where the Moon Says I Love You*. Barrington, RI: Lost Roads Press.

Thoreau, Henry David (1993) Walking. *Civil Disobedience and Other Essays*. New York: Dover.

Williams, Florence (2005) Toxic breast milk? *The New York Times Magazine* (January 9, 2005). Retrieved on 2 November 2017 from http://www.nytimes.com/2005/01/09/magazine/toxic-breast-milk.html

Chapter 12

Experience Investigative Eco-Fiction

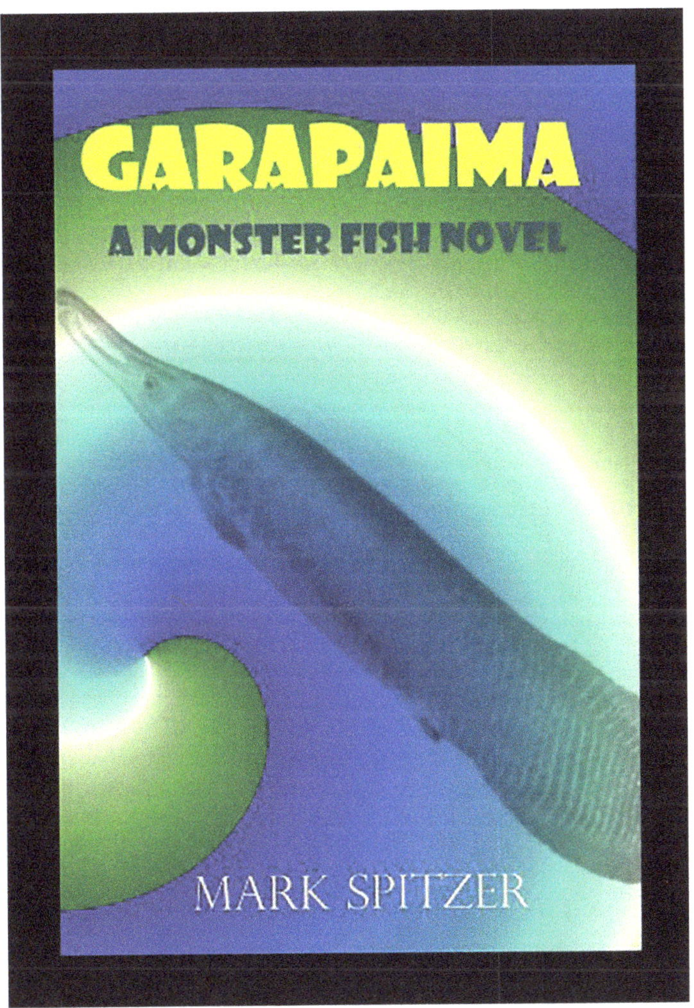

Figure 7. Result of Investigative Eco-Fiction. Image Courtesy of Moon Willow Press.

I show this image for two reasons. First, as shameless promotion for my environmental novel *Garapaima* (Spitzer, 2015), about a misunderstood Frankenfish and a cast of wacky characters fighting to sustain an ecosystem's natural resources. Secondly, to introduce the idea of "investigative eco-fiction," which is a specialized form of "eco-fiction," a term synonymous with "environmental fiction," "ecological fiction," "green fiction" and other forms of storytelling in which real environmental issues provide conflicts for fictional narratives. Examples that come to mind are Edward Abbey's *The Monkey Wrench Gang* (Abbey, 1975), T. C. Boyle's *A Friend of the Earth* (Boyle, 2001), and Ann Pancake's *Strange as This Weather Has Been* (Pancake, 2007). These eco-novels ground readers in specific landscapes and then throw characters into situations in which they partake in guerilla warfare to discourage development in the southwestern United States, deal with futuristic planetary destruction due to the greenhouse effect, and use strip-mining and clear-cutting in Appalachia as occasions for characters to clash. As I've noted before, environmental literature comes from the left and has an agenda. This provides for a subtext that suggests solutions to real eco-problems.

Investigative eco-fiction, however, is a subgenre of eco-fiction. Whereas investigative poetry finds its form in a physical collage constructed from chunks of a subject matter's identity, investigative eco-fiction is more philosophical in its collaging effect. As stated in the Introduction, investigative eco-fiction relies on "montaging moments and memories from one's own experience into a body of fictional prose." At bottom, this approach is about getting out there and investigating in the field. It's about hiking, fishing, kayaking, analyzing water samples, meeting ornithologists, climbing trees, falling out of trees, getting bit by wolverines, whatever writers need to do to gather experiences which lead to discoveries. Then those writers, they take the research they've uncovered, or the adventures they've had, or visions of the natural world, and whatever applicable encounters and thoughts they've collected from an environment, and they use those details to tell a story. And as also noted in the Introduction, investigative eco-fiction advocates "for experiential investigations that immerse and directly involve fiction writers in environmental subject matter … [which] provides writers the opportunity to gather real-life, real-world, real-time information so their final products have the advantage of being narratives informed by genuine experience."

In other words, investigative eco-fiction rejects the idea of researching only through texts for the increasingly hot genre of eco-fiction. Getting information on species, places, current issues, and politics from books, periodicals, databases, and through Internet search engines is always a good place to start, and such texts can be extremely valuable, but the investigative aspect of investigative eco-fiction is about finding a much more intimate connection with the subject matter, which direct experience can provide. In just reading books or magazines to get information, there's no sweat involved nor any risk of getting dirty or lost. Nevertheless, "book learning" and other forms of reading texts can definitely be used along with the much more active approach I suggest. In addition to informing oneself through relevant texts, I'm talking about gathering information that comes straight from being in an environment and from those who are most involved with the subject for the unique perspectives immersion naturally leads to. But more than that, I'm calling for experiential investigations that directly involve writers, thereby providing for a stake in the research focus which transcends applying second-hand information.

It's easy to say, "Get out there and do it." But there's always more involved than just walking out the door. The question is *how* to do it.

What I've found is that my creative nonfiction research on fish and the environment informs my fiction in a way which makes me a participant rather than an observer. This "live action" (Brown, 2011) approach, as Animal Planet's Turtle Man might call it, leads to a much more personal relationship with issues eco-fiction investigates. For example, when I sampled spastic, leaping silver carp with the Kansas Department of Wildlife, Parks and Tourism, this live-action experience gave me the hands-on background to invent the fictional invasive species of dogcarp, which play a role in *Garapaima*.

For others, though, whose fiction isn't a bycatch of their creative nonfiction research or their downtime in the wilderness, I'd say that if you intend to write about place, go to that place. Or if you intend to write about a certain flower or bug, then go to that flower or bug. In other words, design your own "teachable moment" and go for it.

But here's the problem: I recently did some fieldwork with the U.S. Fish & Wildlife Service and the Arkansas Game and Fish Commission on the hellbender salamander for an epic poem I was writing about this creature's relationship to overdevelopment, water quality degradation, an aggressive flesh-eating bacterial disease, and an equally devastating viral infection. A quarter of this poem, now published in its entirety as *GLURK! A Hellbender Odyssey* (Spitzer, 2016), is fictional in that it follows a hellbender experiencing antagonistic fracking forces and pollution due to making

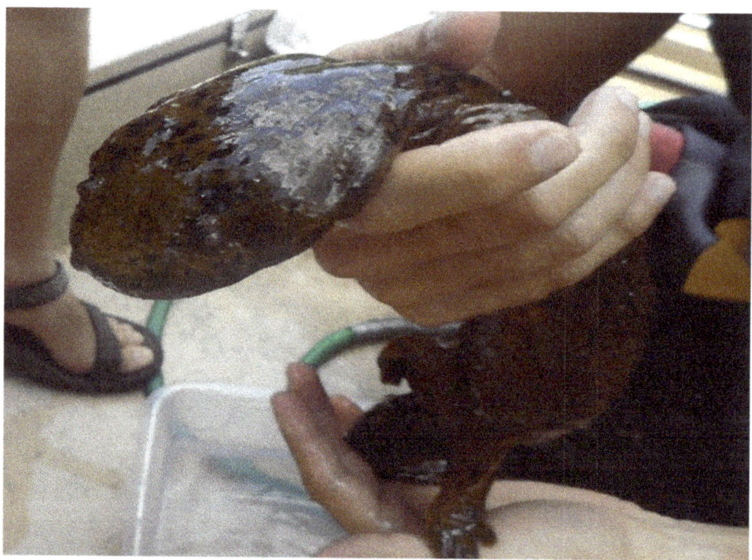

Figure 8. Hellbender from Eleven Point River, Northeast Arkansas. Photo by Mark Spitzer.

meth. But if I had told the state herpetologist that I wanted to join his annual hellbender-hut checking expedition because I was writing fiction in poetry form, he most likely would've laughed in my face and denied me access to the sampling mission he eventually took me on – mostly because I showed up uninvited and imposed myself on his team.

Actively pursuing a subject is something I definitely recommend. If you make the effort to go somewhere, go to the trouble to get licensed for something, or invest yourself in a type of research, the odds are you will form a more profound connection to the subject than if you stayed at home and read a few articles. And if you can impress upon your contacts that you have more than just a fleeting interest in the subject, they might feel an altruistic urge to involve you in publicizing their plight.

But back to the stigma of fiction which the eco-fiction writer has to contend with when addressing real threats to the environment: The best way to avoid looking like some frivolous artist who's there to capitalize on other people's serious research is to bill yourself as a writer or reporter – which you are if you're approaching a subject through investigative eco-fiction. So tell the relevant authorities that you're doing a study or writing a profile or conducting research for scholarship (which you are), but don't volunteer any extra information with the potential to lower your credibility in the eyes of those whose sense of humor might not appreciate the power and reach of alternative forms of literature.

This approach is not deception. It's a practical matter of "creative framing" to facilitate access to knowledge. Billing oneself as an investigative reporter will open a lot of doors for writers working in genres not considered status quo – and there's no deception in going this route if information is what you're after. People love to talk to news people because then they become the news, which helps to disseminate the information they've collected. And there's no reason that eco-fiction can't be a vehicle for the news. If you're working with the press, or a press, or envision working with some sort of press, that makes you a member of the press.

Figure 9. Infiltrate/Investigate. Photo from Burbot Bash by Mark Spitzer.

And since there's no shame in being ambiguously "freelance" or a student (which we all are, even if we're not currently enrolled in any institution), there are creative ways to frame one's urge to investigate.

My monster-fish novel *Garapaima* incorporates an invasive species theme, a subject I could've only approached through speculation and standard research if it were not for direct involvement with the subject matter. Luckily, in addition to sampling invasives in Kansas, I was able to gain further experience with this subject matter through joining an eradication effort for non-native burbot, in Utah and Wyoming. I reached out to the Manila, Utah, Chamber of Commerce, and they helped me infiltrate state wildlife agencies for both states and work directly with their fishery experts. When you do research like this, I've found that you can find yourself digging through buckets of slimy fish, shoulder to shoulder with those who can provide inside information. This means you get to ask questions and receive answers, which is a form of the interview. You also form relationships and make contacts whom you can get in touch with later for more information.

But most of all, when you actively investigate, you get your own experience, which leads directly to revelations that you in fact "own." You can then apply the currency of your own unique reflections and illuminations to eco-fiction, a form of writing which can reach an entirely different audience than those who just want the facts.

Figure 10. Don't Just Sit There, Suggest Solutions. Photo by RJB Photo, reproduced by permission.

Eco-fiction aims to highlight environmental concerns as it entertains and suggests a need for action. If it doesn't offer solutions to environmental problems, though, it can come off as complaining, which can defeat its purpose. For eco-fiction to be as effective as it can, it needs to educate in a timely manner – meaning while environmental problems are problems. For instance, rounding up razorback suckers in Arizona for data with a private native fish lab offered me insight into propagation strategies I never could've imagined from my keyboard in Arkansas. Similarly, taking part in the 2014 Okie Noodling Contest allowed me to directly participate in and witness a destructive overfishing method (noodling) that needs to be more closely examined before genetically jumbo flathead catfish become even more diminished throughout their range. In both cases, what I learned from these investigations made its way to my eco-novel *Garapaima*, and in both cases, practical solutions to pressing environmental problems were hinted at in the text.

By the way, that's me in Figure 10 getting slapped in the face by a thirty-pound catfish, which illustrates what can happen when you take investigative eco-fiction to the streets. This image shows that there are risks involved in getting first-hand experience for your writing. But what's far riskier is when communities fail to heed warnings from those who got slapped in the face for reporting the information we need to make informed decisions regarding the health and safety of our planet.

In the spirit of the advice "Don't just sit there, do something," and assuming you are passionate about what you are researching, here's some bonus advice: Turn your research into interesting travel, even a vacation, or use your travels and vacations as a source of research and experience to feed your writing. Spend money, and write it off if you can. And if you can't, spend spend spend anyway because one day you won't have that chance and you might regret not taking the journey when you had the chance. So why not combine something you are interested in or love to do with travel to gather information (i.e., investigate) to apply to eco-fiction?

Figure 11. Research Travel Can Inform Both Setting and Characters. Photo Courtesy of Mark Spitzer.

For example, I was able to take technical and how-to knowledge from my travel experience catching massive sturgeon in Idaho and apply that to what characters did in *Garapaima* in a believable way. This included everything from how the characters set the drag on their reels, to how they reeled in fish, to understanding where certain fish tend to hide, to knowing the best times certain species feed. When you discover those kinds of details in the field, it may not seem like they have any use at the moment, but later on, those details can be extremely helpful to realizing a text. I'm living proof of that, and I can't stress enough the importance of gathering as much information as you can, even if only one percent of what you collect is eventually applied to your writing.

"Investigative extrapolation" is also a valuable tool to use. My novel *Chum* (Spitzer, 2001), for example, was set in Alaska, a place I've never been. Since I had decades of knowledge about fish and fishing in Washington State's Puget Sound, however, I was able to

Figure 12. Investigative Eco-Fiction as a Tool to Augment Setting. Photo by Kevan Paul, reproduced by permission.

extrapolate the knowledge of those fish into a neighboring region I knew little about in a convincing way. Similarly, in *Garapaima*, I took observations of the flora and fauna in my home state of Minnesota and then applied my knowledge of those trees and fish to the landscape I imagined in Ontario, where the novel is set. I hadn't been to that part of Canada in over twenty years, but my familiarity with a comparable context came off as authentic and made *Garapaima* attractive to a Canadian publisher who bought the book.

Take-Home Message

Those are my primary thoughts on investigative eco-fiction, in which the basic premise is "Get out there and find out what's going on with whatever you're investigating." And when you're out there doing that, take a recording device, a camera, and pen and paper to capture flashes from your experiences as they happen. It can't hurt to ask the experts if you can tag along, and hiring guides can pay off in more than just an afternoon of birdwatching or paddling. Because ultimately, it's not what you get during an experience; it's how you take elements from that experience and plug them into a fictional collage in order to preserve an environment or protect what's in it. And even if you head off to investigate something without any idea of what you're doing or where you're going, you will find direction along the way. Conversely, if you already have direction, direct involvement will give you new direction, will turn you on to something new, something important, something that needs to be placed under the microscope, examined, and discussed in a larger context.

After all, look at the "fieldwork" that Abbey did for his game-changing eco-novel *The Monkey Wrench Gang* (Abbey, 1975). Sabotaging bulldozers, burning billboards, and pulling up survey stakes are all illegal actions, but that's where he got the hands-on experience to write about tactics to discourage development in the American West. Abbey then applied his investigative research to his own eco-fiction, and the results were phenomenal. Activist institutions like Earth First! and the Earth Liberation Front were born from Abbey's connection to place and his involvement with anarchist techniques of "eco-defense." Because of that, a new school of socially conscious literature was born in the United States and persists to this day.

More importantly, the fight for preservation in such works has a highly practical application. Readers are influenced, so readers take action, which is why this genre is no joke. It's one of many attempts to conserve ecosystems during an urgent era of mass extinction, climate change, petro-chemical abuse, and disinformation. The point is that there's a demand for direction right now on how to deal with eco-problems.

So who will supply that direction in the realm of fiction? If you ask me, it's up to the next two or three generations of writers, writing teachers, and writing students because that's all the time we have left. Seriously folks, the ice caps are scheduled to melt in less than a century, and global warming is accelerating so quickly that scientists can't accurately measure it. We are currently heading for unprecedented chaos, which is why investigative eco-fiction is vital not just for contributing to a life-and-death dialogue right now, but it can also be applied as an imperative form of outreach with the potential to influence ecological balance during a time of uncharted planetary crisis.

I know that's a bummer, but it's realistic. We're beyond a manageable carbon dioxide level of 350 parts per million, and we're beyond a pH level of 3.7, the point where everything begins to tip, and we've got conmen and climate deniers running the foremost superpower in history. Investigative eco-fiction, therefore, isn't just one of the most important communication tools we have at our disposal; it's one of the many powerful, progressive, transformative weapons we need to arm ourselves with in a war for survival that needs to be fought on multiple fronts, or else everything – including the world as we know it – goes to waste.

Literally.

References

Abbey, Edward (1975) *The Monkey Wrench Gang*. Philadelphia: J. B. Lippincott.

Boyle, T. C. (2001) *A Friend of the Earth*. New York: Penguin.

Brown, Eddie, Jr. (2011) *Bare-Handing A Snapping Turtle: Call of the Wild Man*. Retrieved on 6 June 2018 from https://www.youtube.com/watch?v=SDh1AxD8J_c

Pancake, Ann (2007) *Strange as This Weather Has Been*. Washington, DC: Shoemaker & Hoard.

Spitzer, Mark (2001) *Chum*. Cambridge, MA: Zoland Books.

Spitzer, Mark (2015) *Garapaima: A Monster Fish Novel*. Coquitlam, British Columbia: Moon Willow Press.

Spitzer, Mark (2016) *GLURK! A Hellbender Odyssey*. Brownsville, TX: Anaphora Literary Press.

Chapter 13

From Wild People to Wilderness:
An Education in Investigating Monsters in Our Midst

As noted in the Introduction, this chapter completes my triumvirate of investigative creative writing pedagogy genres. I've addressed poetry and fiction by touching on the concepts of investigative poetics and investigative eco-fiction. What follows is representative of the subgenre of investigative nonfiction. Whereas investigative poetics creates a physical collage of a subject from various aspects of its identity, the collage effect in investigative eco-fiction has more to do with cutting and pasting moments of memory and experience into a fictional, environmentally oriented text. The collaging in investigative nonfiction, however, happens through combining actual research with actual experience to create a mosaic of nonfictional experience. What makes investigative nonfiction *investigative* is that the act of investigating is central to the discovery process.

Another factor that makes investigative nonfiction investigatory is that it involves *highly active* research. This chapter, which investigates a self-designed education in which I developed a personal aesthetic through decades of research in art history and world lit, is a good example. In the beginning of that journey, I had a host of international research-travel experiences that forged my identity in relationship to the concept of Wildness. Then, twenty-plus years later, I was asked by Marist College in Poughkeepsie, New York, to organize those experiences into a public lecture, which led me to dig up old photographs and undergraduate research which I eventually translated into a PowerPoint presentation. Ultimately, to turn that lecture into a chapter appropriate for publication in this book, I had to revise and secure permissions for images and ground my discoveries in who I am and what my mission is within the constructs of investigative nonfiction.

This brings up the question of how much activity makes an investigation highly active. To provide a solid answer, I'll just state that if any investigation takes you outside yourself or inside yourself to the point where you lose yourself or discover yourself in the creation of a creative nonfiction text, then what you've discovered just might be investigative nonfiction.

Still, what's more important than the question of whether a work of writing fits into a category is what it does. What this chapter does is it follows a progression which led to the most profound discovery in my life: who I am and why I'm that way. For that reason, this chapter is representative of investigative nonfiction. Case closed. Let's move on.

I rarely speak about my studies in medieval and Renaissance art history and literature, which I still return to now and then. My main research these days is on fish. I write environmental fish books about grotesque fish like the alligator gar in Figure 14.

Figures 13 & 14. From Wild People to Wilderness. Photos Courtesy of the Metropolitan Museum of Art, the Cloisters Collection, 1953, and Icon Films.

That six-foot-eight lunker was caught on the Trinity River in Texas during the filming of the "Alligator Gar" episode of Animal Planet's *River Monsters* series in 2008. I've written two books on this primeval leviathan, and one question I'm always asked is how I became so interested in this species. My answer is that I saw a picture in a book as a kid, it blew my mind, and from that moment I was hooked. I wanted to know all I could about that weird and wonderful monster species.

But there's another thing which has been key to my fascination with gar and paddlefish and sturgeon and big ugly catfish, and that's my experience with the icons of the wild man and the wild woman, or wild people, as they're also called. The image in Figure 13 is representative of such a creature. The porcelain pitcher it adorns is believed to have come from Nuremberg, Germany, around the year 1500. It's now housed at the Metropolitan Museum of Art in New York City.

Figure 15. Wild Man and Thistles. Image Courtesy of the Metropolitan Museum of Art. Harris Brisbane Dick Fund, 1922.

The wild man in Figure 13, as you can see, is a fur-covered, half-man, half-beast character. As in most typical medieval depictions from Western Europe, he has long hair, a beard, bald patches on his elbows and knees, and his hands and feet are also bare. He's carrying a club as well, his signature primitive tool, much like the cartoon caveman – which is another incarnation of primitive man created for the pop culture of our imaginations.

So what's the deal with these wild people? That's what I've been asking for over half my life, which is why I'm about to provide a perspective through a condensed version of my own introduction to these fantastical icons. Back in 1988, I was an English major at the University of Minnesota. I wanted to do an independent study, so I approached an ironically named Dr. Edward Savage, who told me about his research with the mythic wild man. Dr. Savage explained how the medieval wild man was frequently depicted with a thistle as in the fifteenth-century engraving in Figure 15, which depicts a wild man climbing around in thistle leaves. Illustrations like these were common in illuminated manuscripts found all across Europe in the Middle Ages, and Dr. Savage theorized that the reason wild folks had a connection with thistles harked back to their legendary reputations as pagan healers who specialized in homeopathic remedies because of their close connection with the wilderness and medicinal plants. Dr. Savage suspected that the pharmaceutical qualities of thistles played a role in healing the Black Plague, which wiped out an estimated 75 to 200 million people in the 1300's, and that wild people had a special connection with this plant. Still, he had to have more proof, and he was looking for a research assistant to search through the Marburger Index, a collection of over one million photographs of art in museums and special collections throughout Germany archived on microfiche at the university library. That sounded strange and colorful and intriguing to me, so I signed up and got to work, printing up relevant photocopies as I discovered them.

I cruised through the whole collection in a few months, and immersed myself in all the books I could find relating to the subject

Figures 16 & 17. The Nordic Pagan Evolution. First Photo by Mark Spitzer. Second Photo Courtesy of the Rijksmuseum, Amsterdam.

matter. In the process, I learned that the evolution of wild people started with pagan vegetation spirits like the jack of the green from the most Nordic parts of Europe, areas which are now Scandinavia. The leafy vegetation spirit in Figure 16 is representative of such wood spirits, commonly found carved into keystones of bridges and adorning buildings. The jack of the green wood spirit was introduced to the body of the continent by the Barbarian tribes that swept south and then westward across the continent during the Dark Ages. This character eventually evolved into the archetype of the green man whose leafiness was pretty much replaced by hair in the 1500's. The illustration in Figure 17, "Wildeman op een eenhoorn" ("Wildman on a unicorn") is from the late 1400's and encapsulates the general idea of the green man.

The leafy aspect of this incarnation symbolizes a connection to the natural world in contrast to the non-leafy and more epidermally bare, citified versions of real humans as they evolved in historical time. The fur motif, in contrast, took wild people in a much more animal-than-vegetable direction. In both cases, artists were depicting folkloric characters that reflected a primitive connection with the wild during a time of increasing urbanization and industry.

Figures 18 & 19. Girls Gone Wild? Images Courtesy of the Metropolitan Museum of Art.

As the Renaissance took root, both wild men and wild women were depicted with bare breasts. Wild people were at their shaggiest in the sixteenth and seventeenth centuries when these icons reached their peak in popularity. At that time, they could be found on murals, in manuscripts, on buildings, tombstones, tapestries, almost anywhere ornamentation was embellished in Europe. The wild woman in Figure 18 is from a German engraving from around 1440 by Martin Schongauer, and the one in Figure 19, by Master E. S., is another German engraving from the same period.

Figures 20 & 21. Wild Men Go Bald – or Hairless. First Photo by Mark Spitzer. Second Photo by RJB Photo, reproduced by permission.

As art became more Baroque and Rococo, or less ostentatiously complex, as the Enlightenment established itself, the furry wild folks from the fifteenth and sixteenth century started losing their body hair. By the end of the 1600's, a more conservative, less shaggy version began to emerge in the communal consciousness, like the wild men shown in Figure 20 on the French coat of arms. By the seventeenth and eighteenth centuries, the wild man evolved into a virtually hairless missing link between primitive and modern humans as seen in the wild people in Figure 21 from Antwerp, Belgium. In fact, pretty much all of the images of wild people from Scotland, at the end of the wild folk migration, lack body hair.

Besides being interested in wild people in art, I was also deep into the literature, which is where most of our cultural understanding of these icons come from. In the case of the wild man, this character has been around as long as literature itself. The first known instance of literature on this planet, *The Gilgamesh Epic* (Sandars, 1972), has been around for at least four thousand years. Written on stone tablets in Babylonia and retold and revised for millennia, this is how I relate the story to my students: There was this hunter out in the woods, and he saw a shaggy wild guy, so he went to King Gilgamesh in the city and told him what he'd seen. Gilgamesh then sent a temple prostitute into the forest, the wild man Enkidu was seduced, and he followed the bait back to the city, where he and Gilgamesh got into a fight. But before the fight was over they were hugging each other like BFFs. Then they went running around together fighting supervillains, like the Bull of Heaven and this giant, symbolic destroyer of trees. Eventually, Enkidu dies, and Gilgamesh goes into the underworld, discovers great knowledge, then returns to the surface world a much wiser king.

The Gilgamesh Epic is the oldest known literary narrative in the world, and what it does is draw a line between Wilderness and civilization, as if these are two different entities to be regarded separately. People had existed in tribes and clans in the Wilderness for centuries, but when they moved from hunter-gatherer-based societies to more agricultural communities, nature started getting thought of as a dangerous place for animals. Conversely, villages and cities began to be thought of as safe places for people. Thus, Enkidu was representative of the Wild, and Gilgamesh was representative of civilization, the primary question being: do we still have a primitive self that can exist outside of society?

This is a question we've been asking ourselves in every culture that has ever existed, most of which have some sort of wild character in their mythologies or religions. Worldwide, there's substantial overlap between wild people narratives. In fact, the *Gilgamesh Epic* includes a story within a story, which is essentially the story of the Deluge and a savior who built an ark and filled it with animals – a narrative which is also recounted in myriad indigenous cultures throughout the world before the Bible ever existed. As a side note, there was also a thistle in *The Gilgamesh Epic*. It was under water and contained knowledge, which explains why the thistle eventually became the logo for *Encyclopedia Britannica*.

Figure 22. Enkidu from the Second Millennium BC. Photo © Iraq National Museum, Baghdad, via Shutterstock.

In the Mesopotamian bas relief pictured in Figure 22, which is over three thousand years old, the wild man Enkidu has a beard and is clutching what looks like a staff: a signature item, in one form or another, that various wild men in various cultures centuries later often have in their hands. If it's not a stick of some kind, it's a club or a cudgel. Enkidu is usually depicted with natural fur or he's wearing furs, and sometimes he has a tail or hooves which hark back to the satyr – a character consistent with all sorts of furry manlike creatures in myriad cultures suggesting links to our more unrestrained sexual selves. Jung, Freud, and the field of psychology made much of such archetypes. The writing of Henry David Thoreau is also relevant to the philosophy of living in the wild versus living in society and how we now differentiate between these extremes in direct contrast to our pastoral histories, when Wildness and domesticity were more connected.

The idea of a wild character hanging out with an urban character was widely adapted as a narrative theme. Many popular tales of similar contrasting characters circulated throughout countless oral

Figure 23. After a Medieval Bruegel Print Based on the Tale of *Valentine and Orson*. Image Courtesy of the Metropolitan Museum of Art, Harris Brisbane Dick Fund, 1926.

traditions, and incarnations of these narratives found their way into tales like *Valentin und Namelos*, which evolved into *Valentine and Orson*, a medieval story of twin brothers separated at birth. One was raised by royalty, the other by bears, so the latter became a "wild man of the woods." Such stories kept popping up through the ages, and these tensions can now be found in children's stories like "The City Mouse and the Country Mouse" and in TV shows like *The Odd Couple*, in which a "civilized" or conservative character ends up being roommates with a freer, "wilder" personality. The Muppet duo Ernie and Bert are a modern derivative of this polarity in a very long line of stories about the two sides of human nature.

Religion, and especially Christianity, had a lot to do with the idea of wild people, or heretical beings living outside of society because they had no concept of God. In prehistoric and ancient times, and continuing into the Middle Ages, the wilderness was something to fear because it was full of beasts, pagans, and sinners. There are many scenarios in medieval religion and art of Adam and Eve being cast out of the Garden of Eden to run around with nothing on but a fig leaf or two, or in some cases, furs. Some artists depicted Adam and Eve as wild people because they were going to hell (as seen in in the thirteenth-century Italian mosaic of Figure 24).

Figures 24 & 25. Out of Grace, Out of Luck. First Image Courtesy of Restored Traditions. Second Image Courtesy of the National Gallery of Art, Ailsa Mellon Bruce Fund (B-30554).

Such social propaganda could also be seen in scenes of wild men fighting Christian knights as pictured on the Hans Burgkmair drawing from about 1500 in Figure 25. Heretical wild men have commonly been depicted abducting maidens or children, or just going ape, conking folks upside their heads. That's what the damned are wont to do, which is why they must be reined in. That was the mentality back then; but of course it would be medieval in this day and age to continue to believe there are heathens among us who must conform to moral directives.

Whereas the Bible tells of King Nebuchadnezzar who lost his mind through hubris, thereby resulting in being reduced to animalistic madness as seen in the William Blake watercolor in Figure 26, the Bible also showcases plenty of stories about saints, hermits, and anchorites who go to the wilderness to pray in isolation. The result is that these characters became furry and wild. Still, these hairy hermits didn't fall out of grace. If anything, their experience with wilderness made them more holy as seen in the example of Saint Onuphrius in Figure 27 from fifteenth-century Germany.

There are two other superheroes from the Bible who earned their wild people wings as well. Mary Magdalene is sometimes portrayed with saintly hermit fur, as in the mid-1400's illuminated

Figures 26 & 27. Hairy Anchorites and Shaggy Saints. First Image © Tate Gallery, London, 2017. Second Image Courtesy of the Metropolitan Museum of Art, Rogers Fund, 1918.

Figures 28 & 29. Holy Hirsutes and Hairsuits! First Image Courtesy of the J. Paul Getty Museum, Los Angeles. Second Photo by Mark Spitzer.

manuscript image from France shown in Figure 28. As in the Italian sculpture of Figure 29, John the Baptist is also sometimes depicted in the wilderness, close to nature, wearing fur to clothe his body and keep warm.

All of this I discovered during my initial research and the writing of my senior thesis (Spitzer, 1989), which – in the spirit of quantity over quality – I deliberately envisioned to be the largest one ever submitted to the University of Minnesota. I never received a trophy for that unofficial record, but it was 400 pages long, and it was written on an old-fashioned electric typewriter. As soon as I turned it in, a new opportunity presented itself. I was informed about an Undergraduate Research Opportunity Project (UROP) grant, which I applied for and got. I received $1500 to supplement a research trip to Europe with my friend Rob Butler, who's now a professional photographer. For a month, we traveled through Hungary, Austria, Germany, France, the Netherlands, Belgium, and the United Kingdom searching for wild people in art.

Figure 30. Scored a UROP Grant to Run Around and Research Wild People. Photo by Mark Spitzer.

In Figure 30, Rob is posing in Canterbury with a statue of a leper, another out-of-favor infidel icon that shares some crossover with wild people. That is, both lepers and wild people were considered out-of-grace rejects of society with no place in the community.

But Rob and I didn't just work. There were nights when we went stumbling through Budapest with Swedish models and Finnish Olympic hockey players, and there were mornings when we woke up in crash pads for bums in Belgium. Shenanigans happened in Amsterdam, and we stowed away on trains in England. I even spent a night in jail in Wales after I got locked out of a youth hostel. The cops said I could sleep in a cell.

We found tons of wild people: on stained glass in France, on confessionals in the Netherlands, and on cornices in Germany. We were so happy to find the one in Figure 32 that I climbed a castle wall in Lubeck, Germany to kiss it, and the police were not amused. I almost got locked up but was saved by a letter from the College of Liberal Arts. Before we left on that trip, I acquired a letter of introduction from my dean to help us get into special collections at museums and archives. It had an official gold stamp on it, and it said I was a serious scholar doing serious research, so

Figures 31 & 32. Fieldwork Finds. Photos by RJB Photo, reproduced by permission.

please provide access. If you're a student thinking of doing similar research, I definitely recommend asking your dean's office for an official letter of introduction, which can help get you through door jambs – and out of jams as well.

Figures 33 & 34. No Better Way to Discover the World and Yourself Than When You Have a Mission to Accomplish. First Photo by RJB Photo, reproduced by permission. Second Photo by Mark Spitzcr.

We also found wild men on church pews and in the streets, which now strikes me as ironic. That is, these personifications of wilderness were primarily found in cities because that's where people keep their art, so that's where we had to go. The countryside, where one would expect wild people to naturally be, hardly yielded such artifacts.

Upon our return, I made a final report, then passed on a lot of the photos to Dr. Savage, who used them in some papers he published. After that, the images we collected were stored away for decades.

But for me the wild people never went away. They stayed with me because all that specialized knowledge I absorbed became part of my identity. The tension between Wilderness and civilization, the question of our primal selves – all became part of my aesthetic and how I viewed the world. No wonder I went off to graduate school at the University of Colorado and studied environmental literature with experts like Linda Hogan, Ed Dorn, Reg Saner, and Lorna Dee Cervantes, then wrote an environmental monster-fish thesis, which was later published as the novel *Bottom Feeder* (Spitzer, 1999), followed by its sequel *Garapaima* (Spitzer, 2015), concerning other monstrous whoppers. It's also not surprising that I went back to graduate school for an MFA and wrote the novel *Chum* (Spitzer, 2001), about grotesque humans and grotesque fish caught up in cycles of primal violence. And then I wrote its prequel *CHODE!* (Spitzer, 2010), which also includes legions of monstrosities. Following that, monsters made their way into my poetry and nonfiction, and even had a presence in my literary trans-lations and memoirs. And no wonder all these works are pinned together by eco-concerns central to the oldest literary conflict in the world (civilization vs. Wilderness) as seen in *The Gilgamesh Epic* (Sandars, 1972).

I kept on studying environmental subject matter until eventually I was teaching it – which, I've realized, might be the most important thing I can do on this planet. Because our planet is in severe decline. The ice caps are melting and the experts agree that we won't have this global cooling device in a century. Climate change, carbon

Figures 35 & 36. When a Study Becomes Part of You, It Manifests Itself in What You Do. First Image by Rex Rose, reproduced with permission. Second Image by Mark Spitzer.

dioxide, and acidification are taking their toll, so if we don't do something soon, we could lose this platform we take for granted – a point I make because I'm scared of what we have to lose. I've made a study of what our greed and ignorance is doing to this planet, and I can see the direction we're going in. Because of that, I'm committed to doing as much as I can to preserve and patch what we have left through the influence I have via my writing and teaching of writing.

That's why my creative nonfiction, especially regarding fish, is actually the most important thing I do. My work in investigative poetics might look like a collage of folklore and history, but beneath that veneer it's actually indirect activism veiling environmental, political messages. But due to the nature of the genre of poetry, those messages don't reach a very wide audience. And neither do the messages embedded in my fiction, which tends to get published by progressive small presses with limited reach. But when it comes to creative nonfiction, eco-topics are hot these days, because the world is getting desperate. We need an understanding of the situation, we need solutions, and there's a socially responsible market out there catering to this growing demand. Which is why, ultimately, I chose the more marketable mode of environmental creative nonfiction to disseminate my ideas on how to proceed. University presses publish these books by the thousands and supply

Figure 37. No Better Way to Become an Authority on Something Than Getting Out There and Doing It. Photo by Eric Tumminia, reproduced by permission.

support teams to get the word out. I tell what the problems have been, I tell what the problems are, and I tell what we can do about them. And this, in turn, gets my messages on TV, the radio, and in newspapers. And those messages, in turn, take me to libraries and colleges and bookstores all over the country, where I talk about what can be done. All those other issues in the world (racism, poverty, human rights, sexism) don't matter if there isn't a planet to apply fixes to. That's my priority, and luckily, I've got fish, an area I am interested in and know a lot about. And luckily, people are interested in fish. Hence, fish have become the messengers for what I've got to say that counts the most.

Lately, I've been expanding my investigations of monstrous fish. I recently published an environmental fish book entitled *Beautifully Grotesque Fish of the American West* (Spitzer, 2017). The University of Nebraska Press came up with those adjectives, and "grotesque," of course, was totally appropriate, given my background in studying wild people and garfish. To research that book, I spent two years traveling throughout the American West investigating eels, burbot, bullheads, bowfin, and about eight other fugly freshwater species. And it was a blast.

More importantly, as noted before, when you get out in the field and work with the experts you get to conduct informal interviews, and when you go to places where history happened, you receive a better understanding of the conditions which allowed for things to happen. For instance, when I went fishing for paddlefish in Missouri, and when I saw how those reservoirs were constructed, I saw with my own eyes how the dams we erect for hydroelectricity and recreation block migrations and cripple reproduction. In Figure 37, that's a five-foot paddlefish caught by snagging, which involves dragging giant treble hooks through schools of fish. That's about the only way you can catch such a fish because they only eat micro-organics.

Similarly, when I went noodling for catfish in the 2014 Okie Noodling Tournament, I saw how the practice of hand-fishing wasn't sustainable. Noodling involves locating active nests, then busting in, and using your body as bait. In defense of its young, a fish attacks a hand or leg and is removed from its nest. In learning this approach, I hauled two thirty-pounders from a river in Oklahoma, and at first I was thrilled. I put the pregnant female back, and I took the male to the tournament. That's where I learned that most of these fish don't always get put back into the

Figure 38. The Catch-and-Release Stewardship Wild People Advocate. Photo by Lea Graham, reproduced by permission.

system, so their eggs often go to waste. That bothered me, and so does the fact that this type of fishing is becoming more and more popular – and because of that there are no hundred-pounders any more (they used to surpass 150 pounds in the 1800's). That's why I called for the hand-fishing community to create and maintain game preserves for giant catfish.

Further, when I studied sturgeon in the Northwest, I learned how overfishing can lead to population crashes that take centuries to recover from, which makes taking preemptive action vital to sustaining ecological balance. I caught and released the sturgeon pictured in Figure 38 on the Snake River in Idaho, and that was the smallest of the three landed that day. The largest one I caught was eight foot one inches long and weighed 250 pounds. But back in the 1880's, white sturgeon reportedly grew twenty feet long. These days, it's doubtful any exist larger than fourteen feet due to the Great Sturgeon Crash of 1892 from which North America is still recovering. As this and many other similar cases illustrate, it pays to monitor the environment and keep looking ahead at what needs to be done to keep things balanced. That's what I write about in my "outreach," which I see as a form of stewardship. This is what wild people are about as ambassadors of Wilderness.

In studying monster muskellunge, I learned how stocking eco-systems takes years of tenacity, which can pay off in healthy sport fisheries that serve as models for preservation of other species – an idea I'm sure wild folk would approve of. Muskies were the hardest fish to catch that I've ever gone after. I had to spend thousands of dollars and work with five guides to finally catch two in Iowa. Lucky for me I can write off a lot of my fishing as professional expenses for research.

One thing I discovered with my fish research is that Americans are fortunate to have taxes to help sustain federal and state fisheries because if we didn't have authorities out there checking into what needs to be done to maintain what remains, we'd be in the same sorry state as many other countries that do not have this oversight. I studied alligator and tropical gar in Nicaragua and Mexico, and

Figures 39 & 40. Using Studies of the Grotesque as a Tool to Get at What We Need to Address Right Now. First Image Courtesy of Anaphora Literary Press, reproduced by permission. Second Photo by Lea Graham, reproduced by permission.

compared to our fisheries in the United States, their fisheries are a travesty. In Central America, I've seen hordes of desperate peasants netting everything they can get and taking immature gar out of the system, which means those fish never reproduce. Alligator gar have very delicate reproductive cycles. In the American South, they only spawn every seven years on average. So reproduction is something we need to be aware of if we want all the links in the food chain to stay as strong as they can be. Because if you take a link out of a chain, the chain is broken. And if the chain is broken, then there's a chain reaction that can easily lead to an eco-disaster.

I have two other books that investigate the grotesque. The first is *GLURK!,* an epic hybrid poem concerning the hellbender salamander (Spitzer, 2016), which is North America's largest, most endangered amphibian. These weird, wiggly "lasagna lizards" are important to other species because they serve as barometers of water quality and biodiversity. They're presently being decimated by the combination of overdevelopment and a toxic flesh-eating fungus. These severe declines in populations are pushing scientists to try all sorts of innovations in propagation. One of the things recently discovered about the endangered Ozark hellbender is that the estimated 590 remaining in the wild actually represent six different separate gene pools, which makes conservation efforts even more urgent to preserve the biodiversity of this species.

Then there's my investigative nonfiction book, *In Search of Monster Fish: Angling for a More Sustainable Planet* (Spitzer, 2019), which looks at various eco-concerns all over the planet. Take the wels catfish, for example, pictured in Figure 40. That fish was caught in Catalonia. It was six foot three inches long and weighed 118 pounds, and that was the smaller of the two I caught. Like humans, this barbelly behemoth is now new to most of its range, and there's a debate raging as to whether these apex predators should be in non-native environments. In contrast, there's hardly ever any discussion of whether humans should be in the environments they've claimed for themselves. Invasive species are a major problem, but one of the questions I'm looking at is, rather than fight losing battles, is there a way we can take these lemons and make lemonade?

My investigative nonfiction projects are driven by the same sort of respect for nature that wild people promote, and a concern for the universal conflicts they've been illustrating for millennia. These days, however, it's not so much a matter of simply warning people about consequences. That time is over because the effects of global warming, over-development, and petro-chemical abuse are rapidly accelerating the destruction of the environment. So what I'm trying to do is get to a more involved discussion of the solutions, which I suggest in the conclusion of *Beautifully Grotesque* (Spitzer, 2017). That's where I note that we've got a planet going down, so we need big ideas fast, minus the unconstructive bickering. I then call for America's history of innovation to be applied to the future. I discuss "iron fertilization," or feeding oceans with iron particles to trigger the growth of blue-green plankton blooms which absorb CO_2 and sunlight. I recommend producing a greener gasoline by growing algae in giant vats. I point to the "monochrome Earth method," in which the idea is to paint roads and roofs white in order to reflect sunlight back into space. I make a case for continuing to invest in wind, geothermal, and other alternative energy sources – and especially solar. I advocate for the working theory of "mariculture," which offers a way to burn a lot less oil on farms and in food-producing industries by growing crops vertically in the ocean rather than horizontally on the land.

Those are just some of the ideas that wild people ultimately led me to and developed in my consciousness. And my consciousness, in return, developed the idea of investigative nonfiction, which is *investigative* in the most traditional sense of the word because it allowed me to get out there and investigate, interrogate, and immerse myself in discovering what the real story is.

This is where wild people exist for me now: as a behind-the-scenes, driving force – not fighting Christian knights and illustrating a division between civilization and Wilderness, but as an informative and symbolic moral source of stewardship. So even though I now concentrate mainly on "monster fish," there are still wild people frolicking invisibly through the thistle leaves of my books. Books which may not be illuminated manuscripts, but nonetheless seek to illuminate through the club I now wield as I crusade for the preservation of monsters in our midst, which make our lives more colorful.

References

Sandars, N. K. (ed.) (1972) *The Epic of Gilgamesh*. London: Penguin.

Spitzer, Mark (1989) *Wild People and Thistles*. Senior thesis. Minneapolis: University of Minnesota.

Spitzer, Mark (1999) *Bottom Feeder*. Berkeley: Creative Arts Book Company.

Spitzer, Mark (2001) *Chum*. Cambridge, MA: Zoland Books.

Spitzer, Mark (2010) *CHODE!* Pittsburgh: Six Gallery Press.

Spitzer, Mark (2015) *Garapaima: A Monster Fish Novel*. Coquitlam, British Columbia: Moon Willow Press.

Spitzer, Mark (2016) *GLURK! A Hellbender Odyssey*. Hephzibah, GA: Anaphora Literary Press.

Spitzer, Mark (2017) *Beautifully Grotesque Fish of the American West*. Lincoln: University of Nebraska Press.

Spitzer, Mark (2019) *In Search of Monster Fish: Angling for a More Sustainable Planet*. Lincoln: University of Nebraska Press.

Part 5

Experiential Exercises

Chapter 14

Seven Investigative Group Exercises

The experiential aspect of investigative creative writing pedagogy makes it fun, but that's no reason to apply it. What's important are the discoveries, and how those discoveries affect both individuals and communities. As noted earlier, teaching provides a way to pass on power, and the most dramatically effective way to teach, I've discovered, is to turn the text-making process into *something else*. When learning becomes an event, it works its magic through transformation; students are transformed, teachers are transformed, and ultimately, expectations are transformed, which leads to better communication and higher objectives. In other words, when writing teachers provide extraordinary experiences, this lights a fire in writing students that stays with them, urges them on, and provides the charge they need to ignite their own self-generated power.

One of my more memorable teachers did just that back in my graduate studies at the University of Colorado. Legendary Western writer Ed Dorn had no hesitation making grandiose if not inflammatory statements in class. Some of these were in regard to his politics, but others were just plain absurd – like how recycling causes pollution, or how the flatulence of vegetarians is destructive to the environment. That approach, of course, was entertainment-driven, but it made students sit up and listen.

More importantly, Dorn demonstrated first-hand that a class can be an event that encapsulates the spirit of *something else*. That class was Literature of the High West, which, from the first day on, was a remarkable experience. I won't get into the many reasons why since they're detailed in depth in my notorious essay "Dinner with Slinger" (Spitzer, 2000), but suffice it to say that Dorn's pedagogy incorporated a collage of both orthodox and unorthodox approaches which always led to his classes being overenrolled.

Dorn had an insanely captivating way of incorporating colorful language and attitude into rambling lectures that never disappointed his audience. He was an expert on the West and had all sorts of interesting historical information to pass on, but that's not why my classmates and I looked forward to the unexpected antics of his class every week. In short, I'll just say that we referred to that class as "The Ed Dorn Show," and that we went to see it for the same reason audiences go to see improv comedy, or the movies, or professional wrestling – which is how he translated his messages to his students: through the theater of himself. Sometimes this involved ranting and raving to scare students out of his class and get the numbers down; other times this involved pacing back and forth while decrying the evils of the first George Bush and his "mutant sons." But whatever the case, he was always entertaining.

About half-way through the semester, students were charged with investigating questions of the American West through messages that took them outside their usual *modi operandi*. For my project, I designed a video investigation about horsepower in the West in which I interviewed motorheads about their muscle cars and recorded poetry screeds in front of dams where security guards ran me off. That was back in the early nineties when video equipment was not as easily available as it is now. To make that video, I bought a video camera at Sears then returned it the next week to the disgruntlement of an irritated salesman who no doubt lost his commission.

My point is that taking Dorn's class was an experience, an event; and subconsciously, it affected me. And the reason I write "subconsciously" is that I didn't even recall how transformative that experience was until I was 95 percent done with this book. In fact, it's all coming back to me on a rainy morning in Arkansas, and these memories are key. That is, they're revealing to me why my teaching style often seems so ridiculously unscripted in the sense that I get up there, gesture emphatically, and take off on tangents. Perhaps I'm emulating or imitating Dorn, or maybe such methods have just became part of me. I don't know, but I do know that Dorn played a major role in informing my pedagogical persona, which is important for what it allows me to offer.

The "Mark Spitzer Show," if you will, gives me a platform for offering *something else* to my own students in my own way so that they can feel empowered to take off on their own self-propelled investigations. It's a show that hinges on investigative activities designed to foster interaction and play. It's a show that incorporates in-class assignments, writing games, and exercises that have proven useful to me in turbo-charging student involvement in the college classroom and creating strong bonds which foster a hunger for more creative writing. At the very least, these activities open up students' imaginations to produce writing that is very different from what students would ordinarily produce, and to think logically and linguistically about the possibilities for far-fetched connections. They also trigger creative processes that result in original work with the potential for publication.

I've used these activities in introductory creative writing courses and in upper-level forms and workshop classes for both poetry and fiction, and I've used some at the graduate level. These entertaining and immersive activities geared toward generating discovery, however, can also be applied to other disciplines (i.e. English, composition, professional writing, communications, even trigonometry), especially as "ice-breakers" that invite students to participate in learning environments which encourage creative approaches.

The investigative processes of the first three assignments (investigative opposites, investigative hypotheticals, and investigative Q & A) hinge on discovering combinations of random phrases in order to create postmodern poems. The freedom involved in the seemingly magical collaging of amusing soundbites is "investigative" because it allows for students to seek answers through creative play. When imaginations are given entertaining problems to solve, they search for entertaining solutions, which lead to juxtapositions which are highly participatory in nature. Just the fact that at least two students created something together, whether it be successful or not, makes the process an interactive event, which is a success in itself. After a few rounds, a rhythm is established, and the calls and responses start coming easier. This benefits students in confidence-building, to know that they can come up with X, add Y, and end up being rewarded with Z – which is especially apparent when students fall out of their chairs laughing. Such events are not that common in my classroom, and when they happen, the result is a yearning for learning. And, as previously noted, learning always works better when it's fun.

Investigative Opposites

To prepare for this writing game, situate students in a circle and distribute index cards (hint: colorful cards may inspire more colorful context). Tell students to write something spontaneous, then hand that card to the next person (clockwise or counter-clockwise, it's up to you; but switch directions on the next round to encourage different tones). Students who receive cards then write on the other side whatever they believe to be the total opposite of the initial message. When everyone's done, pick somebody to read both sides of his/her card and then go around the room. It doesn't matter which side is read first. People will laugh and comment on bizarre connections that magically occur when polarities bounce off each other. Combinations having to do with love and hate, and life and death, and dogs and cats easily occur; but the really surprising stuff happens when students are asked to imagine the opposite of yesterday's news, or a one-eyed lion tamer, or Christmas in Reno.

After a few rounds, the cards begin to pile up, which can lead to a larger purpose for this activity that's especially appropriate for creative writing students, who can take some cards home, and type up combinations to create surreal, experimental poems which they title. I make this a homework assignment, but tell them not to sign the work. Then, to show them how easy and nonthreatening the submission process can be, I bring stamps and envelopes to the next class along with copies of recent *Poet's Markets* (Brewer, 2018) and put them in groups. The groups are instructed to look through the magazines and journals sections for wacky or postmodern titles that are open to poetry by emerging writers. New and punk markets are also good forums to search for. Students then invent a pseudonym for a poet, address envelopes to editors, and prepare self-addressed stamped postcards. I supply my own address for the postcards, but if you're an instructor who's not inclined to give out that information, you can find a student in the class to volunteer his or her address for this purpose – but make sure it's someone who will be at that address for at least a year to receive the reply. I supply a model for cover letters for students to base their own letters on, they whip those up, then stuff the envelopes with their poems. I mail them out, and after a few weeks or months (which is why this exercise works best at the beginning of a semester), the responses start coming in. Students are always psyched to examine the replies and share their amusement in being rejected. Sometimes, though, they get accepted, which pumps up enthusiasm and actually leads to co-publications they can list on their CVs. See Assignment 4 at the end of this chapter for a more detailed description of this particular exercise.

Below is an example of an investigative opposites poem written by undergraduates in a poetry workshop, which broke some students out of a pattern of writing religiously centered poems and led them to another realm:

A Cry for Help

You grow as tall as a tree when you stand next to me
    You shrink down to a seed when you run in place next to your
    doppelganger

The psychedelic possum parachuted at high noon
    The nine-to-five turtle launched during the new moon

Without 90s Grunge and heavily creamed coffee, I am but a spider
in a concrete world
    Drinking loose leaf tea while I listen to Pink Floyd in my yard
    makes me feel
    like a fly in the wind, goin' wherever it takes me

This is a bullshit task because I've been colorblind ever since that
rabbit stole my hat
    This is a useful task because the rabbit has given me my heart back

I never thought I would want to be a character in *Animal Farm*,
but now that I know Leon Trotsky had an affair with Frida Kahlo,
    I can reconsider that I never knew I'd want to be a character in
    1984,
    but now that I know Leon Trotsky didn't have an affair with Frida
    Kahlo,
    I won't reconsider

Dull eyes stare outside of shopping centers, closing at gazelles over
waterfall suns
    Clockwork eyes wander about shopping centers gazing at
    gazelles under
    waterfall moons

Crush my eyeballs with a sledgehammer and I will leak battery acid
    Heal my sight with a feather and I will take in your water

Mocha wisps of a caffeinated breeze slip their way past my nostrils
and into my soul
    Water drops of sleepy stale air block my eyes and my soullessness.

– Hayden Reed
Craig Byers
Victoria Barham
Holly Davis
Annika Warrick
Jordan Willoughby
Noah Freeman

Some of the connections in this poem are obviously more successful than others – but that's to be expected. The point isn't in arriving at the final product; it's in the connecting process, which has the potential to become a transformative event. When that happens, you can usually see a definite effect – an effect that just might serve students more than drafting a generally sound poem that's hard to find fault with. Because what's more important: discovering an entertaining way to investigate with others in order to make poetry that spawns more poetry, or coming up with a poem that ends up being forgotten amidst other poems whose audience is mainly the poets who wrote them?

Investigative Hypotheticals

Investigative hypotheticals is similar to the game above. Students are situated in a circle, index cards are distributed, and students are instructed to write something spontaneous starting with an "If…" The cards are then turned over so that recipients cannot see the propositions as they respond with something that starts with a "Then…" When both sides are filled out, it's good to hand the completed card to a third person so that everyone has a surprise to read. Then, as in investigative opposites, the results are read out loud. Like the previous activity, this one is "investigative" in the sense that the players actively consider causes and effects in their heads, and are subsequently led to literal discoveries. These discoveries are not always logical, but pleasing linguistic surprises do pop up, which often makes the process worth it. Strange juxtapositions are also quite common that create vivid effects in spontaneous ways. Sometimes the best discoveries happen when people are taken to places they never knew existed, where they find something with some mojo.

For instance, when I lived at the bookstore Shakespeare and Company in Paris in the 1990's, I once found myself pulling books off the shelves, picking random words, and building phrases from the luck of the draw – which is a process that's similar to the chance ordering that happens in investigative hypotheticals. One phrase I came up with was "the pigs drink from infinity," a discovery that had metaphoric possibilities. The idea that there are gluttons in the universe hogging an eternity's worth of natural resources led me to consider these words for years, and they eventually served as the title of a poetry book that encapsulated a surreal investigative spirit: *The Pigs Drink from Infinity: Poems 1995–2001* (Spitzer, 2006).

Returning to investigative hypotheticals, one observation I've had from joining in on this experiential process – and I encourage instructors to take part because it helps dissolve the teacher/teachee dichotomy, thereby temporarily placing everyone on the same community-building level – is that after filling out the "If" side of a card, one usually responds on the next card ("Then") according to what one just proposed on the "If" card. For example, if a student proposes an "If" that envisions going to the moon in a rocket, that student is likely to follow up with a "Then" that imagines what will happen when she gets there. This, again, is part of the investigative process, the positing of cause and effect that I wrote of earlier, which leads to discovery. But whatever the case, after the first round of this writing game, as well as in investigative opposites, phrases start coming more freely and increasing in imagination and hilarity.

Another thing to keep in mind is that students who laugh or gasp while reading completed cards to themselves are the most strategic students to end with when they read aloud, since they hold cards in which effects have been created. So when it comes time to read out loud, stack the deck in favor of ending on cards that cause reactions. Such moments will punctuate the ending of poems with finality as well.

Like investigative opposites, the cards can then be converted into poems to be sent out to magazines or journals, thereby exploding the myth that submitting for publication is a complicated, aggravating, or threatening process. And since nothing's at stake when sending out work created by a fictitious poet, this demonstrates how easy it is to stuff envelopes like a machine and shoot them out to faceless entities. Students fearing judgement are often hesitant to risk showing their work to editors, but sending work out anonymously helps illustrate an allusion to a roulette wheel that I use to describe the submission process: The more you spin it, the more likely it is for the ball to land on your number. I tell students that the more they do that, the less they'll stress about what any single editor thinks about their writing. Then, one day, it's payback time, baby!

The poem below is another example of what this investigative activity generated in a poetry workshop. It might at first seem like a silly indulgence, but there are sublime undercurrents here that tell me a lot about what these students feel comfortable revealing about themselves when a ridiculous medium provides the liberty to express amusing connections.

Again, some of the above connections don't work as well as others (like the long one in the middle, which gets bogged down by too much detail), and some work much better than others (like the beginning and ending couplets, in which happenstance led to the lines being extremely appropriate to each other and useful for framing the poem). Also, some connections are more far-fetched or ridiculous than others, and some are more somber in tone. But this mixing of voices and styles and attitudes doesn't have to be the end product. Like investigative opposites, spinning the investigative-hypotheticals roulette wheel can provide opportunities to start other projects.

For example, rather than transforming the cards into poems to send out for publication (or in addition to sending out for publication), student groups can break apart and reorganize lines in order to arrive at more meaningful connections. Students can also investigate the idea of "trimming off the fat," or editing for clarity. Or teachers can lead "what if" discussions – as in "What if we took this adjective here and applied it to that noun there?" or "What if the lack of humor in this stanza was adjusted to match the humor in that stanza?" Another general question which could prove valuable to propose is: "What can we do to synthesize the

What If Madlibs Were Assigned to Me?

Sometimes I think what if my life was different
then I think how everything would change…

If I was seventy but looked like I was twenty
then Johnny Bravo would finally get laid

If I drop just enough acid
then cats would shut up for a change

If a person were to ever give a flying crap
then maybe I wouldn't cry into my Cheetos bag

Maybe, if I drown a fly in a bathtub
then the world would break and bend before me and
everything I have done will lose all meaning

If I built a swing set without a park
then I would cry "Hallelujah!" as
I pet my pet duck's crowned head in my hot tub

If I find out that my shoes are not affected by
The gravity of this earth but pulled by the loneliness
Of the barren rock we call the moon
then we won't believe there is a difference
between religion and burning the cactus

If gargoyles were to fly out of the mayor's ear
then I would jump down the rabbit hole and paint the roses blue

If the octopi stopped drinking Scotch before college football games
then I'll give you three eggs and a ham

Sometimes I think if I never had thoughts like these
then I wouldn't have to visit the shrink.

– Hayden Reed
Craig Byers
Victoria Barham
Annika Warrick
Jordan Willoughby
Noah Freeman
Holly Davis

overall tone of this poem so it looks more like it came from one writer's vision rather than multiple points of view?"

The take-home message for this exercise is that group work can lead to a lot of in-class activity in creative problem-solving that's not only fun to take part in, but can help prepare students for jobs in which communication is currency. First, there's the fact that working and playing together is an exercise in socialization skills which promote camaraderie among team members, and secondly, clearly articulating consequences and results at the sentence level is an ability employers value. Add to that the fact that when students like playing a game in school, they'll play it with their friends when they're not in school, which means that making such connections is more than a game: If anything, it's part of a profound investigation process dedicated to making something worthwhile from chaos. And if you can develop an aptitude for that, especially in this age of overwhelming disinformation, then you're better equipped than most to roll with the punches life deals to everyone.

Investigative Q & A

In investigative Q & A, what matters is how you play the game, and here's how you do it: The instructor situates students in a circle, hands out index cards, and then everyone writes questions. The questions are passed to the left or right, and the receivers, without looking at the questions, provide answers. When it comes time to read the combinations out loud, the next person in line reads both sides of the card. The blind responses often prove to be highly appropriate to what was originally asked. Chance calls the shots and crazy patterns naturally occur – as in the following poem generated from investigative Q & A, which was chosen because it doesn't make sense. Still, there are some moments in it that do make sense. In the spirit of postmodernism, though, process is often more valuable than product. The bottom line being: if you search for meaning and find it in a writing process, and if that discovery

What Happens When I Think

What happens when I chain myself to a tree to save it and
then start to hate the environment & can't get out?
Because the earth really is flat and we've all been lied to.

Why did they take *Dirty Dancing* off of Netflix?
Just giggle and smile and bat your eyes.

How high is Mount Everest?
Because you're no longer attractive.

What if the last possession you had in the world was a Zippo with
no flint?
The destruction of all dolphins on the planet!

What do I do when the drunk old lady who lives down the way
claims to be my father and proceeds to disown me as she calls me
a failure?
Then the bathroom graffiti wouldn't suck so bad! #Thuglife
#Killorbekill

What is the speed of light divided by yogurt?
My favorite color is green.

How can the MLB have a "world series" if it's only open to American
teams?
Good Question. I've been wondering the same thing.
Maybe if we tie ourselves together and count to 5
we'll blast off & be okay.

Why don't you look at me during?
Because illiteracy is cool!

– Hayden Reed
Craig Byers
Victoria Barham
Holly Davis
Annika Warrick
Jordan Willoughby
Noah Freeman

yields something worth the effort to you, then that's an investigative process that just might hold some meaning for others as well.

As in the other investigative activities, the more you do this one, the easier it gets. And the more you do these kinds of activities in class, the more imaginative and expressive students become, and the more they think about how logical and linguistic connections can be made. Like investigative opposites and investigative hypotheticals, the resulting poems can be typed up and sent out to magazines or journals in a following class. Or students can pick one or more lines and use those as starting or ending points for further poems they write on their own or in groups. Like the first two investigative exercises, this one can also generate lines to riff on, elaborate on, or mutate. Toning down or tuning up is also an option for revising poems. Or maybe choose the most colorful lines to inspire one-act plays, or to use as prompts in stream-of-consciousness freewriting or brainstorming lists. As with all the investigative exercises offered in this chapter, the possibilities are as endless as all the investigations chance has to offer creative individuals looking to make something from nothing. In other words, when imaginations are triggered by wordplay, creating something through *something else* offers limitless directions on which to capitalize. And even if the result is disappointing, the time and energy spent on creating order from disorder can only result in the exact opposite. It's the exact same thing as athletes working out. Practice lends to the honing of muscles and minds. Focus and stamina increase, and endurance increases. Even the experience of wiping out, and then getting up again, can be applied to the next race.

Investigative Spy Teams

This is an exercise that I wouldn't blame any cautious teacher from opting out of because it could be considered a bit sketchy. Still, it's worked well for me in creating student camaraderie for more than seventeen years. After hammering my Introduction to Creative Writing students for weeks with writing portraits that show not tell, I put them in what I call "spy teams" of four and send them out of the classroom to literally stalk someone. One team member is charged with taking notes on the person's appearance, another is tasked with taking notes on what the person thinks, another writes notes about his or her past, and somebody else does the same for the subject's future.

I should also note that I prepare students for this assignment by advising that if their subject catches on to being observed, they should run like hell. And if they get caught, then they should reply with the response, "My teacher made me do it."

The thing about this in-class assignment is that after trying and trying to conform to my rules, the students are suddenly encouraged to break the rules. "Rhyme!" I tell them. "And tell not show! Ask questions. Use conditional tenses. Repeat stuff even!"

The point is that to break the rules, you have to know the rules. And you can learn from breaking the rules. However, what I've found is that half-way through a semester, students would rather practice what I preach than break the rules I advocate.

The spy teams have half an hour to run around and collect notes, and usually, some come back with Starbucks coffee. That's fine, since one of the ideas of this investigative exercise (which is literally "investigative" because they invest themselves in getting out in the field and observing a subject) is to get students out of the classroom and provide a sense of freedom. They might stay in the building, or they might not, but since there's a time limit of only half an hour, they won't go far.

When they get back to the classroom, each group is charged with writing an eight-line group poem in which each member donates two lines based on his or her notes. These poems are then read aloud by a team-appointed representative who prefaces the poem with a brief overview of where they went and who they picked and why.

If anything, this experiential project provides for a better sense of my expectations. But does this send a mixed message?

It doesn't matter – because as soon as we're done with that assignment, it's straight back to writing portraits of events in the news in order to identify ambiguous words and install vivid descriptions instead.

The following example, written by a spy team in an Introduction to Creative Writing class, is typical of the not-displeasing

Stalking Mama Jeans

She sat upon the wooden bench wearing faded white leather slippers
with no socks and obviously stinky feet.

She may or may not have noticed that we had passed by her once.
However she sensed us tracking her as her and her best friend
exited Irby.

When she was fifteen her mother got really sick
and then better and then sick again.

Her mama's jeans sagged between her duck-toed gait
nervously fingering the tail of her jacket as she waddled away.

   Should I confront these stalkers?
   Should I tell my best friend?

One time she found a baby shoe in the parking lot
& hid it in her coat & took it home.

Her platonic friend decides today is the day to make a pass at her.

In two years' time the two of them with a combined 82 cats
will travel around the world curing genital herpes one case at a time.

They will cure the worst outbreak the world has ever seen.
Out of gratitude, the villagers will reveal their blood fountain of youth.

– Erika Stanisch
Jason Kidder
David Gomez
Bella Cillia

schizophrenic collages collaborative minds create when you get a bunch of cooks in the kitchen working to put together one main investigative dish. They may have deviated from the assignment a bit, often by adding extra lines, but I always encourage students to take poetic license.

Investigative Manic Cadaver

This is an offshoot of the traditional "exquisite corpse" exercise developed by the surrealists circa 1924. I like to kick this experience off by explaining to the class how there were these avant-garde artists hanging out in salons in France, and they had this parlor game in which somebody would draw or paint someone's head. I draw a cartoon head on the board. "Then," I continue, "that artist would pass the project along to another artist, who would draw the arms." I call a student up to draw goofy arms, and then someone else for the torso, another for the legs, and yet another for the feet. When the portrait is complete, I exclaim, "Voila! Le corpse exquis!"

I go on to explain how the poets had to get in on that action, so they invented their own version of this game by passing a piece of paper around the room on which someone would write something – anything at all – and then somebody else would play off that line and fold the paper so only the last response was visible. The continuously folded piece of paper gets circulated throughout the room with people adding lines and refolding the paper so that only the last line is visible.

To drive students to drive themselves as fast as they can in this exercise, and to be as spontaneous as possible in what they write, I come prepared with two boom boxes and a bunch of old cassette tapes. The students vote on combinations that I will play (i.e. Boston and Van Halen, Jimi Hendrix and Sonic Youth, the Mormon Tabernacle Choir and Stravinsky), and then I put them in groups of four or five. Everyone is instructed to tear a page out of their notebooks and be prepared to start a body of work and to write and respond as fast as they can. If they can't think of anything to write, they should write down what they had for breakfast or something about Harry Potter. I fire up the cacophony, shout "GO!" and the anarchy in the air creates a frenzy that students can't help throwing themselves into. Ideas are released, visions are captured, and students guffaw and shake their heads, as manic cadavers are born.

When they get to the end of the page, that completes the investigative process – which is "investigative" because it spontaneously mirrors the collage aspect so visible in Sanders' model of investigative poetry, while also incorporating the live-action component of search and discovery in the investigative spy-team assignment. More importantly, the investigative manic cadaver teams then work together to identify their best poem (five minutes max), and then a representative reads the winner aloud to the class. I ask them to sign the winning poem and turn it in, and then we do another round; but this time they hand their poems in the opposite direction and write them in reverse, starting with the last line and working their way up to the title. They pick the best one, read those aloud as well, and again, they sign the winners and turn them in to me.

I then submit their manic cadavers to the school newspaper, some local weekly, or a website that's open to undergraduate work. Not only is this method excellent for creating excitement and suspense for following classes and gaining recruits for the Creative Writing major, it frequently results in students getting published. Why? Heck if I know. Perhaps the silly magic that makes these poems work is just felt by editors who have a respect for surrealism. Or maybe it's the genius that the investigative manic cadaver naturally brings out in students.

But watch out if your school has thin walls! The reverberating combination of Janis Joplin and Fatboy Slim has not always gone over so well with rhetoric professors teaching in adjacent rooms. It's a good idea to warn colleagues that this is coming and will not be a regular thing.

Graduate students in an Advanced Forms and Theory of Poetry class wrote the following example, which I especially appreciate for the profundity of its last two lines:

Operator's Manual

The mountains echo with song
God is the Bounty paper towel man
going to Kansas requires a lot of gasoline
unless you breathe green-glittered dust and the ashes of sisters

Nixon 1973 snow exhaust cigars and Scotch
bites down hard on justice, crunches like a cherry pit
of indifference, reach for it

Grasp a handful of weeds on the lip of the abyss
when you go on a date wear short skirts and perfume
carry a pocketknife like a bouquet of roses

Let the thorns snip your strings
and the knife write your words.

– Briget Laskowski
Callie Smith
Mikayla Davis
Mark Lager
J. J. McNiece

Investigative Manic Flash Fiction

When transitioning from poetry to fiction in intro courses in creative writing, I find it helpful to start off with flash fiction as preparatory work for short stories. It used to be that I'd spend a good fifteen minutes explaining what flash fiction is along with its history and the ideas behind it, but I now have a better method that bypasses a lot of needless information students don't care about. I appropriated this method (shout-out alert!) from Dr. Leigh Graham at Marist College in Poughkeepsie, New York. After creating a character with her Introduction to Creative Writing students with my unusual-characters-have-unusual-names exercise (see Chapter 2), she paired students up and told them that they would now co-write an extremely short story together in class. She let them know they would have to write quickly and switch off with their partners and that this in-class assignment would last five minutes.

Each pair used only one piece of paper. Dr. Graham started them off with the prompt of "It was a dark and stormy night," but for my students I like "It was a crappy day," which invites conflict pronto. Whatever the case, the idea is that one student writes the communal story while the other watches. A plot begins to evolve. But before they can predict what happens next, a monkey wrench is thrown into the mix.

My teaching style is unquestionably a bit more manic than Dr. Graham's. After thirty seconds (which is an adequate chunk of time for the first student to start a line of thought), I shout "Switch!" If I make the situation seem urgent, I've discovered this drives students to pick up the pace. Then, after the other student writes for another thirty seconds, I prompt, "There's a knock on the door!" They incorporate that and keep on trucking. "Switch! Switch!" I yowl in a bit, as if the world will explode if they don't. After another half-minute goes by, I say, "Okay, switch again, and throw in a line from a song." This gets them working together to find a solution. "Switch!" I howl, and at some point I tell them to work in a line from a movie. Eventually, switching back and forth and working together, they're told to end the story. "I lied," I say. "Switch again! Now really end the story!"

Half the stories, I've found, start with strippers and end in murder because that's the go-to protagonist students are prone to create with the interesting-characters-have-interesting-names assignment from Chapter 2, and that's often the default ending students choose when I'm urging them to end a story. The result, of course, is usually pretty wacky. We go around the room and the stories are read out loud.

So that's flash fiction," I tell them. "They're just really, really, short short stories with hardly any character development or setting of scene. You just jump straight into the action and get to the meat of the matter, then end just as swiftly."

I also use this exercise to demonstrate that plots need not follow any logical progression, that they're just a series of events, and then it's over, end of story. As far as I'm concerned, that's all they need to know about the form of flash fiction.

As for what's so "investigative" about investigative manic flash fiction, it's essentially the same thing as it is for investigative hypotheticals, investigative Q & A, and other investigative group assignments mentioned above: searches happen in cerebral ways which lead to discoveries. Again, these discoveries may or may not have value for the writers, but the fact that it's more about the process than the product, and the fact that it's fun, makes this assignment more than just appropriate for inclusion in the practice and teaching of investigative creative writing.

The following two examples were co-written by Introduction to Creative Writing students at the University of Central Arkansas in Spring 2017. These particular examples were selected for their attitude and their simplicity in cutting straight to the chase – in other words, for being good examples of investigative manic flash fiction:

Ajax the Depressed Stripper

It was a crappy day. Ajax Markovich was on his first day of work at the Erect Nip here in the beautiful city of Abilene, Texas. He was having a tough time trying to get tips. Being a male burlesque stripper is tough. His friends began to be worried that he would be homeless. There was a sudden knock on his dressing room door.

A big hairy man asked him, "Do you know what they call a cheese burger in France?"

He responded with "Please go away if you're not gonna give me some crack."

The man walked away and Ajax had to go on stage… poor, sad, and out of drugs.

– Hayden Lindersmith
Logan Kimball

Bleu Bacon Back the One-Legged Stripper

It was a crappy day. Someone had been stealing Bleu's tips before she could hobble over to the edge of her catwalk.

The most likely suspect was Saffron, that bitch. She had been snooping around under people's noses.

"Move bitch, get out of the way," kept reverberating in Bleu's head. But she had a battle plan on how she was gonna get her tip money back.

She heard a knock on the door. It was Saffron.

"Where's my money, slut?"

"You mean this money?"

Saffron pulled out a wad of cash from her bra as Bleu raised her hand to reveal a pistol. Needless to say, Saffron gave up the money.

– Erika Stanisch
Erika Johnson

Investigative Postcard Fiction

To prepare students for small group workshopping in fiction, it pays to put them in groups of four to do some preliminary work in order to establish a micro-community in which creative problem-solving establishes trust and lays the foundation for more interactive play. To do this, I provide each group with a handful of postcards that I've been collecting for years. Most have at least two characters pictured on them, and, of course, each is suggestive of various narratives.

"Okay," I tell them, "look at these cards and brainstorm possible stories." The groups do that, and then they pick the postcard they believe will be the most fun to work on. "Now," I continue, "you're going to write a one-page novel: just two paragraphs with some dialogue in the middle. So you need to decide who will set the scene in the first paragraph and who will write the final paragraph and end the story with a twist. And the other two, you'll do the dialogue in the middle."

Figure 41. Smoking Fish in Minnesota © Paul Stanton, reproduced by permission. Duckboy Cards, www.duckboy.com.

The twist, I explain, is an unexpected ending that keeps narratives from becoming predictable. "Go with your fourth or fifth thought," I add, the idea being to get something really unpredictable because who wants to watch a movie when the ending is obvious?

Students then work together to find a surprise ending. Their discoveries, more times than not, are worth it – if not for the product they end up with, then at least for the process of doing unusual work together and laughing their butts off.

This group writing assignment takes about a half-hour. Introduction to Creative Writing students wrote the following example, which I feel does justice to the image it's based upon.

After students hand their flash fictions in, and after I give them credit for doing their part, I hand the stories back to the groups.

"What are we supposed to do with this?" is usually the question.

"I don't know," I answer. "Put it on your fridge or something."

The real answer, though, is that this process-oriented exercise leads to the small group workshopping my intro students eventually do on their individual, longer short stories. As for the other six exercises in this chapter, they also continue to empower students,

Tommy and the Secret Syrup

Ever since Tommy was a boy he never really understood why everyone seemed to be completely obsessed with Mrs. Sap's Syrup. He absolutely hated syrup and refused to touch the sticky shit. While he gagged at the thought of it, everyone else in town was putting it on their eggs, pizza, macaroni, you name it. This intrigued Tommy and made him curious wondering why everyone was so in love with this syrup. He wanted to get to the bottom of this and dissect that recipe. After months of searching for the elusive recipe, he came across a guy named Serik in the black market who had information on Mrs. Sap's secret recipe. Tommy came to find that the secret was in the fish of the Minnesota rivers. Feeling like he was lied to, he set out to the woods of Minnesota to find the answers himself. At this point, Tommy had gone insane.

"Surely I haven't wasted my life on lies!" Tommy screamed at the fish hanging on the end of his fishing pole.

"Oh but you have, you foolish man," the fish taunted.

Tommy ripped the fish from the line, taking a vicious bite out of its tail before pulling out the blowtorch to smoke out the secret drug of Mrs. Sap's Syrup.

– Cybil Blair
Logan Kimball
Teona Bell

even after the processes are brought to completion. Like phantoms, the specters of these events follow them around for the rest of their lives. But instead of haunting them, these apparitions work to remind imaginations of the fun they had turning learning into an event. Because of that, and because every student eventually becomes a teacher in one way or another, the discoverers of such investigative processes will continue to look for ways to encourage the creation of *something else* in their lives and those of others. The result is some degree of more effective learning in the world, a bit more creativity in written expression in the world, and a lot more voices simply rendering visions and associations through clear and colorful details.

Meanwhile, as the next chapter demonstrates, there are other innovative ways to conjure *something else* through investigative activity. So read on, and gain that power to affect change, not for yourself, but for those who need it more than you.

Assignment 4.

WRTG 3370: Poetry Workshop, Spring Semester 2017 In-Class Sending Out Poetry Group Assignment

The class will be split into groups and given a pile of poems that you wrote together. Your mission is to invent a poet, so think of a name and think up a quick history of this individual. Don't make it too absurd, though, and don't make it too complicated because you want editors to buy your pseudonym.

Then look through the magazine and journals section of the *Poet's Markets* I will distribute. Look for markets that:

- have wacky, punk, or colorful names because it's likely that they will be more open to your work than more conservative or mainstream markets

- are open to emerging writers or undergraduate writers specifically

- list a physical address to send to

When your group has come to an agreement, address your envelope, but instead of using the name of the editor listed in the listing, just write "Poetry Editor" because editors are always in flux and the editor listed might not be there anymore.

Next, your group will write a simple cover letter that shows you know how to play the game. Here's a good general model:

Date

Poetry Editor
Name of Journal
Street Address
City, State, Zip

Dear Poetry Editor:

A sentence that either tells why you think your poetry is appropriate for their publication or a sentence designed to catch their attention. Enclosed, please find X poems. If you would like to publish all of them or just one or two, that would be excellent. These poems have never been submitted anywhere else. I have enclosed a self-addressed postcard for your reply. The submission materials need not be returned.

Then a brief biography (2 or 3 sentences) for your poet. I suggest that your poet have no prior publications because it's unethical to list publications that did not happen.

Thank you for your consideration. I look forward to hearing from you.

Sincerely,

Pseudonym

Pseudonym
Spitzer's Street Address
Spitzer's City, State, Zip

Now order your poems with the one you think they'll appreciate the most on top, followed by the next strongest poems. Then staple your cover letter to the top of that pile, look at how I set up the self-addressed stamped postcard, and write something in that small rectangle I put on the top left corner which will identify the publisher when they send it back (for example, TSR could work for *Toad Suck Review*). Then fold the submission material around the postcard. Stuff and seal envelope and give back to me. I will take them to the post office and mail tomorrow.

Since everyone in this class will be here next semester, I'll contact you through your university emails to let you know about any acceptances. If your pseudonym gets published, that's something you can put on your CV.

Note: Sending physical snail mail is becoming less popular due to the ease of submitting through email or online submission managers, but many publications still employ this old school method, which might even allow submissions via the U.S. Postal Service to stand out from the rest.

It should be noted that the conventional method is to send an SASE (self-addressed stamped envelope) rather than a self-addressed stamped postcard, but a postcard stamp is cheaper and discourages the return of submission materials.

References

Brewer, Robert Lee (2018) *Poet's Market*. Blue Ash, OH: Writer's Digest Books.

Spitzer, Mark (2000) Dinner with slinger. In Andrei Codrescu and Laura Rosenthal (eds.) *Thus Spake the Corpse: An Exquisite Corpse Reader 1988–1998, Vol. 2–Fictions, Travels & Translations* 60–65. Santa Rosa, CA: Black Sparrow Press.

Spitzer, Mark (2006) *The Pigs Drink from Infinity: Poems 1995–2001*. New York: Spuyten Duyvil.

Chapter 15

Four Investigative Exercises for Individual Discovery

As I wrote in the last chapter, it's not the show that's important. What's important are the tools teachers provide in the guise of teaching events which give students the impetus to take off on their own. When students become their own guides, discoveries can be groundbreaking, life-changing, and revolutionary for communities. This chapter brings us one step closer to empowering that goal, by starting projects in the classroom which are then taken out into the world where they become tangible, connectable, and realized.

The following exercises, which can also be viewed as writing games or in-class assignments, have proven useful for pumping up student involvement and creating strong bonds that foster a hunger for more creative writing. Like the group exercises in the previous chapter, these entertaining and immersive activities are geared toward generating discovery and can be applied in other academic disciplines, especially as occasions that encourage students to engage in "teachable moments" which foster creative interaction. I've used these activities in introductory creative writing courses, junior- and senior-level forms and workshop courses in poetry and fiction, and graduate-level creative nonfiction courses. I see no reason why variations on these experiential themes can't be applied to any hands-on, imagination-centered environment where discovery is the objective.

Magic Manic Investigative Cut-Up

I usually start this component in my forms of poetry classes (both graduate and undergraduate) with a discussion of William S. Burroughs' cut-up technique. With the undergraduates, it's mainly an investigation into the process of deriving sense from nonsense, but for graduate students, it's more of a theory-based discussion harking back to surrealism, symbolism, and dadaism. Whatever the case, students read Burroughs' statement regarding his approach to the poem "Fear and the Monkey" (Burroughs, 1998) and then the poem itself. We then try to make sense of the role of the ghost boy and the Ouija board mentioned in Burroughs' statement in relation to his technical approach, which has to do with cutting up texts and arranging words in search of random combinations that work together organically.

The practice of creating collages is explored in more depth with graduate students, who read Burroughs' letter of September 5, 1960 to Allen Ginsberg (Burroughs, 2014), in which the underlying philosophy of the cut-up is explained. In contrast to the "cut-up machine" Burroughs developed in collaboration with the visual artist Brion Gysin, we focus on Burroughs' non-mechanized process, of which he remarks, "The cut up method is a tool which I am learning to use …. Often from a page of cut ups I will use one or two sentences … sifting panning process" (Burroughs, 2014: 8).

The sifting, panning process I promote, however, is more concerned with capturing the most colorful words on the page. When I hand out the scissors, glue sticks, and abandoned books and magazines to dismember, I tell students to look for words that leap from the page. And to kick this assignment off, I crank up Black Sabbath, thereby injecting the manic ghost-presence of Ozzy Osbourne into the process.

The students get down to business, seeking, cutting, and collecting words. They do this for a few minutes, and then, to dial the momentum up even more, I yell for everyone to give the text they're chopping up to the person on their left. Now suddenly everyone has a different voice to work with, which introduces a new linguistic texture into their growing word pools. A couple of minutes later, using the example of offering the word "pygmy" and getting an "Armageddon" in return, I yell for everyone to trade a word with somebody else.

A few minutes after that, I order everyone to get up from their seat and go to somebody else's desk and steal a word. They do that, sometimes lamenting the loss of a "Bolshevik," other times celebrating the abduction of an "incendiary."

The process continues. I blast more Sabbath and they continue cutting and pasting their texts and swiping and exchanging words while I shout for them to put their three favorite words in their pocket so nobody can steal them because more stealing is coming up. Then I tell them to steal a word from somebody and give it to somebody else. Now switch texts with someone! Now tear out a page, make a paper airplane, and fly it to somebody! It's chaos, and the students love it. Words are falling on the floor and students are crawling under desks to get them. And when they collect about forty or fifty words, that's when I put the kibosh on Ozzy. Now it's time for concentrating on their own words and looking for combinations, and listening to lyrics just isn't conducive to that.

The students then glue their words in an order they like to a piece of paper, frequently guffawing at what they've channeled from the poetry gods. The process, though, doesn't end when the last word is glued down. At that point, I tell them to take their cut-ups home and study them, then add and delete and rearrange more, because as Burroughs advises, "Use of cut ups of course increases ability to cut with the eyes, that is to make 'natural cut ups' …. That is having cut with the eyes there is always extension of awareness possible with scissors cut" (Burroughs, 2014: 8). Thus, to realize the final form of their poems, students type up their cut-ups. Another level of cutting up then naturally happens through word processing. This action leads to the discovery of texts students never envisioned envisioning, in which the ordering of nonsense leads to sublayers that actually make sense.

As I explain in my poem "Manifesto 1349," which I published a decade before I ever read Burroughs' theory of the cut-up:

in the school of sensible nonsense
visions
make sense to the imaginer
and their connections are linked
through wordplay

it is self delusion
to the point of practice
on paper
achieving
something
more
than nothing

(Spitzer, 2006: 117)

Still, the trick with this approach is to arrive at a "something more than nothing" that's worth it for others. Otherwise, the objective of achieving *something else* might only work for yourself – which is not without its own value, especially if it leads to useful or therapeutic discoveries that are worth your time. The test of it being worth your time is: if any moment from a cut-up is memorable enough to burn itself into your brain, such that you find yourself repeating your own words to yourself when you're walking down the street, then there's a reason for the arrangement of those words.

As an interesting twist on this cut-up technique, the award definitely goes to Shua (short for Joshua) Miller, who was a graduate student in an Advanced Poetry Workshop I taught in Fall 2015. Rather than actually cutting out words, Shua began by using an online search engine to collect the top porn-words Googled state by state. He then cut and pasted those words into an actual bouquet of paper flowers, a sort of 3D-sculpture stage for a XXX-vocab collage.

Figure 42. Porn Carnation Incarnation by Shua Miller. Photo by Mark Spitzer.

This beautiful mutant of a cut-up was definitely a hit in the next class when Shua turned his homework in. Not only had his vision found a pleasingly tangible form that students passed around the room and appreciated, Shua had created a provocatively flowering literal cut-up. His bouquet of commentary effectually invited immediate discussion, including comments about exploitation, human trafficking, race relations, gay rights, and much more

– which means that ultimately, the novelty discovered in Shua's investigation was worth it for others and himself.

Investigative OED Poetry

In *Ordinary Genius: A Guide for the Poet Within,* poet Kim Addonizio advises, "Look up a word's roots, and write a poem that explores or includes that information" (Addonizio, 2009: 45). She then provides the example of A. Van Jordan's prose poem "after glow," which is set up like a dictionary definition starting with the noun designation and providing two different meanings.

Poet Lea Graham (a.k.a. Dr. Leigh Graham at Marist College) then took this exercise a few steps further with her poetry students. She developed "The OED Poem Form," which relies on research using *The Oxford English Dictionary* – which, of course, is the world's best source for an understanding of a word in all its linguistic context. As Graham (2017) explains in her instructions to this assignment:

> I use this form regularly in my poetry workshops because it gives students an immediate place to start and with a form that looks familiar to them. Additionally, it teaches them about the *Oxford English Dictionary* and how they might use it for later assignments.

Directions:

Choose a word that you have some attachment to or choose a word that you didn't know, then look for it in the *Oxford English Dictionary* …

Consider the following things about your word:

a) <u>Its (multiple) definitions</u>: If it has several functions – as a noun and verb, for example, you want to consider how you might play with both. (Example: "dive" – we might automatically think about its function as a verb, the synonym of "jumping head-first," but what about its colloquial use as a noun and adjective? "Let's go back to that dive (bar) where they had the pickled eggs in a jar."

b) <u>Its etymologies</u>: Where does the word come from? Has it traveled in its meanings? (Example: the word "sad" shares the same root as "satisfied" and used to mean "fullness" or "enoughness." It then shifted to mean "somber" and "steadfast" before … meaning "sorrow" – how we understand it today).

c) <u>Connotations</u>: What associations or "baggage" does the word carry? Some of these might be public, but you also might have your own private associations with a word. (Example, the word "doubloon" is associated with pirates, but often, students say that they associate it with the cartoon *Sponge Bob Square Pants*).

d) <u>What does the word sound like</u>? What do the sounds remind you of? (Example, many students say that they choose words because of the use of "special letters" in them like "z" or "q." Some say they like the difference between the long or short vowel sound and hard consonant – like "tulip" or "gut").

e) <u>What does it rhyme with?</u> You might consider how it doesn't have to be a perfect rhyme, but can be an off-rhyme in some way (Example: "sacristy" sounds close to "elasticity" or "passivity").

f) <u>Are there words within the word?</u> (Example: "gorgeous" contains the word "gorge," "or" and "us" within it … how does that literally enlarge the word's meaning for us?).

The main thing to think about are the various approaches to your words. Too often, we think only about definition in a singular way. The considerations I've listed give you different ways of thinking and writing about your words so that the poems will never get boring and become lifeless for lack of ways to approach the words.

Form:

I suggest … the prose block as the form … use slashes (/) as a way to give more of a pause (like a line break) in the line. You may also use the conventions of the dictionary entry by using the abbreviations for the various functions (n., v., etc.) and numbering the entries of the meanings as dictionary entries often do. I find this is a great beginning exercise for students who might not yet understand how to break lines effectively. They may feel that the prose block is familiar and then need to consider the ways that sounds and silence can be shown.

Since being introduced to this OED assignment, I've incorporated my own version of this exercise into my poetry forms courses. The result has been a flurry of highly sophisticated investigations into root-words and their associations, which is always a discovery for the self. In my classes, we cruise through dictionaries and texts in class looking for words rich in possibility, which gets students brainstorming among themselves. Students are then charged with taking their larval ideas home and working them into the form of dictionary poems. When combined with a degree of self-reflection, this exercise can't help but lead to an even more profound level of discovery – as seen in the three poems below written by MFA students in Advanced Forms and Theory of Poetry. I chose these poems because they clearly show how poetry can investigate the self and lead to articulations that are well worth the effort:

Dancing on Cobwebs

Gossamer *n.* 1. From the Middle English for goose and summer. How do goose and summer come to mean this filmy, flyaway substance? 2. Cobweb. One of Titania's magical companions who was commanded to worship and subject herself to an ass of a man. Must have been thinking of goose down / plucked from the eider duck's breast / to fill the eiderdown that I slept under as a child / I would pull the stray quills / poking through the fabric that bound them / as Cobweb crept into my room / draped the filmy substance of sleep / across my willing eyelids / to dream of geese / or eider ducks dancing on cobwebs in the summer.

– Briget Laskowski

sil-ver-back *n. Gorilla gorilla.* dominant male mountain mammal with primate, *hominidae* tendencies – pec pounding, poacher punching patriarch who trains for snares tearing at bear traps. stardust-sprinkled scar. laboratory-made monster who seeks revenge on his creator. convict with a magic mirror. learner of sign language. orchid bike enthusiast. flower weaver. parachute for caterpillars.

– J. J. McNiece

Sa tur nine < medieval Latin *Saturninus,* <*Saturnus* SATURN> A. *adj.* a. *Astrol.* Born under or affected by the influence of Saturn. b. Melancholy and gloomy in temperament. c. Dark in coloring or moody and mysterious. B. The ninth day of the ninth month, i.e., the ninth day of November according to the Roman calendar. a. The death day of Apollinaire (November 9, 1918) by the Spanish influenza epidemic two days before the armistice which ended World War I. b. The death day of Dylan Thomas (November 9, 1953) by pneumonia and alcoholism in the hospital of St. Vincent. C. Cypresses in cemeteries; Cyprus Commandaria wine; Cronus' sickle and Andreas Vesalius' crusted skeleton in caves of Corfu. D. Dante's Dark Wood of Error; Dark Night of the Soul; Blind Willie Johnson's "Dark Was The Night, Cold Was The Ground." E. Edgar Allan Poe's opium delirium of Ligeia. F. Franz Schubert's *Winterreise.* G. Georges Bataille's graveyard groping, penetrating, dirt sea of stars candles on tombs in Trier; Goethe's Gretchen drowning her child while Faust frolics in the fever sweat orgy of Walpurgisnacht. H. Hallucinations, Aurelia, asylum, she haunts Nerval. I. I, yes, I, I dream of digging up the corpses of my ancestors' lovers. J. Johannes Kepler's mother Katharina tortured as a witch, he sheds tears shatter six sided snowflakes.

– Mark Lager

As can be seen in Briget's poem, her associations range from Shakespearian context to personal self-reflections, the ultimate discovery being a dreamy lyrical tone that muses on a word and leaves readers with a feeling to consider. J. J., on the other hand, uses a gorilla motif to explore his own surreal psychology. The "parachute for caterpillars" moment might not make sense to anyone else, but from directing his thesis, I know that this instance of self-reflection was instrumental in cryptically articulating an approach to self-expression in which "A poem is not forced / It is cajoled" (McNiece, 2018: 24). Mark's OED poem then uses a range of associations to reflect on melancholy themes in literature. Since the poet is reflecting outward rather than inward, the self-reflection in this one is a lot less than in the other two examples provided, yet the fact that these factors are part of his consciousness reflects on what he thinks and how he views the world. Just as Saturn is part of a solar system, Mark's reflections on poetic themes of gloom and madness in Western lit find a sort of harmonic convergence which appeals to readers.

The question then becomes what the value of poetry having value is in a world where there might already be too many poets overwhelming the market with work that tends to be ignored. My answer to that is that in addition to poems having their own intrinsic value, the more poets there are in the world, the more hope there is for sustaining creative human life. Because the more poets there are in the world, the more creative ways of seeing things there are in the world. And the more creative ways of seeing things there are in all sectors of society, the better our thinking, problem-solving, and communication will be in order to find creative solutions to the problems that dog us. That's just the way it is.

Investigative Character Development

Time is often scarce in the semester by the time I require my introductory students to write a five- to ten-page short story, and since they're starting to get burned out by their academic studies and life is slapping them around as well, it's sometimes hard to get everyone to synchronize bringing their stories in at the same time for their small-group workshopping. Since I reserve a week for students to read and workshop three peer stories in class during what I call "Fiction Workshopping Week," I prepare them for the writing weekend they'll need before their stories are due by assigning a one-paragraph plot proposal as homework the week before. This gets students thinking about setting, point of view, voice, style, and characters.

It's not uncommon for creative writing teachers to ask students to juxtapose their characters into unfamiliar situations to see how their creations behave. The logic is the more time you spend with a character, the better grasp you'll have of what makes that character tick. But as I noted above, time is tight, and even though inserting your characters into another storyline can prove useful, I find it more useful to get to know them in a more visual, time-crunch-conscious way by literally illustrating their character traits. Therefore, right after my students draft a synopsis of their plots, I have them draw pictures of their characters. With basic traits fresh in their minds, it only takes fifteen minutes at the end of a class session for students to welcome a low-pressure break from their scholastic demands by taking out a piece of paper and drawing pictures of the personalities they're about to essentially throw to the lions. When students are on the verge of introducing characters into an interactive arena, it's not just a different thing to do to actually draw character traits, it's an entertaining and informative exercise as well.

"But I suck as an artist," someone will no doubt opine.

"That doesn't matter," I reply. "Stick people are sufficient."

But here's what makes this exercise an investigation that leads to discovery: I require that students apply six arrows with descriptions to each character. These arrows can point to things like "cool shoes" or "hipster glasses" or "an angry unibrow," or they can point straight into people's brains and indicate things like "he thinks he's hot but he's not." These characteristics are things that students discover about their characters, which lead to character development.

This is definitely an assignment which students envision as easy – and it is. But here's the thing: If teachers get students to brainstorm character traits right before they draft their stories, they'll incorporate details and traits like purple dresses and yo-yos and the politics of their characters into their narratives.

When it comes time for students to hand their pictures in, I don't collect their work. Instead, I go around and mark in my grade book that they have done the work, so that they can keep their illustrations and put them to use as soon as possible. When students sit down to draft their stories, it helps to have the characteristics designed specifically for their characters right next to their plot summaries.

I always hope students will continue to develop those characters and embellish a little or a lot. As I tell them, "Fiction is your license to lie, so throw in a murder or a mystery or even an alien. Embracing your license to lie is fun and something to take advantage of."

Typically, some students will want to write realism-based stories that center on believable characters like family members eating dinner or friends on a road trip, which I always try to discourage. "Remember," I tell them, "this is your chance to make stuff up, and you want to hold your readers' attention. So make the ride unusual, colorful, and full of action they don't expect. Use your imaginations and have fun. We've got plenty of real stories about real people on this planet, and we don't need any more. What we need are shrunken heads, time travel, invisible pixies, whatever you dream up."

But do I really believe this is what the world needs? No, but incorporating unusual details makes students' stories more interesting for me, for them, and for everyone else who reads their work. Also, there's a certain freedom that readers discover when they suspend their disbelief – a freedom which comes straight from what fiction writers discover in what their characters encounter. Since investigative character development has definitely helped my introductory students transform arbitrary characteristics into complex, colorful characters, I see no reason why this method can't work for PhD candidates just as much as children who are just learning to draw and spell.

I offer the following student examples of what can come from the investigative character development assignment, not for any qualities of artistic skill, but because the characters are large and highly visible as are the words identifying their characteristics. The biggest value in this approach, especially for those who've never written a story in their lives, is that students can take real qualities from real people, then shuffle those qualities around to comment on the way things are even if the scenarios require some suspension of disbelief. And the value in this is that it helps developing imaginations become more legitimate investigators of why people do what they do. Such discoveries make fiction writers more empathetic, more insightful, and more precise in their handling of details.

Figures 43 & 44. Investigative Character Development. First Illustration by Landon Kirkland, reproduced by permission. Second Illustration by Olivia Coleman, reproduced by permission.

Spontaneous Investigative Prose

Once, in a graduate-level Creative Nonfiction Workshop, after the class was past the standard discussions of what CNF is, where to draw the line between fiction and nonfiction, and how much bending of the truth is permissible, I decided to try an experiment in stream-of-consciousness writing. After studying and discussing Jack Kerouac's "Essentials of Spontaneous Prose" (Kerouac, 1993) in relationship to Charles Olson's concept of "projective verse" (Olson, 1950), I had students respond as furiously as they could to some list-making prompts provided in class. The idea was to start the improvisational process of "sketching language … [as] undisturbed flow from the mind of personal secret idea-words, *blowing* (as per jazz musician) on subject of image" (Kerouac, 1993: 69). I gave them one minute to respond in writing to each prompt, which were as follows:

- times when you were moving fast
- times when you were on the run
- car accidents
- run-ins with authority
- fights you've been in or witnessed
- memories of chasing an animal or being chased by an animal
- memories of chasing a human or being chased by a human
- other action-packed moments

I chose these prompts for the momentum I knew they would inspire in the next step of this in-class assignment. I wanted them to really get into Olson's advice of "keep moving, keep in, speed, the nerves, their speed, the perceptions, theirs, the acts, the split second acts, the whole business, keep it moving as fast as you can, citizen" (Olson, 1950). So after those students made their lists, I had them pick a line of thought they felt would make for an action-packed session of generating spontaneous prose.

To get their blood pumping and their adrenaline shooting through their tubeways, I then had them stand up and do jumping jacks. Then running in place. Then the washing machine. I led them in these exercises, which lasted less than a minute.

The students were then instructed to sit down and "write like crazy" about the subject they picked, and to apply Kerouac's advice of "No periods separating sentence-structures …. following free deviation (association) of mind into limitless blow-on-subject seas of thought …. No pause to think of proper word …. *no revisions* …. 'without consciousness in semi-trance'" (Kerouac, 1993: 69).

To drive students to drive themselves, I fired up the smartboard, went to YouTube, played Primal Scream's "Kowalski," and cranked the volume up to eleven. I then joined them in the frenzy, writing freehand as the head-nodding rhythm spurred us on.

The spontaneous texts created in class were to be considered first drafts rather than final products. They had the necessary energy captured on the page, but now they needed to rein that energy in. So after urging students to consider the texts they created as starting points, I sent them home to revise, the assignment being to edit what they had written, to refine its shape and language, then type it up and print it out to be handed in.

The following is an example of spontaneous investigative prose written by a student in that class. The process didn't reveal anything she didn't know, but I'd argue that the act of getting this narrative down on paper was an accomplishment in discovery, since a mode was definitely discovered and employed for mapping the psychological travails of the self. I might also add that this graduate student, who eventually wrote and defended her creative nonfiction thesis under my direction, was searching for a voice and style at the time to address and make sense of a phantasmagorical orgy of unconventional memories and relationships, and that this particular act of discovery was just one step in deciphering the complexity of her life. Her writing, including parts not shared here, demonstrate that this type of investigative creative writing can be an effective portal to graphic self-discovery:

I opened the door and there my mom was covered in a cloud and I could smell that peppery smell and I knew I just knew and she was smiling like a dodo and I thought all the things I didn't say about what a hypocrite she was to give us all that DARE bullshit about never doing drugs and here she was stowing away in her own bedroom by herself like an addict and I bet you can be addicted to anything because she sure seemed hooked and she was smiling but the whole thing was pathetic but I didn't feel any pathos, only roiling anger, and for the first time in my life I ran away from home – I fled the scene and didn't tell a single person where I was going or who I'd be with or how late I'd be until. I called up my one and only true best friend and soon to be lover Skip Harvey who lived forty minutes away but arrived in twenty and out the door I went and breathless jumped into his car and he said "Where to" and I said "Anywhere but here" and he drove and it squealed and we didn't care and we blasted new versions of old Beatles songs done in effigy mixed with the hardest stuff we knew of and I was wearing my gothic Lolita knee-length layers of crushed red velvet over silky black shift over lacey white slip and I had on my dog collar and leash and I said "Take me somewhere and parade me around" and he said "I know just the place" and we walked right into that bookstore with me on the lead and him pulling it and my hair a mess and my eyes covered in a stick of dollar black liner from Walmart and we were pumped up with sex and rebellion and hatred for all the ways our parents fucked up and we were laughing and if someone got too close I growled and barked at them and as we were walking out two jocks were walking in with those stupid smiles and one was like "Whoa I gotta get me one of them" and Skip Harvey what a gem said "There's none like her"…

– Jobe

Such "possession" (that is, being possessed by an ultra-energetic, hypnotic drive to generate writing) is a quality that always reminds me of a passage attributed to Plato in Enid Starkie's biography of Arthur Rimbaud, in which the word "poet" can be easily exchanged for "writer": "All great poets, said Socrates … [compose] because they are inspired and possessed. And as Corybantian revelers when they dance are not in their right mind, so lyric poets are not in their right mind when they are … falling under the power of music and metre" (Plato, as qtd. in Starkie, 1961: 120). Plato follows that there is "no invention" in the poet until he is "out of his senses,"[1] which gives the poet the freedom to discover.

Jobe's spontaneous investigative prose was not an uncommon response to a push for students to write in a fast and furious state of "possession." I've been employing a similar high-energy-flow approach for my own work for at least a quarter-century; and it has been extremely useful for me. I first seriously applied it back in the early 1990's when I was desperately trying to pound out a memoir. After numerous attempts and numerous failures to start a spontaneous narrative concerning some very important events in my life that I was delusionally convinced had to be put down on paper or someone would die, I decided to start in the middle of the action and just go go go rather than following a traditional chronology. Armed with REO Speedwagon's live long version of "Riding the Storm Out" (Kevin Cronin era) taped on a loop to play over and over again, I cranked the volume to the max and threw myself into the writing process. The pounding rhythm propelled me like a missile, and I soon lost all sense of time and any consideration for those around me. After a week of riding that frantic storm out, I finally got the story down; but as the eco-writer David Gessner, my housemate at the time, later wrote regarding having to listen to a solid week of repetitive music thumping up from my room, "I want to break his neck" (Gessner, 1995: 3).

My point is that spontaneous investigative prose works for the purpose of discovery, whether one uses music or not. What I'm talking about is getting into "The Zone." It's how Kerouac discovered his revolutionary, stylistic technique for drafting *On the Road* (Kerouac, 1957), and it's the vehicle that allowed me to document the events in *After the Orange Glow* (Spitzer, 2010) and other books of mine.

Now, however, I want it to be quiet when I write.

Yet the fact remains that spontaneous investigative prose was useful for me and then my students who discovered how writing can be an incredibly physical phenomenon. With or without loud music, when you're charged up on endorphins, which stimulate the body's opiate receptors and lead to an analgesic effect, two things are definitely possible: you might stay up for three days straight satisfying the stereotype of "the mad writer," or you might pound out a highly revisable text that ultimately expresses what you're seeking to express.

But be careful with this addictive method because it can sometimes lead to too much fun, too much escape, or too much oblivion. Writers can become so fascinated by the rush of discovery that suddenly it's time to cook dinner, or pick up the kids, or go to bed and get up and do it again. And if that's the case, when priorities get placed on the back burner, watch out! Either that, or proceed to the next chapter, which literally spells out why there's a larger reason for writers to engage in investigative power grabs.

Note

1   Footnote in Starkie reads "Jowett's translation quoted by Read in *Surrealism*, pp. 31–2."

References

Addonizio, Kim (2009) *Ordinary Genius: A Guide for the Poet Within.* New York: W. W. Norton & Company.

Burroughs, William S. (1998) Fear and the monkey. In Jerome Rothenberg and Pierre Joris (eds.) *Poems for the Millennium: The University of California Book of Modern and Postmodern Poetry, Vol. 2: From Postwar to Millennium* 364–365. Berkeley: University of California Press.

Burroughs, William S. (2014) Lost Burroughs. *Toad Suck Review 4*: 8–14.

Gessner, David (1995) Spitzer's peaceable kingdom. *Exquisite Corpse 51*: 3–4.

Graham, Leigh (2017) The O.E.D. poem form. Introduction to creative writing and poetry workshop assignment, English Department, Marist College, Poughkeepsie, NY.

Kerouac, Jack (1957) *On the Road*. New York: Viking.

Kerouac, Jack (1993) Essentials of spontaneous prose. *Good Blonde & Others*; 69–71. San Francisco: Grey Fox.

McNiece, J. J. (2018) *Gussenstein's Galaxies*. MFA thesis. Conway, AR: University of Central Arkansas.

Olson, Charles (1950) Projective verse. Original circulated in pamphlet form. Retrieved on 20 August 2019 from https://www. poetryfoundation.org/articles/69406/projective-verse. Later published as a book (*Projective Verse*, New York: Totem, 1959).

Spitzer, Mark (2006) *The Pigs Drink from Infinity*. New York: Spuyten Duyvil.

Spitzer, Mark (2010) *After the Orange Glow*. Denver: Monkey Puzzle Press.

Starkie, Enid (1961) *Arthur Rimbaud*. New York: New Directions.

Chapter 16

Six Investigative Homework Exercises
for Encouraging Literary Citizenship

Usually the term "power grab" has a negative connotation. A political leader makes a move that allows him to capitalize on something at the expense of others. A country revises its borders to make use of another country's resources. These are typical examples of what people usually think of as "power grabs." But what I'm talking about in this chapter and throughout this book is grabbing something that empowers people in order to make a difference for communities – which can be an act of both selfishness and selflessness at the same time, especially if socially responsible outcomes are the product of one's passion. Not that I believe writers must be responsible, but because I know that the most we can do as writers is to order words responsibly in order to make things better. If that isn't the ultimate discovery about what can be done with writing power, then I don't know what is.

One discovery for me as a teacher is that students sometimes need to be drawn out of their own worlds and into unfamiliar realms. It's what we all have to do to learn and grow and not stagnate on the virtual couches of our existences. But the thing is, you don't even have to get off the couch to go somewhere exotic or new. Because there's this thing called reading, which has the potential to be transformative. Reading can transform writing, transform lives, and transform the world due to what comes from investigating unknown terrain (Pennington and Waxler, 2018). It's not searching that leads to enlightenment; it's when you find something worthy of review, so then you look it over again, which turns searching into *re-searching*, also known as researching. And the more you look at something, the tighter your observations become.

As noted before, I have students in my Introduction to Creative Writing classes write what I call "portraits." The idea is for developing writers to describe people, places, and things in detail; to use the five senses to create vivid images and associations for readers. As I've found out, students can pick their own subject matter – or not. But if they pick their own subject matter, they're liable to focus on the one thing that connects them to the world the most: their cellphones.

Okay, that's a vast generalization, and in fact, it's not always the case. Still, I use this stereotype to illustrate that students will often gravitate toward the known when picking subject matter to write about. They'll choose family members, friends, the house they grew up in, their cars, or recurring memories. That's fine. But when the instructor provides a bit of unexpected direction that leads to exploring previously unexplored galaxies, the growth which takes place isn't based on nostalgia or a desire for security. It's intellectual.

There's another reason for drawing students out of themselves. As Tim Mayers writes in his essay "Reading as a Writer, Writing as a Reader," "If your work is to succeed with readers, you will need to know – or at least convince your readers that you know – about the things, places, activities, and kinds of people that appear in your work" (Mayers, 2016: 36–37). That's why I'm prone to providing a little shove in prompting students to research things they don't know about. I'm not talking about kicking students out of airplanes to parachute into hostile jungles; what I'm talking about needs no metaphor. It's what it is: plain old reading something to discover something new, which is an exercise in being responsible. Because if you don't open your eyes to new horizons, then you're staring at the same old walls – which is of little use to anyone, especially yourself – and reading can help with that. Moreover, reading isn't just something passive; it's an investigative action which allows readers to experience something different, something that bursts the bubbles they confine themselves in.

Hence, the six assignments below for encouraging literary citizenship.

Don't Write About the News, Write About Something New in the News

When writing portraits, I start my students off in familiar territory. This is always advisable at the beginning of a semester when the idea of "comfort zones" is a factor. But in the third week, I come along with my felt-tip pen and start circling vague words that tell not show, like "cool" and "good" and "beautiful." As stated earlier, this is a period of *unlearning*, and because of the natural confusion venturing into the unknown creates, it's important to remain aware of this so as not to freak students out.

After a couple portrait assignments we move on to writing about events in the news. This exercise always draws students out of themselves by placing the focus on something outside of their experience, which makes this assignment intriguing to me for a few reasons. First of all, I love watching the news. It's something that's familiar to me that I used to do with my family as a kid, and something I still do ritualistically every time I get the chance. Secondly, it's a way to stay informed as citizens even if all the networks focus on the same stories. But thirdly, when my students report on reporting, I sometimes learn about things I didn't know were happening – which is the exact kind of discovery I want my students to have for themselves. I want them to discover something they don't know about and write about that. Because investigating what you don't know is the equivalent of steroids for the intellect.

Back in the 1980's, novelist Ken Kesey tried an experiment in a graduate workshop at the University of Oregon. Bored with writing based on what students knew, Kesey posited the idea of writing about what you don't know to force imaginations into unfamiliar labyrinths where discoveries outside one's self offer beaucoup possibilities. These are my words, not his, but since I've been thinking about this approach for almost thirty years, that's how I see Kesey's vision of focusing on material which no one in the class knew anything about. His students settled on the theme of spelunking, and from there on out different students wrote different chapters, and they collaborated on character development and synthesis of voice. The result was a novel entitled *Caverns* (Levon, 1989), published under the pseudonym O. U. Levon – which is "Novel UO" (University of Oregon) spelled backwards.

As for the process of writing the novel, students were not allowed to discuss the details with anyone outside of class. They voted together on developing the plotline, and to keep democracy from dictating the direction of the narration, Kesey's vote counted for fifty percent. Also, there was to be no writing outside of class. In the end, the method for writing was to pass a tape recorder around a table. People spoke their assigned parts into it and the chapters were transcribed later.

It was a novel approach to the novel, even though the concept of "the composite novel" (or "collaborative fiction") has been around for over a century and a half. Harriet Beecher Stowe once co-wrote a book with five other writers entitled *Six of One by Half a Dozen of the Other* (Stowe et al., 1872), but it could also be argued that the Bible was a work of a collaborative prose, since it's made up of books allegedly made legible by numerous apostles, and perhaps thirty to forty additional contributors ranging from random monks to Moses and King David. My point is that Kesey's experiment in this tradition got noticed, even if the book's critical reception wasn't spectacular.

For my students, though, the value of writing about what you don't know is that the experience of immersing themselves in an alien environment helps them discover what they don't know. That's why I tell my students not to just write about any old thing in the news, but to search through the news and find something that's news to them. Otherwise, I'll just get a lot of stuff about whatever the President Tweeted or whatever's trending on social media or the latest video gone viral. Hence, I steer their portraits toward world events that have some sort of international intrigue in order to give this exercise a political or cultural context.

In other words, I'm saying write about what you don't know until you do. Which is why I also developed the following assignments.

Get Thee to Afghanistan, Kazakhstan, and Beyond

When the University of Central Arkansas decreed that the Gen Ed curriculum of core courses should be made even more complicated by requiring students to take a variety of courses with designations like critical inquiry, communication, responsible living, and diversity, my soul actually groaned. This meant that our faculty would have to pick certain courses for lower- and upper-division requirements, and that we would have to pilot specific assignments geared toward investigating topics I felt took away from academic freedom. The meetings and paperwork would no doubt be an annoyance that would take time away from writing. However, as I later discovered, developing assignments based on research (rather than just mining the imagination) wasn't just useful for the intellectual growth of students: it helped my own pedagogy to evolve.

When the time came, I had to come up with an assignment for my undergraduate Forms of Poetry course that introduced students to an aspect of another culture, and since the surrealism-based assignments I had already developed weren't multicultural enough to satisfy the idea of "cultural diversity," I began searching for a more foreign form to incorporate. Eventually, I ran across a video entitled *Ancient Afghan Poetry Form Adapts to Portray Modern Life* (News Hour, 2013), which investigated a couplet called the "landays" used by women in Afghanistan to secretly communicate highly sensitive concerns. My ultimate discovery here was that unlike poetry in Western countries, this type of subversive expression had the potential to get someone killed.

I therefore asked my Forms of Poetry class to think about what they could write that could get them killed. This may or may not have been helpful for the landays-writing assignment I gave out after showing them the video and discussing the form in depth, but the act of analyzing such cultural content did just what it was designed to do for the purposes of the Gen Ed curriculum. Along with a good dose of critical inquiry, it provided some sophisticated social context for the course and enriched the global consciousness of both my students and myself.

In other words, just thinking about communication conflicts in other countries added to the "literary citizenship" of this micro-community. As Donna Steiner remarks in her essay "Literary Citizenship: How You Can Contribute to the Literary Community and Why You Should," "Literary citizenship asks that you think about connections" (Steiner, 2016: 133), which is the first step in actually doing anything with information gleaned from investigative research.

The definition I prefer for "literary citizenship," however, isn't so much the idea as it relates to fostering literary activity at the micro-community level. I'm talking about the larger picture: being a citizen at the most idealistic level, in which arguments are made by citizens and unto citizens in order to sustain environments that make citizenship possible. As Lori A. May writes in "AWP: An Opportunity to Exercise Literary Citizenship," literary citizenship is a term for "engaging in the community with the intent of giving as much as, if not more … than we take … [L]iterary citizenship calls on our acts of giving, of giving back to the ecosystem so that we may actively ensure its sustainability" (May, 2014).

Consequently, I found the landays assignment to be a valuable tool not only for engaging in the concept of literary citizenship, but a solid way to support the university's mission to help students "experience cultural activities as they grow in their appreciation for the diversity of ideas and peoples, both inside and outside the classroom" (UCA, 2011). I also felt this exercise was necessary during an era of rising xenophobia, especially in regard to Arab and Hispanic cultures. So I adopted a politically correct stance, in a sense, by placing the consideration of human rights on the table for evolving writers to examine regardless of whether they formed an opinion on the matter.

Some might say it's not the teacher's role to nudge students toward any ideology, but as the employee of a state institution which champions the values of diversity and critical thinking to the point that it asks its faculty to make such considerations part of the Gen Ed curriculum, I see this matter as something reaching beyond the concept of literary citizenship. This is a matter of *citizen citizenship* – and one that I'm glad my university had me address in order to matriculate a wider pool of well-rounded critical thinkers.

Not too long after being asked to think about critical inquiry and diversity in upper-level creative writing courses, our faculty was asked to consider such components in our lower-level Gen Ed curriculum for our majors and minors in creative writing. We weren't required to immediately provide critical inquiry and diversity assignments, but I became excited about the idea of working an exercise into the fiction component of my intro courses that satisfied such aspects. For years I'd been employing a flash-fiction writing exercise that wasn't working very well. It was an in-class assignment in which students wrote one paragraph per class for four consecutive classes, and complications were not uncommon, with absences. Since I found myself having to constantly re-explain the assignment every class session, I could see it was time to revise the way I handled this groundwork for writing short stories.

So I came up with a brilliant plan (which wasn't even really that brilliant): I'd have them write their flash fictions in just one shot and get that assignment over with. Rather than having them come up with their own subject matter, I decided it would be beneficial to draw them out of themselves by investigating new cultural context.

Thinking back to my days in the PhD program in creative writing at the University of Louisiana at Lafayette twenty years ago, I was reminded of an undergraduate who lived next door. We once had a conversation about a composition course she was taking in which the research focus was cryogenically frozen heads. I'd been extremely intrigued by the fact that an instructor who knew nothing about cryogenics had assigned this specific topic for a series of papers.

"Why'd he make that the focus," I had asked, "rather than something standard like race or nutrition?"

"He just wanted to know more about it," she replied.

Flash forward to Spring 2017: I'm sitting at my desk thinking about what assignment I could offer that could kill two birds with one stone, when it hits me: Kazakhstan! Yes! Perfect! It was a place I didn't know anything about and could barely even spell. But since it was also a place I wanted to know more about, I figured I could have my students do the research for me. I mean, apparently that's what that comp instructor did with the cryogenically frozen heads, so why shouldn't I do the same? Additionally, this was a subject in which my students also had a dearth of knowledge, so this was something we could all use some schooling on. More importantly, during a time of ever-increasing calls for walls, Muslim bans, and the demonization of the mainstream media as "fake news," I knew it wouldn't hurt to provide my predominantly Christian, red-state students with some insight into an intentionally vilified culture to expand their awareness of people and politics. After all, as the university mission statement states, "We seek to enhance interaction and understanding among diverse groups and cultivate enriched learning opportunities in a global community" (UCA, 2011).

The idea was simple: I'd require students to print up three pages of information on Kazakhstan, and then I'd have them write a one-page, double-spaced flash fiction piece about someone growing up over there. That's what I told them to do, and that's what they did. The results varied widely. Some students wrote about impoverished families affected by the economy, others wrote about the military, some explored the geography, and a couple focused on athletes competing in international competitions. And me, I learned about Kazakhstan.

Talk about discovery! By drawing students out of themselves and into the real world via real details, these literary citizens not only expanded their own worldviews, they expanded mine as well.

Next time, I think I'll have students investigate Turkey. Or Botswana? Or why not Swaziland?

Investigating Investigative Poetry

Here's where the book goes full circle, returning to the idea of investigative poetry, which inspired much of what's behind the concept of investigative creative writing pedagogy. There comes a point in my poetry courses, both graduate and undergraduate, when I essentially proclaim, "Citizens, now is the time to trigger thy bias!" Then, envisioning a transformative phoenix of investigative verse arising from the ashes of their discontent, I provide passages from Ed Sanders' *America: A History in Verse* series so they can witness the master in action. I find *1968* (Sanders, 2000) to be the best text for this job because of the political nature of that inflammatory year. Whereas other books in this series span several decades (i.e. vol. 1, 1900–1939; vol. 2, 1940–1961), the epic poem *1968: A History in Verse* zeros straight in on making sense out of some of the most contentious events in U.S. history. Civil rights, Vietnam, MLK, the CIA, the FBI, the Black Panthers, the Democratic Convention in Chicago – it's all in there burning with liberal bias.

Investigative poetry, being poetry, can therefore employ poetic license. It's a quixotic form, but it's not unrealistic. As a form that struts "through the time-track / daring to be part / of the history / of the era" (Sanders, 2000: 6), I picture investigative poetry as a tool to infuse poetry with attitude, which provides position and actively involves its handlers in the discussion.

"Citizens," I therefore proclaim, "pick an issue, any issue, then study that issue. In fact, find three sources that shine a light on that issue, then work data and quotes and history and images and politics and science and whatever useful info you can find from those sources into a flash of your own blatantly opinionated investigative poetics!"

For me, this assignment has nothing to do with recruiting support for any side of any issue. It's about engaging in what's going on. It's about being part of arguments, be they either pro or con – which is why UCA's creative writing faculty used my argument for this assignment to justify our Poetry Workshop course as fulfilling the critical inquiry criteria for our upper-division Gen Ed curriculum.

And here's a fun bonus fact: When literary citizens investigate an issue, then render it in something as abstract as poetry, they will automatically discover, whether they want to or not, the articulation of an attitude based on facts. The following example of student work does an excellent job at addressing an historical oppression. In fact, this piece later found its way into an MFA thesis under my direction:

removal

they prod the flocks forward like diseased cattle
hoping that ice and hunger will shorten the trip
    that their enlistments will end
    before they reach
    the run for cover windstorms
    of the Territories.

from Georgia to Oklahoma
slack jawed soldiers
pus ripe blisters blooming around their sweaty crotches,
    Union Blue

balls brushing the supple leather saddles of their mounts,
veterans of expansion, marauders of the Negro Fort,
slave-traders and tribe herders,
drive the Five Civilized Nations
the Seminole, the Choctaw, the Cherokee, the Chickasaw, the
Muscogee
off of fertile eastern lands,
over the Mississippi
before the planting season.

      white knuckled bullies
      lean forward in their stirrups
      whining about the long ride
      bored with the Swiss cheese reek
      of their own hands in the night.

   they slip into the native camps
   to satisfy themselves.

in the morning
they remount
wearing fresh fleshy flowers
vaginal lips folded
into bleeding corsages
that they pin across the brims of their Kepi caps

      they send letters back to Jackson
      drunk in the cadence of a stallion's hips
      to brag about the fires they're lighting
      about the fertile ashes of the dead
      pollinating the muddy stretches of the delta
      about myths and alibis
      for the sordid labor of
      fore-fathering.

                                 – Scotty Lewis

Applying Polar Approaches for Finding Voice in Creative Nonfiction

Speaking of citizenship, there are two specific exercises I assign in my creative nonfiction courses which are designed to play off each other just as much as they're meant to butt heads. To summarize, I have students study an issue, then rant their heads off about it. This assignment is then followed by the opposite extreme, in which they rationally argue a point in a manner meant to be persuasive. In contrasting these extremes, students gain insight (a.k.a. discovery) into which technique works best for their particular voices. Also, in contrasting the approaches of working from the outside (protest) vs. working from the inside (influence), this assignment has led to students getting published.

Let's begin with the rant, which might be the most knee-slappingest exercise I assign to my creative nonfiction students since it grants them absolute permission to express themselves in a non-academic, humorous, or fiery format which pushes the limits of what is permissible. First of all, I provide Hunter S. Thompson's abusive letter to Holly Sorenson as both a positive and negative example of how to use a rant. It starts out, "Okay, you lazy bitch, I'm getting tired of this waterhead fuckaround that you're doing with *The Rum Diary*" (Thompson, 2001) and ends with him threatening to chop off her hands. That's the negative aspect because it relies on name-calling and violence. The positive aspect can be seen in arguments in which Thompson expresses his viewpoint colorfully and fervently. We discuss both sides of that coin and the efficacy of both approaches, then move on to the infamous New York City subway rant that went viral in 2007. This anonymous post to *Craigslist* is a hilarious case of stereotyping subway riders into categories like "Asshole with the book bag" and "Ghostfarter" (Anonymous, 2007), and it cracks students up. And finally, we review what's commonly referred to as "the viral sorority rant" (Sorority Girl, 2013), a one-page email in which the F-bomb is dropped forty times in a quasi-valley-girl voice and leaves half the class rolling on the floor.

Students are then told to adapt the epistolary form of CNF to their own rants in response to a political or environmental problem. However, there are some rules for this assignment. First, the trick is to not rely on name-calling because that's just juvenile. Despite whatever acrobatics we see on the surface, I tell them, a mature rant should make people reflect. Secondly, because humor is more effective than hatred, I advocate the former approach rather than the latter, which can alienate members of an audience. And thirdly, beneath all that dramatic bluster I want there to be some substantial meat to their arguments, so I ask for practical solutions be offered. That way, their rants won't come off as stupid or uninformed but as energized expressions in which serious intellectual underpinnings are clearly visible – as in the following student example that demonstrates what can arise from the rant. In this case, it's a momentum-filled condemnation of the prison system in Arkansas based on research involving politicians and policy:

Conspiracy Theory Mang

Y'all are killing me, mang! Show'em the big picture – the illuminati shit. Hutto gets Arkansas moving in the right direction – by getting the guns out of the hands of the fuckers serving time – separating the meal from the meal worms – literally – sure – but what is he really up to, mang? Improving conditions? Maybe as a side-effect – but his real project – his real project, mang – is the industrial revolution of a feudal state prison-industrial-complex – BAM! – He was burning down the baronies so the petty bourgeoisie can finally have its day in the sun – The ADC was a shit show of a state-run institution – with a revolving door at the top and dead prisoners piling up on the bottom – READ about it, mang – THOMAS MURTON, mang – "Accomplices to the Crime," mang – The truth is out there – and Hutto saw it on those ever-crumbling walls – He saw it and it burned him up – It burned him, mang – working for a "state" that was burying its bodies in shallow unmarked graves – instead of cemeteries – Hutto saw it, mang – He saw it – and started formulating his new system, mang – right here in Arkansas – refined it in Virginia – and then signed on with Tom Beasley and Doctor Crants – DOCTOR Crants, mang – Doctor is his first name – no shit – not a title – to start the first private prison company in America, mang. Y'all think "Clinton" pushed Hutto out, mang – for making with his "bad faith" comments? – naw – Hutto and Clinton were Arkansas Democrats – through and through, mang – right at that time when the "Dems of Arkansas" were taking the white hoods off and – finally – picking up the protest signs – You think they weren't in on it together, mang? – Weren't "in collusion," mang? – That is some bullshit – Clinton goes on to get crowned "the first black president" of the united states – by none other than Toni Morrison – fuckin' TONI MORRISON herself – and what does he do, mang? – but oversee the largest growth ever in the privatization of state and federal prisons – while Hutto's company rises – it rises, mang – and he becomes – like – the profiteer-in-chief of the private-public partnership. But it doesn't stops there, mang – Oh no – You think this shit isn't still going on? – Within just the last three months, mang – CCA – the Correction Corporation of America – has "rebranded" itself into – into "CoreCivic" – so it can: *provide three distinct site-specific management services to national and state governmental agencies* – that should be "international," mang – because their "correctional facilities" are all over the globe, mang – and "services," Ha! We could own and manage all government infrastructure – so the State pays us to manage all their *"site-specific management services"* – Y'all we've gotta help the people, mang!

– Benjamin C. Roy Cory Garrett

We then do a full reversal and tackle what I call the "be-good-for-something assignment," which is based on the Henry David Thoreau quote of "Be not simply good – be good for something" (Thoreau, 1848), which is central to the primary reason why I teach environmental subject matter. I start off by providing the example of how it's not just possible to fight City Hall; it's possible to shut it down. That's where I bring in my personal story of how a letter I wrote sparked intense, effective, small-town outrage in Kirksville, Missouri. The problem was cattle pollution due to the illegal sale of a greenbelt surrounding a municipal drinking water supply which was not equipped to completely filter out coliforms known for causing E.coli and cryptosporidium. Cow-poop contamination being a huge public safety concern, this informative letter fomented so much fury that the corrupt mayor canceled not one but two town hall meetings and refused to meet with the people. The letter, "Mayor's Actions Put City at Risk" (Spitzer, 2011a), originally published in a local newspaper, was then supplied to my students to study as a way for literary citizens to be good for something.

An even more fact-filled letter to the director of the Missouri Department of Natural Resources (Spitzer, 2011b) citing specific laws and violations and including a list of watershed polluters then followed this model, thereby providing another example of how to creatively call attention to a problem and get results. I actually got a hundred local educators to sign that letter with me, which was also published in a local paper. These measures were successful in getting the Missouri Department of Natural Resources to review a video I sent documenting cow pies all over the place, and it eventually led to the assistant attorney general of the state coming up for a fecal tour of the Hazel Creek Reservoir.

Some colleagues might criticize me for using my own letters as models, but other colleagues encourage teaching what you know best. And since I know my own work better than that of anyone else's (just like you), it made sense for me to use my own work as a prototype. Thus, the next example I showed the class was a letter to the editor I wrote to a widely published weekly in Arkansas regarding the construction of a sewage plant in one of the last remaining traditional spawning grounds for alligator gar in the state. That letter (Spitzer, 2010) got picked up by other media outlets, including the local NPR affiliate, and it exposed the fact that a proper environmental impact study was being bypassed so the local utility company could build a chemical-spewing, water-quality-disrupting sewage plant in the habitat of a species threatened throughout its range.

I then made a case for selling out to publishers by writing in the language of publishers, which can be characterized as ordinary language that simply conveys information with no need for any fancy bells and whistles or stylistic effects. My point was clear: If you write a letter that's appropriate to the forum you are targeting and in the expected language, you can reach thousands of citizens. And if you can do that, you can educate people, change minds, spread awareness, and (back to my initial point) actually fight City Hall.

This unapologetically activist assignment inspires reasons for people to get off their butts and *do* something. Students can approach it through a journalistic work, a column or blog post, an opinion piece, or a letter to the editor, but they have to include some heavy-hitting facts in there and some stats to boost authority. Incorporating numbers and name-dropping experts are also encouraged. Then they're directed to send those letters out.

A graduate student of mine, Heather Steadham, wrote an essay that definitely satisfied this assignment. "Firepower" is a truly investigative piece that takes an insider look at gun culture in the Fort Smith area of the Oklahoma/Arkansas border. The narrative is framed by a first-person account of taking a concealed handgun training course at Big Jake's Steakhouse in Van Buren, while continually flashing back to a family history of firearm mishaps. Grandpa Wilson gets shot while playing with friends and almost dies. The narrator's mother, as a child, is blinded by her brother messing around with a BB gun. Her father goes rabbit hunting with his cousin, who ends up in the hospital when a shotgun accidentally goes off. Cousin John still openly wears his pistol at Christmas dinner, even after the shooting of a vicious dog led to him fumbling a gun and shooting himself.

I first read this essay during a time of increasing pressure from the National Rifle Association on the Arkansas State Legislature. It was a time when legalizing concealed weapons in public schools and public institutions was being shoved down the throats of constituents, and even the police forces throughout the state objected to arming students, staff, teachers, and anyone who steps foot in a school. This post-Sandy Hook conflict mirrors a larger national conflict, in which the right to bear arms on campuses and now also in public schools is gradually becoming a terrifying reality for citizens from coast to coast – the primary question being: "Will having guns in our schools make students safer?" It's a question which Heather addressed as well by telling her family stories and ultimately asking, "Does the true threat come from outside or from within?" (Steadham, 2015). She concludes:

> I have no special gun pocket in my purse.
>
> My dad and every one of his three siblings all have guns. My mom and every one of her three siblings all have guns.
>
> Google "Why own a gun?" The top answer will be "for protection." But who are we protecting ourselves from?…
>
> I tell my dad I've decided against getting a gun right now.
>
> "I hope someone doesn't break in and kill your whole damn family," he replies.
>
> Well, hell, I hope that too. That's something I can't really anticipate. But I can at least stop my kids from repeating my family's history in the confines of my own home.
>
> (Steadham, 2015)

Heather's essay is successful in driving home the message that guns don't always make families safer, especially when people inside families are shooting up family members more than anyone from the outside is. Good point! If this doesn't demonstrate an application for investigative nonfiction in the name of making the planet safer, then nothing does.

As Heather demonstrated, the be-good-for-something assignment is effective in expanding literary citizenship since it directly involves and informs writers as well as their audiences in the consideration of issues as vital as life and death and public safety. Considering such considerations, which aim to empower citizens with the real firepower humans need to progress as progressively as possible, it's clear that writing discoveries which preserve and propagate level-headed, educated perspectives are the apex of what writers can achieve in protecting this planet from insanity.

Applying Writing Superpowers as a Progressive Literary Citizen

And that, folks, is what I have to say about the practice and pedagogy of investigative creative writing. It's a creature I discovered from my experience teaching subjects that involve writing, so now I'm setting it free to swim wherever it goes.

As I've noted throughout this book, because these approaches have worked for me and my students, they can therefore work for other writers, teachers, and students. More importantly, after inspiration leads to discoveries in voice, style, and expression, it's the dedicated practice that comes from bolting down and cranking it out which can lead to creating *something else* in the classroom and on the page. And if a writer can create something of value to others or affect progressive change in the world, that's a bonus for all of us.

Personally, the most rewarding results I've experienced from my own writing weren't in crafting entertaining narratives or poetry which readers appreciate, but in actually creating works that protect fish, humans, and the environment. I've experienced my writing calling attention to pollution and abuses of power, which led citizens to unite and fight as a collective front. I've read from and discussed my gar books in various venues, and I've had old timers approach me to let me know they won't continue wiping out this vital link in the food chain anymore. Likewise, I get regular emails from grateful readers all over the world asking what more can be done about our ecological crisis and how they can get involved. Also, because of the reach of my investigations into water quality issues, community members have asked me to speak on their behalf in city forums, and I have. In combination with other factors, my writing experience played a part in lessening a senseless demonization and passing new state regulations for the protection of a threatened species, which other states have followed suit on. When my research on the alligator gar was incorporated into shows like *River Monsters* and *Monster Fish,* which led to more TV and radio shows to spread awareness of an ecological vulnerability that needs to be treated with serious respect, my messages concerning this niche ended up informing millions of viewers and listeners on the dangers we are currently facing. And hopefully, the international work I'm doing now investigating "grotesque" and "monster" fish will lead to the widespread sharing of highly practical eco-solutions that can help sustain not just fisheries but all life on this planet.

These are not bragging points. These are the measurements by which I see investigative poetics, investigative eco-fiction, and investigative nonfiction really working their magic. Since the methods I teach my students rub off on me, these approaches inform every single vision I envision and every sentence I write while continuing to drive further investigations. That's my experience, and because of that, I can look in the mirror and not feel any regrets about who I see staring back. Not because I publish investigative creative writing, but because I made use of writing tools that are good for something – which, now, hopefully, will also be good for *something else.* At this point, though, it's not about ending the final chapter in an academic study; it's about starting a conversation in which an intersection of experiential writing and literary citizenship is investigated for its proven possibilities.

Thus, this book is an argument for making use of a power that writers need to hone (which rhymes with "own") in order to take the act and art of writing to the next level. It's a power that illustrates an area in which Spiderman and Thoreau agree with me and you, or else you wouldn't be reading this. It's a power which every following generation must discover or we don't meet our full potential. And if that's the case, why even try? But ultimately, it's an overview on how to catch and release a superpower in which the imagination is given license to do the most it can do.

So, literary citizen, make that power grab. And while you're at it, make a difference. Because if an overgrown juvenile delinquent like me can be provided a platform to influence writers and teachers and students to harness writing superpowers, then you can too! But more than that, by applying investigative creative writing practices and pedagogies, you can do something similar but different, something of your own, something in which the discoveries you make have the potential to be progressively transformative.

That's what I'm talking about.

References

Anonymous (2007) NYC subway rant: Jesus Christ! Retrieved on 20 April 2017 from https://www.craigslist.org/about/best/nyc/390658591.html?lang=en&cc=us

Levon, O. U. (1989) *Caverns*. New York: Penguin.

May, Lori A. (2014) AWP: An opportunity to exercise literary citizenship. *The Write Life*. Retrieved on 27 April 2017 from https://wileswritelife.wordpress.com/2014/01/22/awp-an-opportnity-to-exercise-literary-citizenship

Mayers, Tim (2016) Reading as a writer, writing as a reader. In Stephanie Vanderslice (ed.) *Studying Creative Writing – Successfully* 30–38. Suffolk, UK: Frontinus Ltd.

News Hour (2013) PBS. *Ancient Afghan Poetry Form Adapts to Portray Modern Life* (June 18, 2013). Retrieved on 18 April 2017 from https://www.pbs.org/newshour/show/ancient-afghan-poetry-form-adapts-to-portray-modern-life

Pennington, Martha C. and Waxler, Robert P. (2017) *Why Reading Books Still Matters*. New York: Routledge.

Sanders, Ed (2000) *1968: A History in Verse*. Santa Rosa, CA: Black Sparrow Press.

Sorority Girl (2013) Viral sorority rant. Retrieved on 20 April 2017 from http://gawker.com/5994974/the-most-deranged-sorority-girl-email-you-will-ever-read

Spitzer, Mark (2010) Save the garfish. *Arkansas Times* (Sunday August 29, 2010). Retrieved on 20 April 2017 from https://www.arktimes.com/ArkansasBlog/archives/2010/08/29/save-the-garfish

Spitzer, Mark (2011a) Mayor's actions put city at risk. *Proze Attack: Selected Essay, Reviews, Polemics, Rants & Red-Headed Step-Fictions 2004–2010* 186–187. Pittsburgh: Six Gallery Press.

Spitzer, Mark (2011b) To the DNR. *Proze Attack: Selected Essay, Reviews, Polemics, Rants & Red-Headed Step-Fictions 2004–2010* 177–182. Pittsburgh: Six Gallery Press.

Steadham, Heather (2015) Firepower. *The Toast* (April 27, 2015). Retrieved on 16 April 2017 from http://the-toast.net/2015/04/27/firepower

Steiner, Donna (2016) Literary citizenship: How you can contribute to the literary community and why you should. In Stephanie Vanderslice (ed.) *Studying Creative Writing – Successfully* 132–146. Suffolk, UK: Frontinus Ltd.

Stowe, Harriett Beecher, Whitney, Adeline D. T., Hale, Lucretia P., Loring, Frederic W., Perkins, Frederic B., and Hale, Edward E. (1872) *Six of One by Half a Dozen of the Other: An Every Day Novel*. Boston: Roberts Brothers.

Thompson, Hunter S. (2001) This exists: Hunter S. Thompson's profane studio exec rant. *Mediaite*. Retrieved on 21 April 2017 from http://www.mediaite.com/print/this-exists-hunter-s-thompsons-profane-studio-exec-rant

Thoreau, Henry David (1848) Henry David Thoreau to Harrison Blake. Retrieved on 21 April 2017 from http://theamericanreader.com/27-march-1848-henry-david-thoreau-to-harrison-blake

UCA Mission Statement (2011) Board of Trustees. Conway, AR: University of Central Arkansas. Retrieved on 19 April 2017 from uca.edu/about/mission